PRIVATE PILOT HANDBOOK

Comprehensive Guide for Flight Training

UMIT OZTURK, PhD
ATP-A/H, CFII

PRIVATE PILOT HANDBOOK

PRIVATE PILOT HANDBOOK

PREFACE

The Private Pilot Handbook is designed for student pilots, ground instructors, flight instructors, and others with special interest in aviation. The main topics in private pilot training are briefly explained on a need-to-know basis, while topics students frequently have the most difficulty in are covered in detail. Every pilot should be familiar with and use the current FAR-AIM, Pilot Operation Handbook (POH), and Aircraft Flight Manual (AFM). The main sources used in the preparation of the Private Pilot Handbook are the aviation publications put forth in the Airmen Certification Standards (ACS) in Figure 2B. For testing guidance, "_underlined text and notes_" cover questions asked in the written and practice exams.

Copyright © by ProActive Aviation
First Edition, 2020, Illustrated *by A.Atakan OZTURK*
www.flighttrainingshop.com
By UMIT OZTURK, PhD, CFII (FAA-ICAO), ATP (A/H).

All rights reserved. No part of this book shall be reproduced, stored in any retrieval system, or transmitted in any form or by any means, electronic, mechanical, recording, photocopying, or otherwise, without written permission from the publisher. Any questions or comments regarding this handbook can be sent to: info@proactiveavia.com

ISBN:978-1-7350573-0-9

PRIVATE PILOT HANDBOOK

TABLE OF CONTENTS

Student Pilot Certificate/Checklist 1
Things to be done before starting flight 1
Medical Certificate..2
Ground Lessons 2
Student Pilot Certificate 3
Private Pilot Practical Exam (Checkride) Requirements........................3
Private Pilot Certificate Logbook Requirements 3
Private Pilot Airmen Certification Standards (ACS) 5
Introduction to Human Factors 10
English Language Proficiency (Level 4) 10
Airplane Structure/Systems 11
Airplane System-related Malfunctions 12
Flight/Engine Instruments 13
Flight/Engine Instruments 13
Analog (Round-Dial) or Glass Cockpits 15
International Standard Atmosphere (ISA)...16
Type of Altitudes/Airspeeds... 17
Airplane Primary Flight Instruments 18
Engine Instruments 20
Aerodynamic Principles 20
The Axes of the Airplane and Stability 25
Aerodynamic Forces in Flight Maneuvers 26
Forces in Turns and Turn Performance..26
Coordinated Turns, Sliding/Skidding 27
Forces in Climbs and Descends 28
Left-Turning Tendencies 29
Load Factor..30
Traffic Pattern 30
Airspace Classifications 33
How to read a sectional chart 34
Taxiing in Wind... 38
Run-Up Checks... 39
Basic Maneuvers (Air Work- The Four Fundamentals) 39
Constant Airspeed Climbs and Level Off/ Climbing Turns......................40
Constant Airspeed Descends and Level Off/Descending 40
Turns to Headings 40
Visualized Flight Training Maneuvers 41
Normal Landing/ Stabilized Approach/Flare Altitude..............................42
Takeoffs-Rejected Takeoff and Engine failure in takeoff 42
Important Notes for A Safe Approach and Landing................................44

Forward Slip.	44
Go Around	45
Crosswind Takeoff	46
Crosswind Landing: (Wing-Low Landing)	47
How to calculate Crosswind Component	48
Short Field Takeoff and Max. Performance Climb	50
Short Field Approach and Landing	51
Soft Field Takeoff/Ground Effect	51
Soft Field Landing	53
Practicing Area Maneuvers	54
Slow Flight	54
Steep Turns	55
Stalls	57
Power-Off Stalls (Approach to Landing Stall)	57
Power-On Stalls: (Departure Stall)	59
Accelerated Stall	60
Basic Instrument Maneuvers	61
Turns-Ground Reference Maneuvers	62
Turns Around a Point	62
Rectangular Course	63
"S" Turns	64
Emergency Operations	65
Engine-Out (Engine failure) Procedures in Flight	65
Engine Failure During Flight (Restart Procedures)	65
Simulated Forced Landing to Best Place	66
Engine-Out (Engine failure) Procedures After Takeoff	66
Engine Fire In-Flight	67
System and Equipment Malfunctions	67
Pre-Solo Preparation	68
Required Requirements / Maneuvers	69
Pre-Solo Written Exam	70
Pre-Solo Flight Review	75
Weight and Balance (W&B)	76
Center of Gravity Limitations	77
Weight and Balance Sheet	77
Center of Gravity/ Moment Envelope	79
Performance Charts	80
Flight Planning and VFR Navigation Log	81
Sapmle VFR Flight Planning- Orlando (KISM to KORL)	81
How to prepare VFR Navigation Sheet	83
Private Pilot Oral Exam Preperation	86
Wind Aloft/Temp. Data	84

Compas Deviation Table	84
Cruise Preformance (True Air Speed, Fuel Consumption)	85
Private Pilot Written Exam Hints	117
Private Pilot Checkride	116
Common Mistakes During A Checkride	118
ATC Glossary	119
Traffic Pattern Communication Procedures	140
Controlled Airspace, Traffic Pattern Procedures	140
Untowered Airports Communication Procedures	148
Overflying the Airport	151
Requesting Flight Following	152
PAPI/VASI	153
Airport Signs and Runway Markings	154
Runway Lights	155
Airport Operations, Runway Holding Position Markings	156
Private Pilot Dictionary	157
Aviation Alphabet and Practice	185
TAF/METAR Abreviations	186
Aircraft Right-of-Way Rules	187
Supplemental Oxygen Requirements	187
ATC Tower Light Gun Signals	188
Flight Plan Form	188
Weather Fronts, Isobars, High/Low Pressure Systems	189
VFR Cross Country Planning Checklist	190
Abbreviations	191
Figures	194
Index	196

Student Pilot Preperation Checklist :

Preflight Actions :

- **Materials to be supplied: Student pilot must purchase following items.**

No	Name	Piece
1	Aviation Head Set	1
2	Kneeboard *(to copy radio transmissions and write down instructions of Instructor)*	1
3	Private Pilot Textbook, FAR AIM, POH.	Set
4	E6B- Flight Computer or Electronic Flight Computer	1
5	VFR Sectional Charts	1
6	EFB application (Electronic Flight Bag)	1
7	Flashlight *(preferably a head lamp with red and white LEDs)*	1
8	Hood *(Foggles//view limiting device)*	1
9	Multi-tool Set	1
10	Fuel Tester *(fuel strainer)*	1
11	Logbook	1
12	Pilot Operating Handbook (POH)	1
13	Small Student Pilot Bag	1

Figure-1 Start-up Materials for Private Pilot Training

- **Private Pilot Test, Written Exam (Airman Knowkedge Test) Studying Materials, Where to begin..**

Software is probably the best way to go as it allows you to take tests and repeat them with randomly generated questions. *(Ask your Flight School and CFI which software they recommend.)* Other options for self-study are ASA, GLEIM, JEPPESEN, and King School text books. All text books use the same test prep resources. Regardless of your source of study, the Knowledge Test Preparation Source should provide you with the easiest, fastest, and least expensive means to pass the FAA Private Pilot Airplane knowledge test.

Note: All applicants must establish an FTN number, by creating a profile in the Integrated Airman Certification and Rating Application (IACRA) System, PRIOR TO taking an FAA Airman Knowledge Test.

- **Medical Certificate:**

In order to begin flying, the Student Pilot must have a valid Medical Certificate.

There are 2 steps to initially obtain your First Medical Certificate from an AME:

* Visit the Web Page and subscribe: medxpress.faa.gov (official FAA Online Database)

* Visit the nearest Aviation Medical Examiner (AME) to complete your Medical Exam (3rd Class).

A new FAA Regulation called Part 68 BasicMed privileges and limitations have made the medical check easier. *(If the pilot has no issue in three areas: Psychiatric, Neurological and Cardiac.)*

Note: While operating under BasicMed, the pilot in command must have visited their primary care physician within the preceding 48 calendar months. See Pg.97

If you are unsure whether a medication you are taking might prevent you from flying, contact an Aviation Medical Examiner *(AME).*

- **Ground Lessons:**

In order to become a Private Pilot, you need to receive both ground and flight training. Flight Schools and Institutes provide you with ground training, they teach you the theory that is required to pass the FAA Written Exam. If you are unable to attend a ground school, the self-study method can be satisfactory. Haphazard or disorganized study habits usually result in an unsatisfactory score on the FAA Written Exam.

Obtain the POH (Pilot's Operating Handbook) and FAR-AIM (Federal Aviation Regulations and Airman's Information Manual) for self-study. You will need to focus on FAR Parts 61-91 and subscribe to a YouTube "private pilot ground school course." Start your training by becoming acquainted with the applicable FAA knowledge test. The knowledge test has 60-questions with a 2 h. 30 m. time limit. The questions are multiple-choice with three answer choices. In order to pass, you'll need to score 70% or higher. The more you take the online practice tests, the more familiar you will become with the types of questions asked.

Note: To get the most out of your flight training, be prepared for each ground and flight lesson. Practice procedures at home by "chair flying," pay attention to small details, and do what the CFI tells you. Finally, practice all maneuvers until they are a reflex. To achieve an optimum score, it is recommended that the knowledge test be taken after the student has completed a solo X-C flight. This way, the operational knowledge gained by the experience can be used to your advantage on the knowledge test.

- **Student Pilot Certificate**:

A student pilot certificate allows you to receive flight instruction from a Certified Flight Instructor (CFI). This is the first step you will take toward earning a Private Pilot License (PPL). To obtain a Student Pilot Certificate, you must meet some basic eligibility requirements. First, in order to obtain a Private Pilot License you must be at least 17 years of age, however, you may receive a student pilot certificate at the age of 16. Additionally, you must be able to proficiently **_"read, speak, and understand English"_**. Student pilots also need to enlist a CFI to supervise their training and endorse their logbooks.

Next, you will complete the Integrated Airman Certification and Rating Application (IACRA). Your application will be processed and submitted with the required documents to the Airmen Certification Branch (ACB). Once it has been reviewed by ACB, you can expect to receive your student pilot certificate by mail in approximately three weeks. The plastic U.S. student pilot certificate never expires.

You must submit this form electronically to Certified Flight Instructor (CFI) and an FAA Designated Pilot Examiner (DPE) before the check ride (Practical Exam).

When you have your student pilot certificate and medical certificate, you are ready to begin training.

- **Private Pilot Practical Exam (Check ride) Requirements:**

In order to take the Check Ride with a DPE *(FAA Designated Pilot Examiner) you must achieve:*

- A Private Pilot Written Exam Result of at least 70%, requires CFI endorsement addressing the questions which were answered incorrectly during the FAA Written Exam.
- Valid Medical Class III Exam. (3rd Class)
- Logbook and IACRA endorsed by CFI,
- Valid Driver License or Passport.
- Current publications and documents such as the FAR/AIM, Airport/Facility Directory and VFR sectional charts.
- Collect engine, airframe and propeller maintenance logs.

- **Private Pilot Certificate Logbook Requirements:**

What does it take to become a private pilot? Considerable interest, time, dedicated work, commitment, and most important of all, money. Flight Requirements (ground and flight training) to be certified by the FAA as a Private Pilot have been determined in the 61.109(a)(1-5)

Private pilots usually must complete a minimum 40 hours of flight time consisting of: *(Figure-2A)*

Flight Training	Fight Hours	Recommended FAA Logbook Requirements and Endorsements
Dual Flight Training	20 H (Min. Flight Training)	- 15 H. Pattern Work *(Figure-15)* - 5 H. VFR Navigation, Preparation to X-C See Figures-48, 70 - 15/20 H. Air Work *Figures 20-41.* - 3. H. Hood, *flight training by reference to instruments, Pg.61* - 3 H. Night *(100 NM, 10 T/O and Landings to a full stop.)* Total: 36-41 H.

Student Solo	10 H. (Min.)	- 5-10 H Solo Flights (In-pattern)
		- 5 H. Solo X-C
		  * Solo X-C *(150 NM, 3 points, 50 NM between the T/O and landings) (3-4 H.)*
		  * 3 T/O and Landings at controlled airport. *(1 H)*
		Total: 10-15 H.

Check ride with DPE	3+ 2 H.	Oral Part of Exam 3 H. *(See Pg.6, 116)* Practical Part of Exam 2 H. *(See Pg.6, 42,116)* Emergency Procedures *(See Pg.66)*
Flight Instructor Endorsements		- Knowledge Test Endorsement - Initial Solo Endorsement *(61.87)* - Solo X-C Endorsement *(61.93)* - Additional Airport Endorsement W/IN 25 NM. *(61.93)*
Note: *3 hours of flight training in a single engine airplane within the 60 days prior to the Private Pilot Check Ride.*		

Figure-2A Private Pilot Logbook Requirements and Endorsements.
Note: The number of flight hours aforementioned to meet the requirements

for the check ride will vary with each student's level of dedication. The national average indicates most pilots require 55-65 hours of flight training.

- **Private Pilot Airmen Certification Standards (ACS) :**
  - The goal of the airman certification process is to ensure that the student pilot possesses the required knowledge, ability to manage risks, and skill consistent with the privileges of the certificate or rating to be exercised.
  - The Airman Certification Standards (ACS) is the guide for aviation students, instructors, and FAA-designated examiners to know what pilot and industry license applicants must ***know, do,*** and ***consider*** for their FAA Knowledge Exam and practical exam (check ride) to earn a certificate or rating.
  - During the ground and flight portion of the practical test, the FAA expects evaluators (DPE's) to assess the student pilot's mastery of the topic in accordance with the level of understanding most appropriate for the specified task. The oral questioning will continue throughout the entire practical test and will relate to the ACS Subject Titles. (Figure-2C)
  - The FAA has set forth these maneuvers in the Airplane Airman Certification Standards (ACS) since 2017. The ACS details critical ***task, objectives, skills, risk factors***, and the pass/fail requirements for each maneuver. If you are unable to complete any of the associated tasks, you will fail the Practical Test (check ride). This is known as a *"letter of discontinuance"* and you will need to test again.
  - What is the core professional pilot skills? The skills of coordination, timing, decision making, precise control, and airspeed awareness in addition to the fine motor skills required to fly an aircraft.
  - As a student pilot, it is a must to read carefully and be fully aware of ACS "task/objectives/knowledge/risk management/skills" determined by the FAA. *(See Figure-2B, 2C and Student Pilot Certification Standard Checklist, Pg.6)*

Note:(1) In summary, the ACS provides a single-source set of standards for both the knowledge exam and the practical test.
(2) Risk management, as part of the aeronautical decision making (ADM) process, relies on "situational awareness, problem recognition, and good judgment."
(3) A pilot who tries to exhibit "the right stuff", can effect safety by generating tendencies that lead to practices that are dangerous, often illegal, and may lead to a mishap.

(4) A pilot who allows himself to get behind the aircraft, can easily lose situational awareness.

Figure-2B Airman Certification Standarts Coding System

VII. Slow Flight and Stalls

Task	A. **Maneuvering During Slow Flight**
References	FAA-H-8083-2, FAA-H-8083-3, FAA-H-8083-25; POH/AFM
Objective	To determine that the applicant exhibits satisfactory knowledge, risk management, and skills associated with maneuvering during slow flight. *Note: See Appendix 6: Safety of Flight and Appendix 7: Aircraft, Equipment, and Operational Requirements & Limitations*
Knowledge	The applicant demonstrates understanding of:
PA.VII.A.K1	Aerodynamics associated with slow flight in various airplane configurations, to include the relationship between angle of attack, airspeed, load factor, power setting, airplane weight and center of gravity, airplane attitude, and yaw effects.
Risk Management	The applicant demonstrates the ability to identify, assess and mitigate risks, encompassing:
PA.VII.A.R1	Inadvertent slow flight and flight with a stall warning, which could lead to loss of control.
PA.VII.A.R2	Range and limitations of stall warning indicators (e.g., airplane buffet, stall horn, etc.).
PA.VII.A.R3	Failure to maintain coordinated flight.
PA.VII.A.R4	Effect of environmental elements on airplane performance (e.g., turbulence, microbursts, and high-density altitude).
PA.VII.A.R5	Collision hazards, to include aircraft, terrain, obstacles, and wires.
PA.VII.A.R6	Distractions, loss of situational awareness, or improper task management.
Skills	The applicant demonstrates the ability to:
PA.VII.A.S1	Clear the area.
PA.VII.A.S2	Select an entry altitude that will allow the Task to be completed no lower than 1,500 feet AGL (ASEL, ASES) or 3,000 feet AGL (AMEL, AMES).
PA.VII.A.S3	Establish and maintain an airspeed at which any further increase in angle of attack, increase in load factor, or reduction in power, would result in a stall warning (e.g., airplane buffet, stall horn, etc.).
PA.VII.A.S4	Accomplish coordinated straight-and-level flight, turns, climbs, and descents with the airplane configured as specified by the evaluator without a stall warning (e.g., airplane buffet, stall horn, etc.).
PA.VII.A.S5	Maintain the specified altitude, ±100 feet; specified heading, ±10°; airspeed, +10/-0 knots; and specified angle of bank, ±10°.

PA.VII.A.S4
- PA : Private Pilot Airplane (Applicable ACS)
- VI : Slow Flights and Stalls (Area of Operation)
- A : Maneuvering During Slow Flight (Task)
- S4 : Elements of Slow Flight and Stalls (Task Element)

Private Pilot Airmen Certification Standards (ACS)
Student Pilot Certification Standard Checklist (Task/Objectives)
I. Preflight Preperation *(Pg.116, Check out POH/AFM)*

    a. Pilot Qualifications
    b. Airworthiness Requirements
    c. Weather Information
    d. Cross-Country Flight Planning

e. National Airspace System (NAS)
   f. Performance and Limitations *(Weather, Pilot Technique, A/C Configuration, Airport Environment, Loading (CG Limitations), W&B)*
   g. Operation of Systems
   h. Human Factors
II. Preflight Procedures
   a. Preflight Assesment
   b. Flight Deck Management
   c. Engine Starting
   d. Taxiing
   e. Before Takeoff Check
III. Airport Operations
   a. Communications, Light Signals, and Runway Lightning Systems
   b. Traffic Pattern
IV. Takeoffs, Landings, and Go-Arounds
   a. Normal Takeoff and Climb (+10/-5 KIAS)
   b. Normal Approach and Landing
   c. Soft-Field Takeoff and Climb (+10/-5 KIAS)
   d. Soft-Field Approach and Landing
   e. Short-Field Takeoff and Max. Performance Climb (+10/-5 KIAS)
   f. Short-Field Approach and Landing *(within 200 feet beyond or at)*
   g. Forward Slip to a Landing (+400)
   h. Go-Around/Rejected Landing (+10/-5 KIAS, min. loss of altitude)
V. Performance and Ground Reference Maneuvers
   a. Steep Turns (45° bank ±5°, Va, ±100' Alt, ±10 KIAS, roll out ±10°)
   b. Ground Reference Maneuvers
      * S-Turns (±100', ±10 KIAS) * Rectangular Course (±100', ±10 KIAS)   * Turns Around a Point (±100', ±10 KIAS)
VI. Navigation
   a. Pilotage and Dead Reckoning
   b. Navigation Systems and Radar Services (±200', ±15°)
   c. Diversion (heading, ground speed, ETA, fuel burn)
   d. Lost Procedures.
VII. Slow Flight and Stalls
   a. Maneuvering During Slow Flight (±100', ±10 KIAS)
   b. Power-Off Stalls
   c. Power-On Stalls
   d. Spin Awareness
VIII. Basic Instrument Maneuvers
   a. Straight-and-Level Flight (±200', HD ±20°, ±10 KIAS)
   b. Constant Airspeed Climbs (±200', HD ±20°, ±10 KIAS)
   c. Constant Airspeed Descents (±200', HD ±20°, ±10 KIAS)

d. Turns to Headings (±200', HD ±20°, ±10 KIAS)
e. Recovery from Unusual Flight Attitudes.
f. Radio Communications, Navigation Systems/Facilities, and Radar Services.

IX. Emergency Operations
a. Emergency Approach and Landing (Simulated) (±10 KIAS)
b. Systems and Equipment Malfunctions *(Pg.66,114)*
c. Emergency Equipment and Survival Gear.

X. Night Operation
Night Preparation *(Avoid bright white lights <u>at least 30 min before</u>)*

XI. Postflight Procedures
After Landing, Parking, and Securing the Airplane.

Critical Tasks / Risk Management Factors
1. Positive Aircraft Control *(Coordinated Flight)*
2. Procedure for Positive Exchange of Flight Controls
3. Stall/Spin Awareness *(Situational Awareness, Disorientation, Loss of Control)*
4. Collision Avoidance
5. Wake Turbulence Avoidance
6. Land and Hold Short Operations (LAHSO)
7. Runway Incursion Avoidance
8. Controlled Flight into Terrain (CFIT)
9. Aeronautical Decision Making (ADM) and Risk Management. *(Human Factors)*
10. Environment (Weather, Airports, Airspace, Tarrain, Obstacles)
11. Appropriate Checklist Usage
12. Temporary Flight Restrictions (TFRs)
13. Special Use AIRSPACE (SUA)
14. Risk Management Factors (PAVE), Aviation Security Concerns.
15. Single-Pilot Resource Management (SRM).

Note: (1) Safety Concern. During the flight training and testing, the applicant and the instructor or evaluator must always recognize and avoid operations that could lead to an inadvertent stall or spin and inadvertent loss of control.

(2) Flight crewmembers are specifically required to keep <u>their safety belts during takeoff and landing and while enroute</u> and <u>shoulder harnesses during takeoff and landing fastened.</u>

(3) Each person who holds a pilot certificate or a medical certificate shall present it for inspection upon the request of <u>any local law enforcement officer.</u>

Figure-2C Private Pilot Airmen Certification Standards (ACS), FAA-S-ACS-6B, Change 1, June 6, 2019.

Subject Title	Task / Objective	References
Preflight Preparation	Pilot Qualifications, Airworthiness Requirements, Weather Information, Cross-Country Flight Planning, National Airspace System, Performance and Limitations, Operation of Systems, Human Factors.	14 CFR Parts 1, 23, 43, 61, 68, 91; FAA-H-8083-2, FAA-H-8083-25; AC 68-1, 14 CFR part 91; FAA-H-8083-25; AC 00-6, 00-45, 00-54, 60-22, AIM.
Preflight Procedures	Preflight Assessment, Flight Deck Management (Pax. Briefing, Checklist Procedures, Current NAV Data), Engine Starting, Taxiing, Before Takeoff Checklist.	FAA-H-8083-2, FAA-H-8083-3, FAA-H-8083-23; POH/AFM; AC 00-6, AC 91-73, FAA-H-8083-25.
Airport Operations	Communications, Light Signals, and Runway Lightning Systems, Traffic Patterns, Normal Takeoff and Climb, Normal Approach and Landing.	14 CFR part 91; FAA-H-8083-2, FAA-H-8083-25; AIM.
Takeoffs, Landings, and Go-Arounds	Soft Field Takeoff and Climb, Soft-Field Approach and Landing, Short-Field Takeoff and Maximum Performance Climb, Short-Field Approach and Landing, Forward Slip to a Landing, Go-Around/Rejected Landing.	14 CFR part 91; FAA-H-8083-2-3, FAA-H-8083-25; AIM, FAA-H-8083-23; POH/AFM.
Performance and Ground Reference Maneuvers	Steep Turns, Ground Reference Maneuvers (Rectangular course, S turns, and Turns around a point)	14 CFR part 61; FAA-H-8083-2, FAA-H-8083-3; POH/AFM, FAA-H-8083-25.
Navigation	Pilotage and Dead Reckoning, Navigation Systems and Radar Services, Diversion, Lost Procedures.	FAA-H-8083-2, FAA-H-8083-3, FAA-H-8083-6, FAA-H-8083-25, FAA-H-8083-2, FAA-H-8083-25; AIM.
Slow Flight and Stalls	Maneuvering During Slow Flight, Power-Off Stalls, Power-On Stalls, Spin Awareness.	FAA-H-8083-2, FAA-H-8083-3, FAA-H-8083-25 /15; AC 61-67, POH/AFM.
Basic Instrument Maneuvers	Straight-and-Level Flight, Constant Airspeed Climbs, Constant Airspeed Descents, Turns to Headings, Radio Communications, Navigation Systems/Facilities, and Radar Services	FAA-H-8083-2, FAA-H-8083-3, FAA-H-8083-15, FAA-H-8083-25.
Emergency Operations	Emergency Descent, Emergency Approach and Landing (Simulated), Systems and Equipment Malfunctions, Emergency Equipment (ELT) and Survival Gear, Engine Failure During Takeoff Roll (Simulated).	FAA-H-8083-2, FAA-H-8083-3; POH/AFM, FAA-P-8740-66.
Night Operations	Night Preparation (Physiological aspects, Airport-Runway – Taxiway Lighting systems), Night orientation.	FAA-H-8083-2, FAA-H-8083-3, FAA-H-8083-25; AIM; POH/AFM
Postflight Procedures	After Landing, Parking and Securing. (shutdown, securing, and postflight inspection, Documenting in-flight/postflight discrepancies)	FAA-H-8083-2, FAA-H-8083-3; POH/AFM

- **Introduction to Human Factors:**

    As a student pilot, a better understanding of how your mind and physical body function when you fly is as important as knowing how to operate your airplane's systems and equipment. Your ability to make safe decisions as a pilot depends on a number of critical factors. You have to be able to recognize and manage the factors explained below, and learn skills to improve your decision-making ability and judgment.

> **Figure-3** Student Pilot Self-Awareness (Go/No-go) Checklist
> **(Personal airworthiness -(Aeronautical Decision Making-ADM):** There is a self-assessment checklist to assist pilots in determining their own physical and mental health before a flight. *I'M SAFE* Checklist is taught early in training and is used throughout a pilot's professional career to assess their overall readiness for the flight when it comes to Illness, Medication, Stress, Alcohol, Fatigue, and Emotion.
>
> **Ask yourself the following questions before Flight Training:**
>
> - Is there any reason I should NOT today ? (Am I **S-A-F-E**?)
> - Am I willing to devote my full attention to the flight portion?
> - Am I having any healthy and emotional situation that My Flight Instructor (CFI) should know about that?
> - Is there anything about our previous/last flight We need to talk about ? Post-flight Briefing ...
> - Has my Flight Instructor prepared me for today's flight?
> - Am I relaxed?

- **English Language Proficiency (Level 4):**

    In accordance with the requirements of 14 CFR part 61, section 61.13(c) the applicant must demonstrate the ability to read, write, speak, and understand the English language throughout the application and testing process. English language proficiency is required to communicate effectively with Air Traffic Control (ATC), to comply with ATC instructions, and to ensure clear and effective crew communication and coordination. <u>Normal restatement of questions as would be done for a native English speaker is permitted, and does not constitute grounds for disqualification.</u> The FAA Aviation English Language Standard (AELS) is the FAA evaluator's benchmark. It requires the applicant to demonstrate at least the International Civil Aviation Organization (ICAO) *"Level 4 standard".(ICAO Doc 9385, Annex1, Personnel Licensing)*

The standard is to ensure the holder of an FAA certificate or applicant for an FAA certificate or rating must be able to communicate in English with air traffic control (ATC), pilots, and others involved in preparing an aircraft for flight and operating an aircraft in flight. This communication may or may not involve the use of the radio. *(FAA AC 60-28B, Feb.; 2017)*

The FAA AELS (Level 4) proficiency test is based on the standards, including *"pronunciation, structure, vocabulary, fluency, comprehension, interactions"*. DO PRACTICE on Figure-63, Pg.184.

- **Airplane Structure/Systems:**

   This chapter covers the primary systems found on small airplanes. These include the engine (powerplant), propeller, induction, ignition, fuel, lubrication, cooling, electrical, landing gear, and environmental control systems.
   - **Airplane Components:** An airplane is made up of five major parts. *(Figure-4)* Most of the pertinent information about a particular make and model of airplane, including parts, operating limits, can be found in the Pilot's Operating Handbook (POH) and FAA approved Airplane Flight Manual (AFM).
   - **Powerplant and Related Systems:**

   The airplane engine and propeller, often referred to as a powerplant, work in combination to produce the thrust. The powerplant propels the airplane and drives the various systems stated below that support the operation of an airplane. Most small airplanes are designed with reciprocating engines (four-stroke oprating circle).
   - **Engine.** Reciprocating and turbine engines
   - **Propeller.** Fixed-Pitched (Cessna 150,172) or Constant-Speed.
   - **Electrical System.** Alternator, Battery, Ammeter, Circuit Breakers.
   - **Ignition System.** The ignition system is made up of magnetos, spark plugs, interconnecting wires, and the ignition Key/Switch .
   - **Oil Systems.** Engine-driven oil pump, oil sump.
   - **Induction System.** Carburetor or Fuel Injectors.
   - **Fuel System** provides an uninterrupted flow of clean fuel from the fuel tanks to the engine. *(two vented integral fuel tanks, a three-position fuel selector valve, fuel shutoff valve, fuel gauges, sumps and drains,*

auxiliary fuel pump, fuel strainer, fuel primer, fuel/air control unit, engine driven fuel pump, fuel distribution valve and fuel injection nozzles or carburetor)

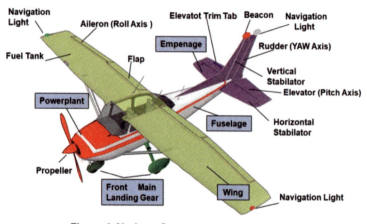

Figure-4 Airplane Components

- **Cooling Systems**. Most small aircraft are air cooled
- **Exhaust System.** Exhaust piping is attached to the cylinders, muffler and muffler shroud for cabin heating. *It eliminates the most of the heat.*

• **Airplane System-Related Malfunctions :**
If you fly an aircraft you should know exactly what all the levers, bells, and whistles do! A light aircraft isn't exactly a complex machine; a good understanding can be accomplished in only a few hours of study. **Read the POH.**

- **Carburator Icing:** The fuel/air mixture can be adjusted from the cockpit with the mixture control. Carburetor ice may be caused by fuel vaporization and decreasing air pressure in the venturi which causes a sharp temperature drop in the carburetor. Carburetor ice is more likely to occur when temperatures are *below 21°C (70°F)* and *relative humidity* is above 80%. To combat the effects of carburetor ice, engines with float-type carburetors employ a carburetor heat system which is designed to eliminate ice by routing air across a heat source before it enters the carburetor. Applying carburetor heat will enrich the fuel/air mixture, and

decrease engine performance. If an aircraft is equipped with a fixed-pitch propeller and a float-type carburetor, the first indication of carburetor ice would most likely be loss of RPM. *(See Pg.114)*
Note: Utilizing carbutetor heat will cause any ice that has formed in the venturi to melt, this will result in engine roughness as the ice becomes water and is ingested into the engine's cylinders.

- **Detonation/Preignition:** *Detonation* occurs when fuel in the cylinders explode instead of burning smoothly. This can be caused by contaminated fuel or by using fuel that is not authourized by the POH.

Preignition is a result of the fuel/air mixture being ignited in advance of the normal timed ignition. See Pg.67

- **Magneto Problem :** The magneto check is one of the first things we learn as student pilots. Run the engine up to a specific rpm and switch to the right mag, back to both, then the left, and finally back to both. If you see a "suitable" drop in the engine's rpm, you're good to go. Or are you? *Figure-20*

If the RPM drop exceeds 125 RPM, Correction Action: Increase power to 2000 RPM, slowly **lean** the mixture until the RPM peaks. Then retard the throttle back to 1,800 RPM, fully enrichen the mixture and repeat the **magneto** drop-off check. If the drop-off does not exceed 175 RPM, the difference between the drop-off values for both magnetos does not exceed 50 RPM, the engine is running smoothly, then the ignition system is operating properly. Ensure the mixture is set to full rich or best power before take-off.

- **Alternator/Generator Problem :** After engine start-up, make sure that battery has a positive charge and no red low voltage light. During the run-up check, check the ammeter and see that it is near "0" or no discharge reading on ammeter *See Pg.114*

- **Vacuum System Problem:** Proper suction is required for reliable operation of the gyroscopic instruments. If the suction reading drops/increases noticeably, it will directly effect the Gyro-driven instruments and result in erroneous indications. *See Pg.114*

Note: If you are flying an aircraft equipped with a G1000 or a similar suite of glass instrumentation, ensure that you understand which instruments are driven by the vacuum system and which recieve their information through the Altitude and Heading Reference System (AHRS) and Air Data Computer (ADC).

Flight/Engine Instruments:
- **Flight Instruments:** *See Figure 5-7*

There are six traditional flight instruments in most aircraft cockpits. The flight instruments are divided into sub-categories according to their method of operation. These six basic flight instruments (Six Pack) are the **"main source of cockpit flight information"** for pilots and are divided into two categories: <u>static (or pitot-static) instruments and gyroscopic instruments.</u> The instruments that reflect your speed (indicated air speed- IAS), rate of climb or descent, and altitude operate on air pressure differentials and are called **"pitot-static instruments."** <u>*(Pitot Pressure is present only an airplane is in motion, Static Pressure always present whether an aircraft is moving or at rest.)*</u> Airplane's attitude, rate of turn and heading Indicators (HI) operate on gyroscopic principles.

Student Pilots must know the operating principles of flight instruments and how to scan, interpret and operate the flight instruments.

A quick scan of the six pack provides the pilot with current information on aircraft speed, altitude, climb/descent, attitude, heading and turning/banking. *(See Figure-5/6)*

- **Pitot-static System**
  - Altimeter (shows the aircraft's altitude above sea-level.)
  - Airspeed İndicator- ASI (shows the aircraft's speed relative to the surrounding air.)
  - Vertical Speed İndicator- VSI (rate of climb/descend indicated in feet per minute (FPM))
- **Gyroscopic System**
  - Attitude Indicator-AI shows the aircraft's orientation relative to the horizon. (AI is the foundation for all instrument flight)
  - Heading Indicator-HI displays the aircraft's heading in compass points.
  - Turn-and-Slip Indicator (Turn Coordinator-TC) (indicates rotation about longitudinal axes, It includes an inclinometer that displays whether the A/C is in coordinated flight, in a slip, or skid.) The turn-and-slip indicator shows the aircrafts rate of turn and indicates <u>indirect</u> bank information.

Note: 1. *Blockage of the pitot tube only effects the <u>airspeed indicator</u>, but a clogged pitot/static port effects <u>all three pitot-static instruments</u>. (Airspeed, altimeter, and vertical speed.)*
2. *The turn coordinator provides a backup source of bank information in the event of attitude indicator (artificial horizon) failure.*

- **Navigational Systems (Flight Director Systems)**
  - Very-High Frequency Omnidirectional Range (VOR)

- Nondirectional Radio Beacon (NDB)

Note: The magnetic compass is the simplest, most primitive, and sensitive instrument available in the aircraft by which the pilot can determine the direction of flight. It shows the aircraft's heading relative to magnetic north.

Because of the Earth's magnetic field, compass turning error are most apparent when turning through headings close to north and south. Turning Error Memory Aids: **_UNOS_** for Northern Hemisphere. Undershoot North, Overshoot South.

* Smooth turns made on east and west headings will allow for reasonably accurate compass indications. However, the only time a compass can be considered accurate is when the aircraft is in level, unaccelerated flight.

Analog (Round-Dial) or Glass Cockpits:

Differences between Glass Cockpit and Steam Gauges (6-Pack)

Conventional Cockpit:
1. Airspeed Indicator (ASI)
2. Attitude Indicator
3. Altimeter
4. Turn-and-Slip Indicator (Inclinometer)
5. Heading Indicator (HI)
6. Vertical Speed Indicator (VSI)
7. Engine Tachometer (RPMx100)
8-9-10 VOR and ADF
11 Fuel Indicator
12 Fuel Flow/EGT Gauges
13 Oil Pressure/Temperature
14 Vacuum/Ampermetre

Glass Cockpit:
1. Airspeed Indicator (Vertical Tape)
2. Attitude Indicator (AHRS)
3. Altimeter (Vertical Tape)
4. Turn-and-Slip Indicator (Inclinometer, on top of the HSI)
5. Heading Indicator (HI)
6. Vertical Speed Indicator (VSI)
7. Navigational Systems VOR/NDB/GPS

Figure-5 Flight and Engine Instruments 6-Pack and G1000 (Glass Cockpit)

Glass or Analog (Steam) gauges? Both are great for primary flight training. it is a good idea to start off with the classic 6-pack to get an idea/feel for the basics of flying *(Private Pilot/ Instrument Pilot)*, and then switch to the G1000 *(Commercial Pilot)*. In terms of practicality for the future, you are going to have advanced avionics similar the G1000 in front of you.

I'm a proponent of starting with analog instrumentation. I really think that the 6 pack helps you understand the concepts of instrument flight much more and teaches you a scan/multitasking approach that you would never learn via glass/G1000. Ultimately, the choice is up to you.

Steam Gauges- 6-Pack

Glass Cockpit - Garmin 1000

Figure-6 Flight Instruments: Steam Gouges and Glass Cockpit

International Standard Atmosphere (ISA):
At sea level, the standard atmosphere consists of a barometric pressure of **29.92 in. Hg.** (1013.2 millibars) and a temperature of **15°C** (59°F). Standard atmospheric pressure is defined as "a measure of the force onto a surface" based on the weight (density) of the air above the surface. As the aircrafts altitude increases, air gets thinner due to the change in density of the air. (Less dense air, fewer air molecules), The most dense/heavy air and greatest pressure is at sea level.

Air density has a direct effect on aerodynamic (airframe, propeller, and airfoil) and engine performance.

Type of Altitudes/Airspeeds:
- **Altitudes:**

- **Indicated Altitude:** Indicated altitude is the altitude measured by your altitude indicator (altimeter). During flight, you will always use Indicated Altitude.

- **Pressure Altitude (PA):** Height above the standard datum plane (SDP). If you set your altimeter to the standard _sea level (SL) atmospheric pressure of 29.92 in. Hg._ or 1013 Mb., your indicated altitude will be equivalent to _Pressure Altitude (PA)._

- **Density Altitude (DA):** Density altitude is pressure altitude corrected for nonstandard temperature. Density altitude increases as ambient temperature increases. Be aware of its effects on hot days at high altitudes, especially relating to takeoff and landing roll.

- **Absolute Altitude:** Constantly changing, absolute altitude is the distance measurement of your airplane above the ground. Expressed in "feet AGL" (above ground level), you can also find many obstacles and airspace classifications that exist in feet above the ground. A radar altimeter gives the Absolute Altitude Reading.

- **True Altitude:** True altitude is the _vertical distance of the aircraft above sea level (ASL)._

- **Airspeed Indicator:**

The airspeed indicator is the only instrument which uses ram-air pressure from the pitot tube. The airspeed indicator is divided into color-coded arcs which define speed ranges for different stages of flight. The upper and lower limits of the arcs correspond to particular airspeed limitations, called V-speeds. *See Figure-7.*

White Arc: (Full Flap Operating Speed Range from Vso to Vfe),

Green Arc: The Green Arc on the Airspeed Indicator depicts the normal operating airspeed range. (_Normal Operating Speed Range_ from Vsi to Vno),

Yellow Arc: (Caution Speed Range, Smooth Air Operating Range from Vno to Vne) The speed range marked by the Yellow Arc is the Caution Speed Range. Flight Operations in the Yellow speed range are to be conducted in Smooth Air only!

Vr: Rotation Speed

Va : Manuevering Speed (Va changes with aircraft weight and is not depicted _(no code)_ on the Airspeed Indicator.

Vfe: Flap Extention Speed: Bottom of the white arc.

Vne: Never Exceeding Speed. The Red Line at the top of the Yellow Arc.

Vso: Stall Dirty – Stuff Out (Landing Confugration Stalling Speed)

Vsi: Stall Clean- Stuff In.

Vno: Normal Operational Speed, the top of the green arc is the Velocity (V) of Normal (N) Operations (O) or Vno. Operation of the Aircraft at the Vno speed, and lower, is within the certified range for operations within gusts. _(Vno-maximum structural cruising speed within gusts)_

• **Type of Airspeeds:**

- **Indicated Airspeed (IAS)** : IAS is the direct airspeed reading shown by an airspeed indicator.

- **Calibrated Airspeed (CAS):** Calibrated airspeed is indicated airspeed corrected for instrument and positional errors.

- **True Airspeed (TAS):** True airspeed is equivalent to CAS corrected for non-standard temperature and pressure.

- **Groundspeed (GS):** It's true airspeed corrected for wind. (Speed across the ground.)

- **Mach Number:** Mach number is the ratio of the TAS of the aircraft to the speed of sound in the same atmospheric conditions.

- **Maneuvering Speed (Va):** It is the max speed at which you may apply full and abrupt control inputs without causing structural damage. Va changes with aircraft weight. It s highest at an airplane's maximum gross weight. Light weight results in a lower maneuvering speed.

Note: As altitude increases, the indicated airspeed at which a given airplane stalls in a particular configuration will **remain the same** regardless of altitude.

• Airplane Primary Flight Instruments

In order to safely fly any aircraft, a pilot must understand how to interpret and operate the flight instruments. The pilot also needs to be able to recognize associated errors and malfunctions of these instruments. Figure-7 defines the _color codes of speeds,_ indicators of instruments and how to set the instruments and read the figures. Not only is it important for a pilot to know the aircraft's geographical position, but it is also important he/she understand what is happening in terms of aircraft flight heading, altitude and attitude and the future impact these characteristics will have on the flight.

Airplane Flight Instruments		
Airspeed Indicator- ASI		Pitot Pressure
Nu.1	Vso- Stall Speed with Flaps- Stuff Out	Landing Configuration Speed, Flaps Down
Nu.2	Vsi-Stall Speed – Stuff In	(Spesific, Clean Configuration)
Nu.3	Vfe – Max. Flap Extended Speed	Top of White Arch
Nu.4	Vno- Max. Structural Cruising Speed	Top of the Green Arch
Nu.5	Red Line- Vne	Never Exceed Speed
Attitude indicator (Artificial horizon) informs the pilot of the AC orientation to earth's horizon		Gyroscopic System (GS), principle of precession
Nu.6	Pointer-Index and Roll Pointer	Direction/degree of bank (Angle of Lateral Axis)
Nu.7	Pitch Lines, long :10°, short: 5°	Top (Blue), bottom (Brown)
Nu.8	Miniature Aircraft (Aircraft Symbol)	lateral axis indicates pitch
Nu.9	Artificial Horizon	gives immediate indication
Nu.10	Adjustment Knob	controls the artificial horizon
Nu.11	Banking Scale	10°, 20°, 30°, 60°, 90°
Turn and Slip Indicator		Gyroscopic System (GS)
Nu.12	Turn Needle (Airplane replica)	sensing rate-of-turn and roll.
Nu.13	Rolling Scale	
Nu.14	Inclinometer	
Nu.15	2-MIN, completes a 360° turn in 2 min.	_3° per second turn_.
Nu.16	Ball (for a coordinated flight.)	It has to be in the middle of tube.
Heading Indicator (HI)		Gyroscopic System (GS)
Nu.17	HI Manual Setting Knob	It needs to _be adjusted with Magnetic Compass_
Nu.18	Heading Indicator- Heading Bug	Manual Set
Vertical Speed Indicator (VSI)		Pitot-static System, shows rate of climb/descend, feet per minute (FPM)
Nu.19	Vertical Speed Indicator Needle	
Altitude Indicator (AI)		
Nu.20	Barometric Pressure twisting knob	Setting window (Inch-Hg or Milibar)
Nu.21	Altimeter Kollsman Window	

PRIVATE PILOT HANDBOOK

Figure-7 Airplane Primary Flight Instruments

Engine Instruments:

After starting engine, first action is <u>to adjust the RPM and monitor the oil pressure/temperature gauges</u> *(Figure-5, Nu.13)* to check if there is abnormal engine instrument indication. if the oil pressure doesn't begin to rise immediatly after an engine start in warm weather, the engine must be shutdown to avoid irreperable damage as the engine lubrication system is not operating properly. During the flight, You must monitor both the oil pressure and oil temperature gauges periodically to see if they remain within the normal operating range. <u>(If the oil level is too low, It may cause high oil temperature)</u>

The cylinder head temperature gauge provides a direct temperature reading from one or all of the cylinders.

Note: If the engine oil temperature and cylinder head temperature gauges have exceeded their normal operating range, avoid using <u>excess power and fully enrich the mixture, as fuel acts as a coolant. Land as soon as practicable.</u>

Aerodynamic Principles:
- **Introduction to Aerodynamics and First Flight :**

Aerodynamics is the study of objects in motion through the air and the forces that produce or change such motion. The theory of aerodynamics began with prehistoric man's desire to immitate the actions of birds and fly through the air. During the Renaissance, **Leonardo Da Vinci** foresaw the shape of things to come. Da Vinci correctly concluded that it was the movement of the wing relative to the air and the resulting reaction that produced the lift necessary to fly.

Hezarfen Ahmet Çelebi was the first person, inspired by the designs of Da Vinci, to design and produce a robust aerodynamic structure (eagle wings) like birds in order to fly in the 16th century.

Figure-8 The first flight in the history of the world

Çelebi completed the first flight in the history of the world **from Galata Tower to Uskudar over the Bosphorus in 1632**. The flight, which was welcomed with the intense enthusiasm by the people, stretched 3558 meters or just over two miles. *(Figure-8)*

On December 17, 1903, in North Carolina, Wilbur and Orville Wright *(The Wright Brothers)* made the first powered flight at Kitty Hawk with their first powered aircraft, lasting a mere 120 feet (35 meters). Aviation and aerodynamics have developed rapidly since 1903.

Aerodynamic Forces and Definitions:

Aerodynamics is the way air moves around Aircraft. The four forces of flight are **"lift, weight, thrust and drag."** These forces make an object move up and down, and faster or slower. How much of each force there is changes how the object moves through the air. Weight comes from gravity pulling down on objects. *(F = m x .a)* Lift works opposite of weight. Thrust works opposite of drag. *During* *straight-and-level, unaccelerated flight, the forces of thrust and drag are equal.*

As a promising student of aviation, you must fully understand the basic principles of aerodynamics and their effects on the aircraft and its associated systems, e.g.;

- **Airfoil.** (Lift, Drag, L/D Ratio) (See Figure 9-11)
- **Pressure Altitude (PA)**. When altitude is corrected for nonstandard pressure, the result is pressure altitude. Check Figure-48 and take note of how different pressure altitudes effect the performance of an aircraft; (ground roll at sea level, 30°C is 925 feet, at 2000 Feet, 30°C is 1110 feet.)
- **Newton's Third Law**. For every action, there is an equal and opposite reaction. Thrust *(forward action)*-Drag *(rearward reaction)*
- **Bernoulli's Principle.** Air moving over the curved surface of the wing moves faster than the air below. The fast moving air exerts less pressure on the wing than the slower-moving air below *(Figure-9)* That means there is greater pressure exerted on the bottom of the wing, resulting in lift.
- **Temperature Effects on Density.** Density altitude is the term for pressure altitude that has been corrected for nonstandard temperature. On a hot day the density altitude at an airport may be 1,000 or 2,000 feet higher than the field elevation, this means the airplane will perform as though the airport were at a higher elevation. The higher the te*mp*erature, the faster the molecules are moving. As the air is heated, the molecules speed up and spread out which means they push harder against their surroundings. *(Efficiency is reduced because the propeller exerts less force at high density altitudes and has less air to grab.)*

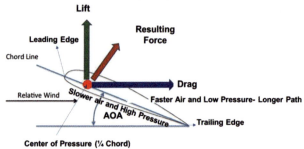

Figure-9 Bernoulli's Equation: Airfoil – Lift – Pressure – Velocity Relation

- **Pressure Effect on Density**. A number of factors -*altitude /pressure, temperature, and humidity)* influence the air density.
- **Angle of Attack (AOA)** is the angle between the oncoming air or relative wind and chord line. *(Figure-9)*
- **Moisture:** The density of the air varies inversely with the humidity. On damp days the air density is less than on dry days. This is because water has a lower molecular weight than nitrogen and oxygen. This means that airplane requires a longer takeoff and landing roll on humid days than it does on dry days.
- **Airfoil:** Airfoil is the wing that provides aerodynamic force once it is in motion through air, and the air is passing above and below the wing. (Figure-9) The differential pressure of air molecules creates a force on the wing that lifts the wing up into the air. The shape of an airplanes' wings is designed to take advantage of both Newton's laws *(minimum drag)* and Bernoulli's principle *(maximum lift)*.

The air pressure on the bottom of the airfoil is higher than on top.

When air passes above and below the airfoil, the air on top moves faster because of the curve (the air molecules must travel a greater distance in the same amount of time), this generates an area of lower air pressure known as Bernoulli's Principle. Bernoulli's principle states, "as the velocity of a fluid (air) increases, its internal pressure decreases. *(Figure-9)*

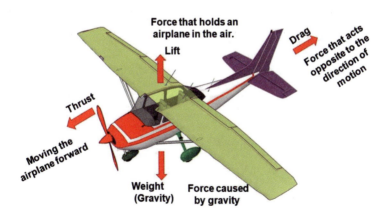

Figure-10 Aerodynamic Forces (4-Force) in Flight

How does this relate to flying an airplane? The air pressure is greater on the bottom side/surface of a wing, so it is pushed upward producing a force known as lift. Once the forces are balanced, a plane flies without

climbing or descending. See Figure-10.
Climb: Lift and Thrust > Weight and Drag
Descend: Weight and Drag > Lift and Thrust.

The amount of lift generated by an airplane is controlled by the pilot by changing the Angle of Attack (AOA), As a pilot, you can change the angle of attack and the airspeed or you can change the shape of the wing by lowering the flaps *(increase the angle of descent without increasing the airspeed.).* To put it simply, the pilot is in a position to manipulate the control of speed, altitude and attitude of the plane.

This balance of forces changes as the airplane climbs and descends, as it speeds up, slows down, and as it turns.

• **Drag:** Drag is the aerodynamic force that opposes an aircraft's motion through the air. Drag is generated by every part of the **airplane** *(even the wings, engines and propellers.)* In order to understand the theory of **Flight**, Aerodynamic forces such as Lift and Drag must be learned very well.

• **Types of Drag:** There are two basic types: Parasite and Induced Drag.

Parasite drag is the drag which is not associated with the production of lift and caused by any aircraft surface which deflects the airflow around the airplane, parasite drag increases with speed *(See Figure-11)*

Three types of Parasite Drag:

Form Drag is because of the shape and size of the aircraft. Flat/ sphere-shaped objects of airplane.

Interference Drag results from the intersection of airstreams that creates small whirlpool currents, turbulence, or restricts smooth airflow. (external tank under wing, wing root,)

Skin Friction Drag is the aerodynamic resistance due to the roughness of the airplane surfaces. Every surface may produce this drag. (e.g. antennas, pitot mast, engine cowling)

Induced drag is byproduct of lift, *decreases with speed.*
High pressure airflow from beneath the wing has the tendency to spill over the wingtips to equalize with the lower pressure above. When this happens, turbulent whirlpools called wingtip vortices form and create drag. Additionally, any time *the angle of attack is increased*, a portion of the wing's lift vector is angled backwards. This too creates more induced drag. *(An increase in the AOA increases the induced drag.)*

• **L/D Ratio (Lift-to-Drag Ratio):** In aerodynamics, the lift-to-drag ratio, or L/D ratio, is the amount of lift generated by a wing divided by the aerodynamic drag it creates by moving through the air. A higher L/D ratio is one of the major goals of aircraft designers.

This is a fundamental characteristic of the aerodynamics of a particular aircraft. L/D ratio varies with airspeed; for determining best engine-out glide performance, the L/D ratio at "best glide airspeed" is used. "Best glide airspeed" is the speed that maximizes the L/D ratio, and this maximum value is known as L/D max. *(Figure-11)*

For a Cessna 172, the L/D ratio (L/Dmax) is about 9, so its glide ratio is approximately 9:1. (This means that it will glide about 9,000 feet for every 1,000 feet of altitude available.)

For a Boeing 747, the L/D ratio (L/Dmax) is about 17 therefore, its glide ratio is about 17:1. Airliners tend to have significantly higher L/D ratios (12-20) than small aircraft.

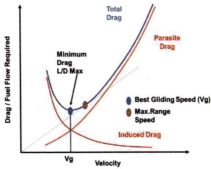

Figure-11 L/D Max (Lift/Drag Ratio)

• **Scientific Approach to Aerodynamic Forces:**

The four aerodynamic forces are in equilibrium during level, unaccelerated flight. The aerodynamic structure of the wing is designed to take advantage of both Newton's laws and Bernoulli's principle. According to Bernoulli's principle, the increase in speed of the air over the top of an airfoil produces a drop in pressure and this lowered pressure is a component of total lift.

The reaction to downwash from the top surface of the wing and the airstream striking the wing's lower surface causes a lifting action in accordance with Newton's third law of motion.

• **The Axes of the Airplane and Stability:**

Each airplane resists or responds to control pressures in different ways. A quick or slow response is related to the features of the plane. These features determine the *"Stability, Maneuverability, and Controllability characteristics of an Airplane"*. In order to better understand the three important factors, each student should be familiar with the basic concept of stability and its axes. Stability is a desirable characteristic of an aircraft in which it is able to maintain uniform flight characteristics or "balance" regardless of changing flight conditions such as movement of the

Center of Gravity (CG), Center of Lift (CL), speeds and attitudes. *(less effort to control.)* Figure-12 explains how to control the stability. Aerodynamic balance and controllability directly depends on the stability of the axes. *(Lateral, Vertical, Longitudinal and changes in the center of pressure of a wing.)*

Lateral Stability-Resistance to roll (fuel imbalance affects roll attitudes) *Lateral or roll stability is normally achieved by the upward angle of the wings, called dihedral.*

Longitudinal Stability–Resistance to pitch (related to CG)
Vertical Stability – Resistance to yaw (related to CG)

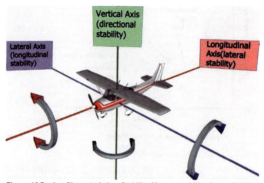

Figure-12 Design Characteristics: Stability, Maneuverability, Controllability..

Aerodynamic Forces in Flight Maneuvers:

- Forces During the Coordinated Turns: From the previous lesson It was given that there are four forces acting on the aircraft, lift, drag, thrust and weight. Figure-13A explains the forces in medium banked turn and steep banked turn. *(have this figure put in your memory for steep turns)*

- As a student pilot, using coordination (ball centered in the slip coordinator/lower part) for balanced turns is one of the simplest and most useful indicatons to determine the forces in turns. *(Slipping/Skidding)*. If the ball is on the inside *(wing down side)* of a turn, the aircraft is slipping, when the ball is on the outside (wing up side) of the turn, the aircraft is skidding

• **Forces in Turns:**

Three types of turns: Shallow (less than 20°), Medium (20° to 45°) and Steep Turns (45° or more). In order to better understand the turn aerodynamics, Pilot should be aware of the changing forces during the turns.

We have also previously discussed the four forces of flight, those being lift and weight that act in a "vertical direction" and thrust and drag in the "horizontal direction".

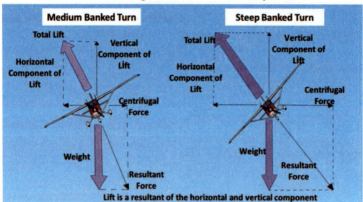

Figure-13A Aerodynamic Forces in Turns

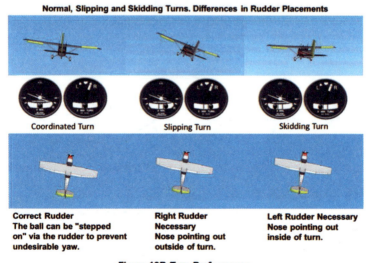

Figure-13B Turn Performance

All forces can be divided into their vertical and horizontal components. In Figure-13A, horizontal and vertical forces are shown to be changing with bank angle.

As long as the aircraft is in coordinated, level flight, these forces will remain balanced. When the aircraft is rolled into a medium/steep bank angle. *See Figure-13A,* the vertical component of lift is less than the weight. Because of this disparity, the greater force exerted by the weight relative to lift will pull the aircraft downward and it is unable to maintain the same altitude. To overcome this behavior a pilot is to pull the yoke *(stick)* back to increase the lift of the plane and maintain the same altitude. *The force turning the airplane is* the horizontal component of lift.

Centrifugal force is the "equal and opposite reaction" of the aircraft to the change in direction and acts equal and opposite to the horizontal component of lift.

How to avoid slipping and skidding in turns: The inability to coordinate during turns lead to both slips and skids. In Figure-13B, A slip is when the ball is to the inside of the turn and a skid is when the ball is to the outside of the turn.

Shortly, if you turn with no rudder, this results in **"SLIP"**, If you turn with much rudder, this results in **"SKID"**, to counteract this tendency, the pilot applies required rudder to balance the forces. *(Figure-13B)*

• **Forces in Climbs and Descends:** (Figure-14) Equilibrium is required for a steady climb and descent.

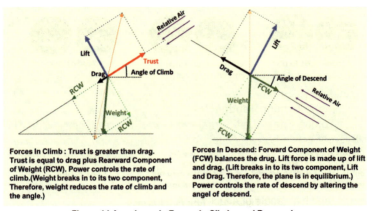

Forces In Climb : Trust is greater than drag. Trust is equal to drag plus Rearward Component of Weight (RCW). Power controls the rate of climb.(Weight breaks in to its two component, Therefore, weight reduces the rate of climb and the angle.)

Forces In Descend: Forward Component of Weight (FCW) balances the drug. Lift force is made up of lift and drag. (Lift breaks in to its two component, Lift and Drag. Therefore, the plane is in equilibrium.) Power controls the rate of descend by altering the angel of descend.

Figure-14 Aerodynamic Forces in Climbs and Descends

Note: During turns, rudder controls and coordination with aileron are very important to keep the airplane stabilized and to avoid slipping and skidding.

When the airplane begins climbing or descending it is necessary for the ratio of these forces to be temporarily altered as more/less thrust is required. Climbing requires an increase in the thrust to compensate for the increased drag associated with the increased angle of the aircraft. Descending requires lowering the nose of the aircraft and results in an angle of descent.

In straight & level flight thrust equals drag (T = D). In a climb, thrust must increase to equal drag plus the rearward component of weight. "thrust is greater than drag." In a descend, thrust must decrease with the nose down for a steady descend. Figure-14 explains the exchange of forces in both climbs and descents.

Constant airspeed descents and climbs are very important during flight in the traffic pattern.

Skills: Transition to the climb/descent pitch attitude, with the application of appropriate power settings, on an assigned heading, using proper instrument cross-check, interpretation, and coordinated flight control application. Pitch – Power – Trim (PPT)

Climb: Increase power smoothly, *(stop the resulting yaw with rudder).* This will cause the nose to pitch up, power and attitude should be considered a coordinated movement. Hold the wings level and trim the airplane to remove excess loads. (You should achieve a steady rate of climb at approximately 500 to 700 ft/min in most planes.)

Descent: Reduce the power, stop adverse yaw condition with rudder. The nose of the aircraft will want to pitch down. Hold the level attitude until the proposed descent airspeed is reached, and then select and hold the attitude for the descent. Use trim to remove any excess loads felt in the control column. Maintain wings level with aileron and balance with rudder.

- **Left-Turning Tendencies:**

<u>Torque Effect</u> (Left Turn Tendency of the airplane/Newton Third Law) Every action has an equal and opposite reaction *(propeller rotates clockwise, cockpit view, fuselage reacts counterclockwise)*, During the takeoff roll, pilot must use right rudder/rudder trim to correct for the torque effect. <u>The effects of torque are greatest at low airspeed, high RPM settings, and high angle of attack (AOA).</u>

P- Factor: Once the airplane flying at a high angle of attack, <u>the downward moving blade of propeller has higher velocity, therefore forming more lift than upward moving blade of propeller.</u> This asymmetrical loading of the propeller, (resulting from the difference in velocity) creates P-Factor, or the tendency of the airplane's nose to pull to the left. A pilot must apply right rudder during the takeoff roll and climb to compensate for P-Factor.

Spiraling Slipstream: The propeller creates a spiral of air that spins about the fuselage of the airplane and contacts the left side of the rudder creating an additional left-turning tendency.

Gyroscopic Precession: A spinning propeller (rotating disc) acts in a similar manner to a gyroscope, a force applied to the disc is felt 90° in the direction of rotation.

- **Load Factor:** *(Aerodynamic lift divided by aircraft weight)*

A Load Factor is <u>the ratio of the lift generated by an aircraft to its weight</u>. For example, a load factor of 3 means that the total load on an airplane's structure (mostly on lifting surfaces) is three times that of its gross weight, known as "3G's" or 3x the force of gravity. In an aircraft subjected to 3G's in pull up maneuver from a dive, the pilot will be pressed down in his/her seat by a force that is three times that of the person's weight in a static condition.

The load factor of an airplane is *determined by bank angle alone* and increases with steep turns *(45° bank turn, 1.5 X CG.)*, and abrupt changes in airplane attitude. Increasing load factor increases the stalling speed.

- **Traffic Pattern (TP):**

The traffic pattern at an airport is a standard path for coordinating the flow of air traffic. An aircraft using the traffic pattern remains close to the airport in a rectangular course sometimes called a racetrack. Airport traffic patterns (left/right hand) are developed to ensure that air traffic is flowing into and out of an airport safely. *(Check out the Airport Facility Directory A/FD, VFR Sectional Chart, See Figure- 16-17)*

Flight schools are mostly located in either Class D (controlled, towered) or Class G (uncontrolled, non-towered) airspace. There are several profound differences in the ways one may approach and enter the pattern. Here is the most pertinent explanation:

"When necessary, the ATC Unit (Tower) will issue clearances or other information for aircraft to follow on a desired flight or taxi path *(e.g., make straight in approach, report at 3 miles, clear left base Runway 10, etc.)*

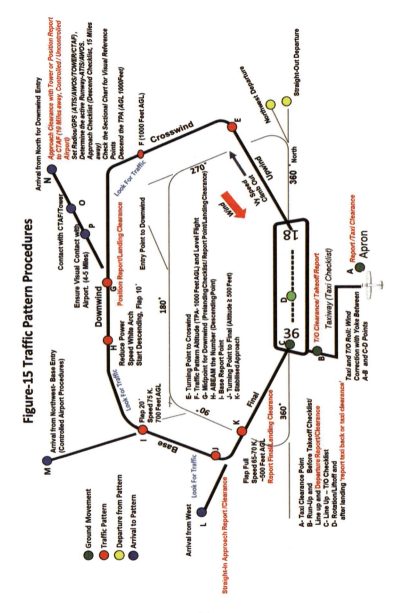

Figure-15 Traffic Pattern Procedures

All the procedures starting with engine start-up, taxiing, run-up checks, line up and take-off, call out points, checklist procedures should be practiced as much as possible during the ground training with CFI or AGI. In the ATC Glossary pages, VFR Communication Procedures including both controlled airspace and uncontrolled airspace have been explained in detail. (See Figure-53-54, Page 145)

During the daily routine training, You will commence the training with traffic pattern and after completing the required air work (or maneuvers) in the practicing area, you will be on the way to return to the airport of departure or in some cases a nearby airport to practice the takeoff and landing in the pattern, briefly, you will have to perform this path several times every day.

Keys to Traffic Pattern Procedures:
Daily Preflight Planning starts with preflight briefing in the flight School *(See Pg.89 for preflight planning)*

Takeoff:
- Airplanes on takeoff should continue straight ahead on the runway heading until beyond the departure end of the runway. Start turning to crosswind leg (X-wind) after reaching 300-500 feet.
- Turning Crosswind. Airplanes remaining in the traffic pattern should not commence a turn to the crosswind leg until beyond the departure end of the runway. *When flying the crosswind leg of a rectangular course the airplane must be crabbed into the wind.*
- Pilots should make the turn to downwind leg at the traffic pattern altitude.

Note: If departing the traffic pattern, continue straight out, or exit with a 45° turn (to the left when in a left-hand traffic pattern; to the right when in a right-hand traffic pattern) beyond the departure end of the runway.

Approach:
- Determination of traffic pattern flow is the vital importance.
- *Entry to the downwind leg should be at a 45° angle abeam the midpoint of the runway to be used for landing.* (1,000' AGL is recommended pattern altitude unless established otherwise. Check out the A/FD)
- Descent and Base Turn. The traffic pattern altitude should be maintained until the aircraft is at least abeam the approach end of the landing runway on the downwind leg. The base leg turn point is

approximately 45° relative bearing from the approach end of the runway. See the runway 45° behind your left shoulder before banking.
- Complete turn to final at least 1/4 mile from the runway and do not overshoot final or continue on a track, which will penetrate the final approach of the parallel runway, During the Pattern Work and Cross Country (XC) Flights, pilots must become familiar with all A/FD information pertinent to the flight route including at the departure/arrival airport, runways, practicing area, frequencies, NOTAMs, Flight School Weather Limitations, Traffic Pattern Altitude (TPA), right or left hand traffic pattern, frequencies, altitude limitations, NOTAM's, TFR and other restriction stated in A/FD, as well as back up plans if the flight can't be completed as planned.

Airspace Classifications:
There are five different classes of controlled airspace: A, B, C, D, and E airspace. Figure-16 defines the color code and altitude and airspeed limitations of airspaces. While operating in controlled airspace (Class A, Class B, Class C, Class D, and Class E) you are subject to certain operating rules,

Class G (Ground) airspace is the only form of "uncontrolled" airspace in the United States. Although ATC has no authority or responsibility to control air traffic, pilots should remember there are visual flight rules (VFR) minimums that apply to Class G airspace.

As a rule of thumb, there is a common question asked by examiner or CFI, by pointing out a spot in the VFR sectional chart, Which air space you are in? Answer: Inside the shaded magenta surface to 700 feet AGL, outside the shaded magenta surface to 1200 AGL. (*Figure-17, KOBE Airport*) (blue and red circles) Class G airspace typically extends from the surface to the base of the overlying controlled airspace.

There are almost no requirements for VFR aircraft flying in Class G airspace, other than certain cloud clearance and visibility requirements. <u>When the weather conditions deteriorate from VFR minimum to IFR,</u> the aircraft either must be flown by instrument-rated pilots in accordance with IFR clearances issued by ATC in controlled airspace or Special VFR (SVFR) must be requested by the pilot & approved by ATC.

The Airman's Information Manual (AIM) describes "Class E airspace may be designated as extensions to Class B, Class C, Class D, and Class E surface areas. (See Figure-16-18) <u>Class E Surface with extension from Class D.</u> The extensions provide controlled airspace to contain standard instrument approach procedures without enforcing a communications requirement on pilots operating under VFR.

Chart Suplement A/FD - Airport Facility Director

Miami, Sectional Chart

Traffic Pattern Altitude,
Fixed Wing 798', Rotary
Wing 498' AGL.

The Airport/Facility Directory (abbreviated A/FD), provides comprehensive information on airports, facilities and operations. Traffic pattern altitudes for propeller-driven aircraft generally extend from 600 feet to as high as 1,500 feet above the ground. Unless otherwise indicated, all turns in the traffic pattern should be made to the left.

A sketch map provides a visual orientation of airport's layout including the runways, nearby obstructions, residential areas, and primarily trees. For more information Refer to A/FD LEGEND (FAA Chart Supplement)

Class D Airspace, Blue dashed lines, from the surface to 2,500 feet AGL. Class D is not always a perfect circle, Because PMP Class D airspace is within the Class B airspace in the Southeast Florida area and close by other Class D Airspace, Its shape has been modified. *(Solid Magenta within 30-Mile Circle)*

Pompano Beach (PMP) Airport Data ,Control Tower Freq.124.5 * Part-time Operation Control Tower, ATIS Freq. 120.55, 29 Elevation in feet, L- Pilot Controlled Lightning /Refer to A/F, 49- Lenght of Longest Runvay- 4900 Feet, 122.95 UNICOM Freq.

Miami Class B airspace, furthest surrounding in the Southeast Florida area. (Thin Solid Magenta within 30-Mile Circle)

Fort Lauderdale Executive Airport (FXE), Class D airspace within the Class C (Fort Lauderdale FLL)and Class B airspace (Miami MIA)

Class D Airport, Pompano Beach (PMP),

Class C Airport, Fort Lauderdale (FLL), designated by solid magenta lines, from the surface up to 4,000'. First Layer from the surface up to 4,000' with a 5-nm radius. Second layer from 1200' to 4000' wirhin 10 nm.

Class B Airport, Miami (MIA), Upside down wedding Cake, from the ground surface up to 7,000 feet MSL, designated by Thick Blue Lines.
ATC Clearance required, two-way radio comm., MODE C Transponder (Altitude Reporting),

Class G, Uncontroled Airport, Miami Homestead General Aviation Airport- X51, ATC has no authority or responsibility, visual flight rules (VFR) minimums that apply to Class G airspace. Inside the shaded magenta surface to 700 feet AGL (blue circle), outside the shaded magenta surface to 1200 AGL (red circle).

Questions to find out how much knowledge you have:
1. You lost 2-way communication? What action should be taken?
2. Which airspace altitude, VFR limitations?
3. Can You plan to make a fuel stop? Why? 4. Which airspace you're in?
What are the VFR Minimums for T/O and landing to Nu.5?
6. Airspace Limitations?
7. What does 100/60 mean?
8. What does 1² mean?
9. Meritt Island Airport, you plan X-C flight from KCOI to KDED to KINF? What kind of facilities are available en route?
10. Is that possible to go for training at LM-ETS, Nu.10?
11. Explain the obstruction, What does 1949 (1874) mean ?

Figure-16 Airport Facility Director- A/FD and Airspace Classifications

PRIVATE PILOT HANDBOOK

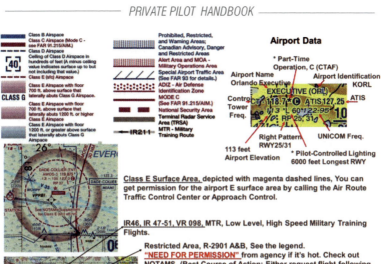

Airport Data

* Part-Time Operation, C (CTAF)
Airport Name — Orlando Executive
Airport Identification — KORL
Control Tower Freq. — 118.7
ATIS — 127.25
Right Pattern RWY25/31
113 feet Airport Elevation
* Pilot-Controlled Lighting 6000 feet Longest RWY
UNICOM Freq.

<u>Class E Surface Area</u>, depicted with magenta dashed lines, You can get permission for the airport E surface area by calling the Air Route Traffic Control Center or Approach Control.

<u>IR46, IR 47-51, VR 098</u>, MTR, Low Level, High Speed Military Training Flights.

Restricted Area, R-2901 A&B, See the legend.
<u>"NEED FOR PERMISSION"</u> from agency if it's hot. Check out NOTAMS. (Best Course of Action: Either request flight following from center or go around.). You cannot fly through the dimensions of a restricted airspace without getting permission from the controlling agency (usually Center, Miami.) If the airspace is <u>*"active," "open," or "hot"*</u> they will deny you permission, and you will have to go around.

MOA, <u>"No Need for Permission"</u> if it's Hot, be cautious.

Untowered Airport, KOBE, Okeechobee, Class G Airspace, typically extends from the surface to the base of the overlying controlled airspace (Class E), Why does the Class E airspace suddenly drop from 1,200 feet AGL to 700 feet AGL in blue circle? Think of it like Class B,C and D airspace, it drops down to protect aircraft on approach or departure to and from airport runways.. Blue Circle (Class G Up to, But Not Including, 1200 feet AGL, Red Circle (Class G Up to, But Not Including,1.200 feet AGL on outside, 700 feet inside the vignette) See Figure-18-19

Prohibited Area, P-50, <u>*"NEVER ENTER N/A"*</u> Check for the details of identification Number (P50) on Sectional Chart, Legend Information.

Untowered Airport, , KCOI, Merritt Island, Class G Airspace. What altitude does Class G extend up to at KCOI ? <u>Up to, but not including, 700 feet AGL.</u> Weather minimums during the day below 1,200' AGL in Class G airspace is 1 mile visibility and clear of clouds. How far out should pilot start announcing his/her position/intentions on CTAF? The AIM recommends Pilots start self-announcing at a distance of 10NM.

Warning Area, blue hatched lines, W-497B, <u>"NO need for permission"</u> if it's Hot, be cautious for aerial gunnery and guided missiles, 3NM outward from the coast of US. Check for the details of identification Number (W-497B) on Sectional Chart, Legend Information.

<u>Air Defense Identification Zones (ADIZs)</u>, All aircraft entering U.S. domestic airspace from points outside must provide for identification prior to entry or exit.

Figure- 17 How To Read A Sectional Chart

35

The airport is a class D (blue dashed line) while the rectangle off of it is Class E Extension (surface to 700 ft AGL) because of the magenta dashed lines. This extension of Class E airspace coincides with an instrument procedure.
The Magenta Vignette is Class E (700ft to 1200ft AGL). The reason why it's only a part-time tower, so an IFR flight can talk to the ATC all the way to the ground. The Class E rectangle is even lined up with the runway. It's also important to know the Class E takes over when the Class D Tower is closed.

This is a group of obstacles with high intensity lights that is higher than 1000 ft AGL (notice the different shape, the top of the M is skinnier and longer). Down in the left hand corner you'll see again the MSL height and (AGL in parentheses.)

This is a group of obstacles (the M shape means more than one). The numbers besides is MSL. The AGL height is not always available due to close by sea level. They are less than 1000ft AGL.

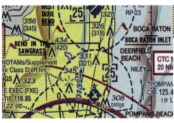

VFR Reporting Point- Magenta Flag Bend In Sawgrass

In black letting is the name of the reporting point. This may be used on the way back to an airport to let ATC know your specific position. It lets Tower know where you are, especially if you don't know the exact mileage away you are.

Merritt Island, COI,This is an uncontrolled airport. You can also see this uncontrolled airport doesn't have a beacon (no star sign). It does have fuel services though. you can see it has AWOS-3 on 119.025, altitude of the airport – 06 ft. It is lighted, which is denoted by the L, the star in front of it means the lighting operations are limited so check the A/FD. 36 is telling you the length of the longest runway in hundreds of feet. Lastly, is the CTAF frequency. The C is denoting it's the CTAF 122.975

Figure- 18 How To Read A Sectional Chart

Figure-19A Airspace Classification

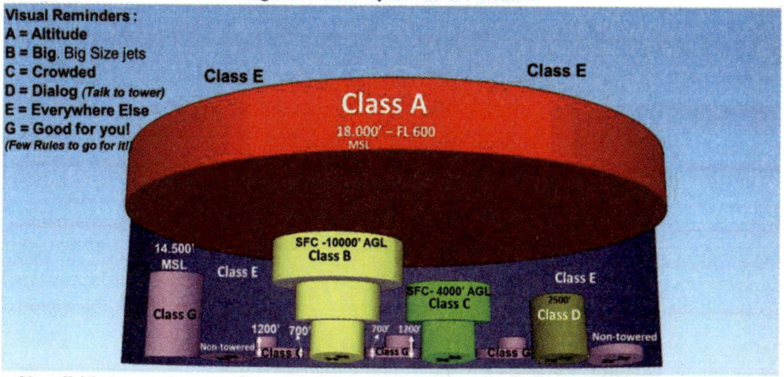
Visual Reminders:
A = Altitude
B = Big. Big Size jets
C = Crowded
D = Dialog (Talk to tower)
E = Everywhere Else
G = Good for you!
(Few Rules to go for it!)
Class E
Class E
Class A
18.000' - FL 600
MSL
14.500'
MSL
Class G
Class E
SFC -10000' AGL
Class B
SFC- 4000' AGL
Class C
Class E
2500'
Class D
1200'
700'
700'
1200'
Non-towered
Class G
Class G
Class G
Non-towered

- Class E All airspace between Class A and G, In most areas, the Class E airspace base is 1,200 feet AGL.
- Class G Uncotrolled, upper-limit varies. Class G airspace extends from the SFC to the base of the overlying Class E airspace.

Airspace VFR Weather Minimums (14 CFR 91.155)			Reminder
Class A			No VFR
Class B			3, CoC
Class C			3, 152's
Class D			3, 152's
Class E	Less than 10,000' MSL		3, 152's
	At or Above 10.000' MSL		5, 111
Class G (Uncontroled)	1,200' or less AGL	Day	1, CoC
		Night	3, 152's
	More than 1200' AGL but less than 10,000 MSL	Day	1, 152's
		Night	3, 152's
	At or Above 10,000'		5,111

CoC: Clear of Clouds.
3, 152's: 3 SM Visibility, 1000' Above, 500' Below, 2000' Horizontal.
5,111 : 5 SM Visibility, 111- 1000' Below, 1000' Above, 1 SM Horizontal.
*** Unless otherwise authorized, maximum indicated airspeed below 10,000 feet MSL is 250 Kt.**

Figure-19B Airspace VFR Weather Minimums

Taxiing in Wind:
The main idea of wind correction by aileron deflection is to prevent the wind from "picking up" a wing or the tail and turning the airplane over as the pilot is taxiing around. You will be expected to show "proper aileron deflection" during your check ride.

For example, How should the flight controls be held while taxiing a tricycle-gear equipped airplane with a left quartering tailwind?

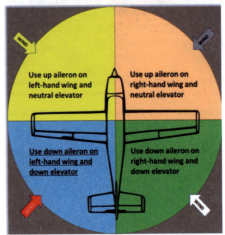

Figure-20 Wind Correction During Taxi, Aileron and Elevator deflection

"Climb into the wind, dive away from the wind"

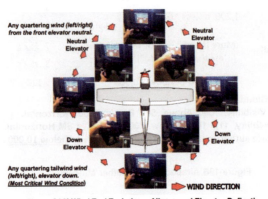

Figure-21 X-Wind Taxi Technique, Aileron and Elevator Deflection

PRIVATE PILOT HANDBOOK

Run-Up Procedure:

(Checklist Items: Checks performed by pilots on an aircraft just prior to take-off.)

The main purpose of run-up checks on a single engine piston aircraft is to test the engine and associated instruments. Engine run-up consists of usually of checking the aircraft's carburetor heat and a quick check of the airplane's magnetos as well as the basic engine instruments such as oil pressure, oil temperature and cylinder head temperature, suction gage and ammeter.

As a student pilot, you're supposed to taxi to the run-up area and stop in the run-up area just short of the active runway to go through the before takeoff checks. You run through the tasks all pilots would associate with this checklist...flight controls, trim set, engine run up with magnetos, carburetor heat check, idle and instrument checks. After bringing the engine to 1000 RPM, you will turn to CFI/DPE and say, **"Run-up check completed, I'm all set...you ready sir?"**

NOTE: Don't forget to lean the mixture before taxi to run-up area. Right sequence of lean procedure: Startup, lean, taxi checklist complete, taxi to the run-up area and perform run-up check and takeoff.

At the core of the run-up procedure is the magneto check, during the magneto check, the drop "must not exceed 50 RPM between magnetos." Check out AFM/POH.

Figure-22 Preflight Magneto Check Key and Engine Tachometer

Basic Maneuvers (Air Work - The Four Fundamentals):

To be a competent pilot requires mastery of the four basic flight maneuvers upon which all flying tasks are based: *straight-and-level flight, turns, climbs, and descents.* Reminder: While flying VFR, instruments are secondary. Outside reference of the aircraft, especially the horizon line, is the primary source for keeping the aircraft straight and level.

The only instrument that displays *an accurate, instantaneous indication of pitch* is the attitude indicator. The four fundamentals demonstrate the coordination between yoke (stick) and rudder (due to P-Factor, Torque Effect) and Power Lever (PPT). Applying with correct trim and power, let the airplane fly hands-off. Training airplanes are built to be very stable to make the training easier. *(the airplane remains stable and responsive.)*

Straight and level flight is flight in which heading and altitude are constantly maintained. If altitude is being gained or lost, the pitch attitude or power should be readjusted in relation to the horizon.

- **Constant Airspeed Climbs and Level Off:** *(PPT- Pitch, Power, Trim)* Clear the area, apply full power, then apply gentle back elevator pressure to initiate and maintain the climb altitude, and the desired climb speed. Before reaching the desired altitude (50 feet before), Apply smooth/steady forward elevator toward level flight altitude and reduce power for the speed desired.

- **Climbing Turns:** Clear the area, establish the climb first by applying gently back elevator pressure and then bank into (roll into) the turn or climb and turn simultaneously. During climbing turns, as in any turn, the decrease in vertical lift component must be compensated by an increase in pitch altitude.

- **Constant Airspeed Descends and Level Off:** Clear the area, Descending action can be commenced by reducing power, lowering the nose to a pitch altitude lower than the level flight altitude,

- **Descending Turns:** Clear the area, establish the descent first by applying gently forward elevator pressure, reduce power and then bank into (roll into) the turn or descend and turn simultaneously.

Note: Lead level-off by 10 percent of the vertical velocity (e.g. 500 foot-per-minute rate of climb/descend on the vertical speed indicator, begin leveling off 50 feet before your desired altitude).

- **Turns to Headings**: Clear the area, before starting the turn to any new direction/heading the pilot should hold the airplane straight and level and determine in which direction the turn is to be made. Roll into the turn by using coordinated aileron and rudder pressure in the direction/heading of the desired turn and establish the desired bank angle.

At approximately 10 degrees before reaching the desired heading *(less lead for small heading changes),* coordinated aileron and rudder pressures should be applied to roll the wings level/stop the turn.

Visualised Flight Training Maneuvers:

Takeoffs: *(Normal Takeoff, Crosswind Takeoff, Short Field /Soft Field Takeoff)*
- **Normal Takeoff.** (FART Checklist: Flap, Aileron, Rudder, Trim)

A normal takeoff is one in which the airplane is headed into the wind, the takeoff surface should be firm and of sufficient length to permit the airplane to reach the rotation speed and gradually accelerate to normal lift-off and climb-out speed,

55/60 knots is considered to be the optimum takeoff (rotation speed) speed. *(Check the POH/AFM)* This speed will allow enough lift under the wings to give a smooth, stall-free takeoff.

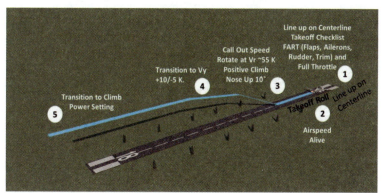

Figure-23 Normal Takeoff, Climb and Rejected Takeoff Procedures

Steps to be followed on Normal Takeoff: *Figure-23*

- Complete the appropriate checklist and make radio calls as appropriate. Verify the assigned/correct runway.
- Clear the area; taxi into takeoff position and align the airplane on the runway centerline
- Confirm takeoff power and proper engine and flight instrument indications prior to rotation
- Monitor positive acceleration on takeoff roll *(Call outs: speed alive, 40,55 and rotate)*

- Rotate and lift off at the recommended airspeed and accelerate to VY (positive rate of climb)
- Climb (transition to Vy (best rate of climb) and flap settings)

- **Rejected Takeoff and Engine Failure in Takeoff/Climb Phase of Flight.**

If we lose engine before the departure, cut the power hold the breaks and exit from runway,

If we lose engine before 1000 feet, turn 20-30 degrees right or left, and land straight ahead.

If we lose above 1000 feet, try get back the airport! At this point, your knowledge of aerodynamics is crucial. As you roll into a turn, your vertical lift decreases and your horizontal lift increases. Which option is safer? Returning the runway or planning a forced landing to the field ahead or either side of the takeoff path!

Note: Discuss the possible conditions with your CFI if you decide to return the runway.

- **Normal Approach and Landing:**

The most difficult part of learning to fly is mastering landings. It takes a long to learn. The proper landing procedure always requires a stabilized approach. For a good landing, you should be familiar with new concepts such as **"peripheral vision, looking sideways, following the horizon to keep the runway centerline and determining the flare altitude."** Therefore, landing includes slow flight, stall and ground reference maneuvers.

Don't Forget **"Learning is a result of experience."** **Practice, Practice, Practice.**

Here are the 5-step on final approach for a safe and perfect landing: Assuming that wind is calm and visibility is OK.

- Complete all pre-landing checklist before turning base leg *(mixture full rich, fuel selector on both, flaps as required, Carb. Heat is Hot (If available), All engine instruments are in green etc.)*
- Stabilized Approach: Turn the final approach, full flap setting,
- Use pitch, power and trim to control the speed and altitude (PPT), airspeed and altitude (glide path) control, direction of aircraft *(keeping the plane aligned with the runway center line).*

If you are high, reduce the power as needed and pitch down to keep the speed in limits.

If you are low, apply power and pitch up as required to keep the Airspeed in limits on final approach.

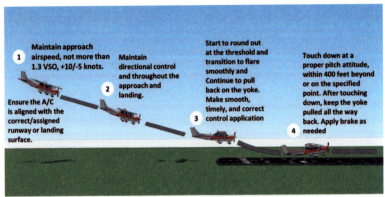

Figure-24 Normal Approach and Landing Procedures

<u>Note:</u> *Number 1-2 : Establish the recommended approach and landing configuration and airspeed, and adjust pitch altitude and power to maintain a stabilized approach. Number 3: Recognize the round-out altitude (10 feet) and swift transition to the flare altitude (3-5 feet) with simultaneous idling of power. Number 4: Look at far end or sideway to get reference how high you are.. If you are over flare, just stop applying additional back pressure.*

Note: Base to final: Keep the altitude more than ~500 ft AGL on your turn to base leg. Keep the speed over 60-65 K. *(See POH or 1.3 Vs)*

 - Flare Altitude: Flare-point recognition is the most important part of safe and perfect landing. When you reach the flare altitude *(3-5 feet off the ground)* gently reduce the power all the way back *(throttle idle cut off)*, keep the plane level by increasing amount of back pressure on the yoke. *Figure-24/4.*

 - During flare, avoid floating, keep final approach speed (VsX1.3)

Notes:
 - *When lining up to take off, note the height of the aircraft above the ground and the picture straight ahead. (just till landing issue is solved)*
 - *Start to round out at the threshold and transition to flare smoothly and continue to pull back on the yoke. (the round out is the transition from the approach glide path to the hold off the runway.(flare))*
 - *At the threshold, look at the far end or sideway to get reference on how*

high you are and decide how to make the landing easy in accordance with the wind, crosswind and, gust conditions.
- If you over 'flare', just stop applying additional back pressure.
- After touching down, keep the yoke pulled all the way back. (To minimize the side loads placed on the landing gear during touchdown, the pilot should keep the longitudinal axis of the aircraft parallel to the direction of its motion.)
- Apply brakes as needed to leave the runway safely until reaching taxi speed (a fast walking pace) and turn off at the nearest taxiway. (Don't stop until you pass the hold short line.)

Important Advice for Stabilized Approach and Landing:

- If you are not stabilized on approach (glidepath, attitude, speed), Do not get focused on recovering from a bad situation – GO AROUND.
- If the aircraft sinks, this indicates you speed is reducing and the need to increase AoA to maintain lift. Keep pitching up until you reach the right glide path *(observe the VASI/PAPI lights).* See Pg. 153
Basic things you have to get across on short final:
  * Reduce the rate of descent gradually so that the impact with the ground is within the limits of the aircraft.
  * Use peripheral vision to judge rate of closure with the ground.
  * Recognize the round-out altitude (10 feet) and rapid, smooth transition to the flare altitude *(3-5 feet)* with simultaneous idling of power.
  * "Flare" is the only way you need to hold the nose up higher to allow the airplane speed to decay.

What is Forward slip? *(Forward slip is to lose altitude)*
    Slip can also be used for final approach to lose the altitude, steepen the approach, where you put the airplane out of balance to increase drag, allowing more rapid descents without increasing airspeed.
    If you realize you're high to final with calm wind, it's time to start a forward slip. What are the inputs?

- Apply full rudder and simultaneously opposite aileron as needed to hold straight path to quickly descend without gaining airspeed.
- Maintain the safety margin above stall speed with full flap setting.
(Check out POH/AFM) Some aircraft cannot be slipped with full flaps.

Overall, it is a very safe maneuver and can be very helpful when done properly.
Note: Configure the airplane for landing with full flaps, determine if any crosswind condition, if there's a crosswind, bank into the wind, yaw the airplane's nose in the opposite direction of bank by applying opposite rudder.

- **Go Arounds:** *(Rejected landings)*

Safety in flight sometime requires you to execute a go-around while on final approach to landing.

Go-around procedures differ based on the aircraft you're flying, but the basic principles are the same: power up, pitch up, clean up. The go-around is not an inherently difficult procedure.

"If you are not stabilized on approach *(glidepath, speed, wind shear etc.),* Do not get focused on recovering a deteriorating situation – GO AROUND". It's as simple as that. Go-arounds are not shameful!

Basic Steps for Safe Go Around:
- Power: Increase to full power (Ensure Carb. Heat is OFF)
- Elevator pressure: Apply

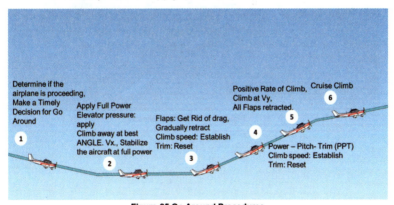

Figure-25 Go Around Procedures

Note: Raising flaps will cause further loss of height (certain amount of sink) until airspeed is increased and a positive climb is established.

- Stabilize the aircraft at full power. Pay attention to lose minimum altitude.
- Flaps: Gradually retract to get rid of drug. *(Do not raise the flaps*

until safely away from the ground)
      - Climb speed: Establish
      - Trim: Reset.

- **Crosswind Takeoff:**

A good crosswind takeoff starts on the ramp by observing the windsock. Every aircraft has crosswind limitations, so, check the wind sock before you throttle up. When the takeoff roll begins, the upwind aileron should be fully deflected in an upward direction *(yoke turned toward the wind)* to prevent the upwind wing from rising in gusts. Reduce the aileron deflection somewhat as the aircraft accelerates and the controls become more responsive.

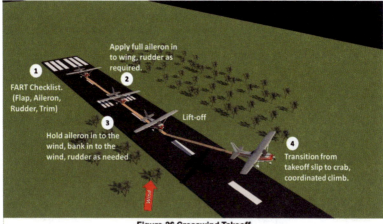

Figure-26 Crosswind Takeoff

The perfect takeoff sequence for a crosswind is: First, nose wheel, second downwind wheel, third upwind wheel in order to keep the airplane centerline after rotation. If you're facing up to a significant crosswind, you have to use the same procedures regardless of the type and weight of the aircraft.

Note: For a perfect croswind takeoff: Aileron position in to the wind should be maintained while the airplane is accelerating until the ailerons become effective and responsive at which time aileron deflection should be decreased to maintain wings level. Be ready to quickly apply whatever rudder pressure/deflection is required to keep the airplane rolling straight down the runway. (Torque Effect and P-Factor)

- **Crosswind Approach and Landing: (Wing-Low Landing)**
Mastering crosswind landing is the key point of training.

Crosswind limits the airplane, crosswind limitations in the POH are not suggestions, they were derived from testing, using average piloting techniques. Crosswind effects which runway is being used for takeoff and landings, how you ll perform the takeoff and landing, and most importantly, whether or not operation is sate to take off and land. (Go/No-go decision)

Crosswind landing technique is the wing-low landing. *(Sideslip technic)* Cross-Control is essential to keep the airplane aligned with the centerline.

Tactics for Perfect Crosswind Landing:
- Crab Method on Final Approach till round out altitude,
- During the transition to flare, use wing-low Landing.
- Just before touchdown, you have to step on the rudder to align your nose with the runway,
- Simultaneously use the ailerons to prevent drifting with the effect of crosswind.
- During all stages, maintain directional control and appropriate crosswind correction throughout the approach and landing.

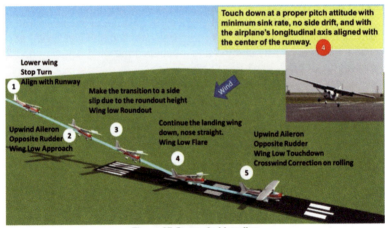

Figure-27 Crosswind Landing

Note: Landing in a strong, gusty crosswind is challenging. Investigation of runway excursions on landing where the crosswind has been a significant factor usually identify the following factors:

- *Inappropriate pilot decision to attempt a landing. (Insufficient judgment)*
- *Insufficient Crosswind Landing Skill.*
- *Incomplete understanding of the aircraft performance limitations.*

Strong crosswinds with gust, low visibility, and turbulence can affect a pilot's ability to execute a smooth landing. Do not attempt to salvage an airplane having <u>severe bouncing, porpoising, floating conditions</u> during landing. Otherwise, these conditions can cause a hard landing. Hard landing is one kind of typical landing incident that airplane hits the ground with a greater vertical speed and force than in a normal landing.

If you are unsure of your setup for landing, immediately execute a go-around.

How to calculate Crosswind Component:

In order to determine the crosswind component of the wind, we need actual wind conditions of airports *(ATIS, AWOS etc.)* and active runway, crosswind graph *(Apply POH/AFM.)*

In the graphic, (Figure-28)

- Curved Lines defines the actual wind speed as mostly knots. (wind 330°/ 20 Knots)
- Diagonal straight lines defines the wind directions relative to the direction of the plane *(angle between wind direction and flight path)* In our example: wind velocity and the angle between the wind direction and the runway is 30° *(330-300:30°)*
- Crosswind Component: 10 K. Headwind Component: 18 K.

Note: (1) Most light aircraft have a demonstrated X-wind figure in the POH. (2) <u>To determine the best runway to land on</u> and take off, <u>divide by the wind direction</u> by ten (330/10:33) and use the runway that is long enough whose name is closest to the result. (Rwy. 30 is the closest the 33.)

— PRIVATE PILOT HANDBOOK —

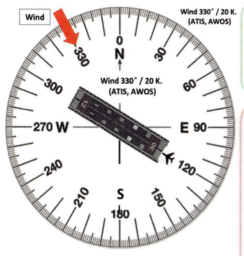

Wind 330° / 20 K. (ATIS, AWOS)

Wind 330° / 20 K. (ATIS, AWOS)

Easy Formula: The crosswind component is equal to the speed (V) of the wind multiplied by the sin ∞ of the angular difference (XWC = V × Sin ∞).
(Sin 30°: ½, Sin 45°: 0.7, Sin 60° : 0.8 Sin 90°: 1)
Therefore, in the example given below (Rwy 30 – W/V 330°/20 K) the angular difference is 30° (330-300), and the Sin ∞ of 30 degrees is 0.5. XWC: 20x0.5: 10 K.

Runway directions 30 and 12 (300° and 120°, truncating the last digit). This's a little confusing for new beginners, Runway we're facing is the direction of Runway for takeoff/landing. In the example, We're facing Runway 30, which means 300° heading on Heading Indicator and Compass. When you line up for Runway 30, HSI/DG and Compass should indicate Runway Direction. If not, set the DG accordingly just before takeoff.
One of the most important checklist Items (Line-up Checklist) before takeoff is to confirm the runway heading.
The main purpose of calculating crosswind component is to <u>find out the most favorable runway for safety</u> flight, especially during the flight training at uncontrolled airport, It is absolutely essential to calculate XWC in terms of safety marjins of airplane stated in the Pilot Operating Handbook (POH)

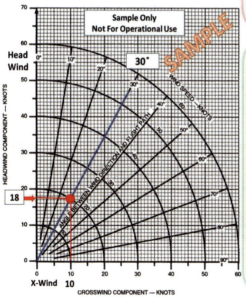

Reported Wind 330° / 20 K.
According to ATIS, the current runway in use is 30. Is this runway acceptable?
How to solve the problem ?
Determine the angular difference between the wind direction and the runway (Angle Between Wind Direction and Flight Path) 330°- 300°: 30°
Find the intersection of the 30° angle radial line and the 20-knot wind speed arc on the graph shown in Figure.
From the intersection ● move straight down to the bottom of the chart and read that the crosswind component equals 10 knots. From the point of intersection move horizontally left and read that the headwind component equals about 18 knots.
Croswind component of current wind conditiĝons is acceptable for Runway 30.
Crosswind Component: 10 K.
Headwind Component: 18 K.
(Note: Refer to the POH/AFM to find out maximum demonstrated crosswind for your aircraft.)

Figure- 28 How to Find a Crosswind Component (XWC)

- **Short Field Takeoff and Max. Performance Climb:** *(shortest ground roll and the steepest angle of climb.)*

When the takeoff area is short or available takeoff area is restricted by obstructions, the pilot should perform the short field takeoff. Let's break it down into six phases: before takeoff, takeoff roll, liftoff, initial climb and climb via runway heading.

- Prior to Takeoff: Flaps-10 degrees, use all available runway, set trim and wind correction. *(FART Checklist: Flaps, Aileron, Rudder, Trim)*
- Hold brakes, Apply full power/check engine instruments.
- Takeoff Roll. Control the elevator by pulling yoke slightly back *(means slightly tail low)*, Don't allow the nose wheel to come off the ground at the beginning of roll.
- Rotation, Liftoff at 50/55 K. *(Refer to the POH/AFM)*
- Initial Climb, monitor positive climb at VSI, pitch for Vx *(best angle of climb)* and smooth transition to Vy *(best rate of climb)* speed *(recommended climbing for Vy 50 feet)* after safely cleared the obstacles, Note: As soon as speed is alive, pull the yoke slightly aft to keep weight off nose wheel.

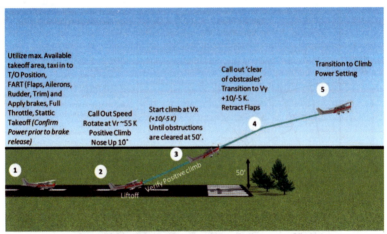

Figure-29 Short Field Takeoff and Max. Performance Climb

- Retract the Flaps according to the Airplane's POH. Then normal climb out.

- **Short Field Approach and Landing:**
(Descent at Minimum Safe Airspeed, 1.3 Vso +5/10 Kt.)
Short-field landing is a challenging procedure for pilots when the length of the runway or landing area is relatively short, or where obstacles in close vicinity to the landing approach limit the available landing area and mostly the runway have a displaced threshold.

4-Step for Stabil Short Field Approach and Landing:
- Set the final approach speed – 55/65 Kt. *(fly no faster than 1.3 VSO.)* Until Flare *(Apply POH/AFM)*. Advise the CFI/DPE the aiming point to touch. *(select the most suitable touchdown point. Mostly touchdown zone marking or designation marking.(+200/-50 feet) See Figure-60)*

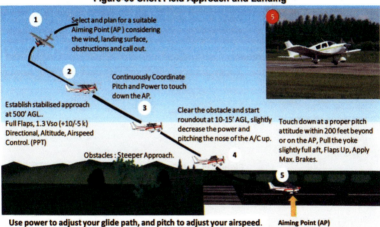

Figure-30 Short Field Approach and Landing

Use power to adjust your glide path, and pitch to adjust your airspeed.   Aiming Point (AP)

Start descending the glide path, Set elevator trim - just high enough to clear obstacle at approach end of runway. *(Figure-30)*

- Power – Reduce to idle after clearing obstacle and Flare - minimum float.

- After touchdown *(within 200 feet beyond or on the specified point)*, Flaps up, Maximum braking, Control wheel full aft.

- **Soft Field Takeoff:**
In a soft-field takeoff, your objective is to get the wheels off the ground as soon as possible, eliminating the surface drag and lightening the load on the landing gear due to increased drug with snowy, tall grassy or muddy runway surface, not paved and smooth runway ahead of you.

Here are the phases for a perfect Soft Field Takeoff: takeoff roll, liftoff and ground effect and initial climb.

 - Prior to Takeoff: Flaps - 10 degrees, set trim and wind correction *(FART Checklist),* apply full power without stopping and check engine instruments.
 - Takeoff Roll. Full aft elevator while taxiing and during initial takeoff roll.

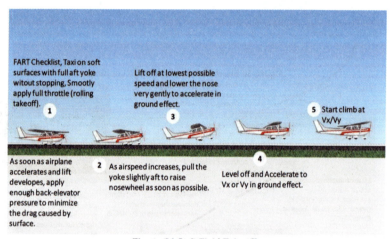

Figure-31 Soft Field Takeoff

Note: Establish and maintain a pitch altitude that will transfer the weight of the airplane from the wheels to the wings ASAP. Apply very fine control touch.

 - As nose wheel lifts off, reduce elevator slightly to avoid tail striking ground,
 - As aircraft becomes airborne, level off in ground effect and transition to Vx or Vy . (If no obstacle ahead of you, direct to Vy Speed.) then normal climb out
 - Retract the flaps according to the POH.

Note: During Taxi on soft surfaces, Apply full aft yoke.

* Ground Effect *is the increased lift (force) and decreased aerodynamic drag that an aircraft's wings generate when they are close to a fixed surface. This results in becoming airborne before reaching liftoff speed.*

- **Soft Field Landing:**
Soft field landings are pretty much the same as normal landings, till reaching the runway threshold. Flare and fly in the ground effect, transfer the aircraft weight from the wings to the main wheels as gently as possible. *(See Figure-32)*

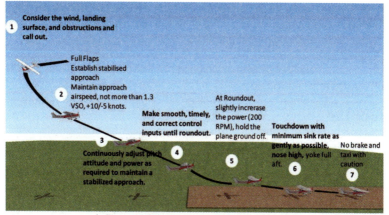

Figure-32 Soft Field Approach and Landing

Note: Soft Field landing is same as normal landing technique during the approach, At flare, hold the airplane 2 feet off the surface as long as possible while dissipating airspeed. Add slightly power to control minimum sink rate.

5-Step for Stabil Soft Field Approach and Landing:
- Normal approach configuration (not more than 1.3 VSO)
- During flare - maintain nose high altitude
- Add power during flare before touchdown to keep elevator effective to help keep weight off nosewheel. Touchdown is as soft as possible, and that is achieved through energy management.
- During rollout, power to idle and gradually increase back elevator to keep weight off nosewheel, taxi with caution because of soft surface.
- No braking action during roll out.

Note: You should add or keep a bit of power in the flare to avoid touching down too firmly.

Practicing Area Maneuvers:

Everyone is taught to make clearing turns in pilot training, to "clear" the blind spots above and below your aircraft, especially during climb, descent and climbing/descending turns you need to bank in both directions, removing them. Practicing area maneuvers requires "Clearing Turns" (two separate 90° turns for collision avoidance). Clearing turns to precede each maneuver requiring pitch changes such as slow flight, steep turns, stalls and engine out practices.

Procedure
 - Visually clear area in direction of first turn and lift wing to check for traffic (check blind spot)
 - Commence first turn using 30° of bank and check mixture rich during turn.
 - Resume second turn and reduce power for desired airspeed.

Slow Flight:

Slow Flight is one of the leading maneuvers that increases the pilot's ability and self-confidence to control the airplane in variable conditions, including the relationship between angle of attack (AOA), airspeed, load factor, power setting, airplane weight and center of gravity (CG), airplane altitude, and yaw effects. When practicing slow flight, a pilot learns to divide attention between aircraft control and other demands. It develops the ability to recognize changes in aircraft flight characteristics and control effectiveness at critically slow airspeeds.

Note: Establish and maintain an airspeed at which any further increase in angle of attack, increase in load factor, or reduction in power, would result in a stall warning (e.g., airplane buffet, stall horn, etc.).

Stall horn is a stall warning indicator. It activates at least 5 Knots above stall speed.

In slow flight, prior to a stalled condition, <u>the controls start to feel mushy- not as responsive.</u>

Entry:
 - Throttle- 1500 RPM, 10° flap within white arc. (Increase pitch to maintain altitude as airspeed decreases – TRIM)

Figure-33 Slow Flight

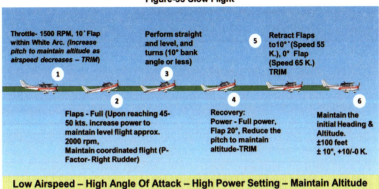

Note: The applicant should demonstrate slow flight with no stall horn annunciating. (ACS)

- Flaps - Full *(Upon reaching 45-50 Kt., increase power to maintain level flight approx. 2000 rpm, maintain coordinated flight (P-Factor- right rudder)*
- Perform straight and level, and turns (10° bank angle or less)

Recovery:
- Power - Apply Full power, Flap 20°, reduce the pitch to maintain altitude-TRIM
- Respectively, retract flaps to 10° *(speed 55 Kt.)*, 0° Flap *(speed 65 Kt.)* TRIM
- Accelerate to normal cruise speed and TRIM. Maintain the initial heading & altitude. *(Airman Certification Standards: Maintain the specified altitude, ±100 feet; specified heading, ±10°; airspeed, +10/-0 knots; and specified angle of bank, ±10°.)*

- **Steep Turns:**

In this performance maneuver, trim and horizon are always your best friends! TRIM and HORIZON.

Firstly, roll into bank, apply power (100 RPM more) and trim right away. This will help you reduce the majority of back pressure. *(develop a formula how much trim you put on trim wheel - 2/3 rolls of trim, make little corrections immediately as needed.)* Secondly, while keeping a quick visual scan over the instruments, keep your eyes outside *(70-80 %)*, keep the nose where you want it relative to the horizon.

Main purpose of steep turns associated with aerodynamic is to

increase the ability to control all axes of plane and better understand the,
- Coordinated and uncoordinated flight,
- Overbanking tendencies,
- Maneuvering speed, including the impact of weight changes,
- Load factor and accelerated stalls,
- Rate and radius of turn.

When performing steep turns, pilots may be exposing to higher load factors, *(The load factor for any airplane in <u>a 60˚ bank angle is 2G's</u>)*. Because of the loss of vertical component of lift, the need for substantial pitch control pressures with trimtab, and the need for additional power setting to maintain altitude and airspeed.

Keep in mind the flight heading *(Use the cardinal headings or outside visual reference point)* and initial start-up altitude.

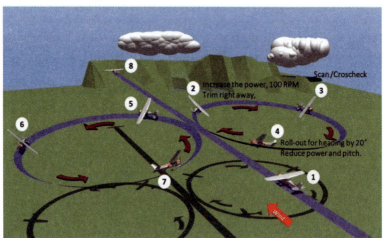

Figure-34 Steep Turns

Nu.1- Clear the area, select entry altitude (1500' AGL), cardinal heading and outside visual reference points.

Nu.2-3-4 - Roll into a coordinated 360° steep turn with approximately a 45° bank.

Nu. 5-6-7- Perform the task in the opposite direction, as specified by evaluator.

Nu. 8 - 5 <u>Maintain the entry altitude ±100 feet,</u> airspeed ±10 knots, bank ±5°, and roll out on the entry heading ±10°.

> **How to master steep turns.** *(Recommended Techniques.)*
> Establish airspeed at 90-95 K. approx. 2200-2300 rpm. *(PPT)*
> Roll into a 45° bank turn *(Pls pay attention to the tendency to either loss or gain altitude.*
> *Increase back pressure and power to maintain altitude and airspeed)*
> Continuous scan and crosscheck (horizon-out front, VSI, altimeter, airspeed indicator)
> Begin rolling out for heading by approx. 20° (through 30 ° bank, start decreasing the RPM, pitch and TRIM)
> Reduce power and pitch as necessary to maintain altitude and airspeed *(Refer to the POH/AFM ~ 90-95 K.).*
> Immediately roll into a bank in the opposite direction.

Note: FAA's Airman Certification Standards use 45 ° of bank as a target for private pilot practical tests.

- **Stalls:**

A stall is a loss of lift and increase in drag, disruption of the smooth air over the airplane wing. It's an indication that the airplane's wings are approaching their <u>critical angle of attack</u>—the angle of attack that, when reached, results in a stall. *(<u>The point at which the wing will stall.)</u>*

<u>Critical angle of attack is the same regardless of airspeed, weight and configuration.</u>

In order to become proficient in exercising Power On/Power Off Stalls, you have to be aware of the flight conditions that are conducive to stalls and know how to apply the necessary corrective action. Indicators of impending stall should be recognized by sight, sound, and feel.

<u>An airplane can stall at any flight attitude, any airspeed and any power setting.</u> So, stall recognition, prevention and recovery must be critical core skills for any pilot to master. *(Execute a stall recovery in accordance with procedures set forth in the POH/AFM.)*

Power-Off Stalls: (Approach to Landing Stall)

Landing Stalls (can be classified as power-off stalls) are practiced to simulate normal approach-to-landing conditions and configuration.

Entry:
- Clear the area, select an altitude -1500' AGL.

- Perform clearing turns.
- Reduce power to 1800 RPM by adjusting pitch to maintain altitude.

Figure-35 Power Off Stall (Landing Stall)

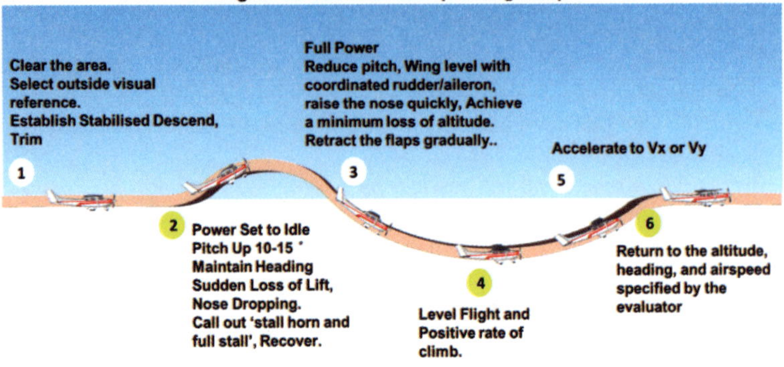

1. Clear the area. Select outside visual reference. Establish Stabilised Descend, Trim
2. Power Set to Idle Pitch Up 10-15° Maintain Heading Sudden Loss of Lift, Nose Dropping. Call out 'stall horn and full stall', Recover.
3. Full Power Reduce pitch, Wing level with coordinated rudder/aileron, raise the nose quickly, Achieve a minimum loss of altitude. Retract the flaps gradually..
4. Level Flight and Positive rate of climb.
5. Accelerate to Vx or Vy
6. Return to the altitude, heading, and airspeed specified by the evaluator

Note: During the training, recoveries should be done until student pilot exhibits skills in automatic reaction.

- Extend full flaps and establish 1500rpm/65 K. descent (configure the airplane in the approach or landing configuration, establish the stabilized descend.)
- Power set to idle and apply back pressure, pitch up 10-15° *(Transition smoothly from the approach or landing attitude to a pitch attitude that will induce a stall.)*
- Call out **"imminent stall"** at stall warning horn.

After a full stall occurs, recover promptly and accordingly.

Recovery: *(Execute a stall recovery in accordance with procedures stated in the POH/AFM.)*
- Simultaneously, reduce pitch, full power, wings level with coordinated rudder and aileron.
- Retract flaps to 20° establish climb pitch attitude, speed more than 50 K.
- Retract flaps to 10° accelerating through 55 Kt. TRIM
- Retract flaps to 0° accelerating through 60 Kt. TRIM
- Accelerate to Vx/Vy before the final flap retraction and normal cruise speed and TRIM.
- Maintain the heading & altitude, airspeed specified by examiner.

- Level off as briefed.

Note: Aerodynamics associated with stalls in various airplane configurations, to include the relationship between angle of attack (AOA), airspeed, load factor, power setting, airplane weight and center of gravity, airplane altitude, and yaw effects.

- **Power-On Stalls:** *(Departure Stall)*

Power-on stalls simulate a stall from normal takeoff, main purpose is to develop the pilot's ability to recognize an approaching stall by sound, sight, and feel; familiarize the pilot with the conditions that produce power-on stall.

Entry:
- Select an altitude -1500' AGL.
- Perform clearing turns.
- Reduce power to 1500 RPM, Slow to rotation speed 55 Kt.
- Add power to 2000 rpm.
- Smoothly increase the pitch to induce stall.
- Call Out **"imminent stall"** at stall warning horn
- Call out **"stall"** when stall occurs

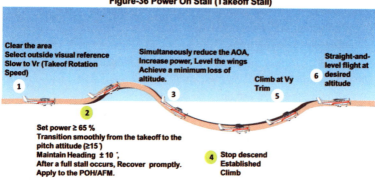

Figure-36 Power On Stall (Takeoff Stall)

Acknowledge cues of the impending stall (buffeting, shaking), Indicators of intentional stalls should be recognized by sight, sound, and feel.

Recovery:
- Full power, reduce pitch then establish Vy pitch attitude.

59

- Accelerate to Vx/Vy and normal cruise speed and TRIM.
- Maintain the heading & altitude, airspeed specified by CFI/DPE.
- Level off as briefed.

Note: In a power-on stall, it requires significant amount of right rudder to compensate for the left-turning tendencies while holding aft elevator to hold a high altitude and induce the stall.

How to access to spin: If you do not use any right rudder to keep the ball centered and pull the yoke completely aft, stall the airplane, and let the left wing start to drop. The aircraft will roll to the direction in which the rudder is deflected. It is strongly possible airplane will be ready to start spinning. If it happens inadvertently, immediately **Power idle, apply right rudder** to stop the wing from dropping, followed by **unloading the yoke, neutralize the rudder.** *During a spin to the left, both wings are stalled.*

Accelerated Stall:

Accelerated stalls occur at higher than normal airspeeds when excessive maneuvering loads are imposed by steep turns, pull ups or other abrupt changes in flight path. As mentioned before, stall speed increases with load factor due to a loss in the vertical component of lift. <u>So, stall can occur at any airspeed, attitude, power setting.</u> The stall speed at any given angle of bank can be predicted simply by multiplying the stall speed. As an example, an aircraft with a normal stall speed of 45 knots would stall at about 64 knots in a 60-degree banked turn.

Entry:

- Select an altitude -1500' AGL.
- Perform clearing turns.
- Reduce power to allow the plane to decelerate to cruise speed *(below Va due to increasing load factor in a 45° bank.)*
- Ensure the flaps are up.
- Establish a 45° bank to the left/right
- Reduce power to idle, adjusting the pitch to maintain altitude.
- Once reduced the airspeed approximately 15/25 knots, smoothly/firmly increase elevator back-pressure, callout "**stalling**".

Note: Nose will fall down abruptly to the side of bank. So, first attempts should be "full power and level the wings to balance the vertical/ horizontal component of lift. Failure to take immediate action may result in complete loss of flight control, notably, power-on stall and spin due to excessive yaw in to the side of roll.

Recovery:
- Simultaneously, add full power, wings level with coordinated rudder and aileron, reduce pitch *(AOA to the horizon or slightly below to build airspeed.)*
- Establish climb pitch attitude,
- Accelerate normal cruise speed and TRIM.
- Maintain the heading & altitude, airspeed specified by CFI/DPE.

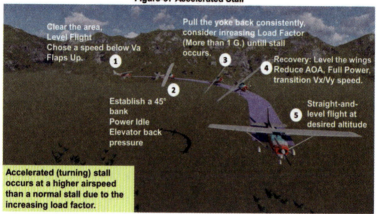

Figure-37 Accelerated Stall

Note: * Slow flight and Power-on stalls are the maneuverers which will be resulting in an accelerated stall.
** Principally, private pilots don't have to demonstrate accelerated (turning) stalls on the practical test, but the Private Pilot Airman Certification Standard (ACS) lists it in both the knowledge and risk management sections of steep turns and power-on stalls.
*** The onset of this stall develops abruptly and too much rudder on the inside of the turn will cause a spin.

Basic Instrument Maneuvers: (3 H.)
This includes straight and level, climbs and descents, climbing/descending turns, turns to headings at 15° bank angle, VOR orientation, bearing/radial to the fix, and unusual attitude recovery. Comply with ATC Instructions, maintain altitude ±200 feet, heading ±20°, and airspeed ±10 knots.

You aren't expected to know or follow all the many instrument flight rules. There's no partial-panel training required, or any coverage of the IFR rules.

Very simple, wear a hood/foggles and fly with instruments, level, climbs and descents, climbing/descending turns. This is called as "flight by reference to instruments in simulated IMS" *(Instrument Meteorological Conditions).*

<u>Note: If you accidentally fly into IMC weather as a VFR pilot, do a 180° turn and exit the IMC. Don't think that It will be clear in a few moments.</u>

- **Turns -Ground Reference Maneuvers**
  (Turns Around a Point, Rectangular Course, "S" Turns)

The main aim of ground reference maneuvers is to develop the wind and ground track awareness and student's self-confidence maneuvering low to the ground. DPE will request at least one maneuver for the applicant to demonstrate.

Note: *During the ground reference maneuvers, you are supposed to calculate the pivotal altitude before starting the maneuvers. Pivotal Altitude: square the groundspeed and then divide by 15 if you use mph, or 11.3 if you prefer knots. That will provide a starting altitude. For example, 90 mph times 100 equals 9,000, divided by 15 equals 600 feet approximate pivotal altitude.*

- Clear the area, choose forced landing area before starting the maneuvers.

- Apply steeper bank angles for higher ground speeds, shallow bank angles for slower groundspeeds.

- Maintain altitude ±100 feet; maintain airspeed ±10 knots.

Turns Around a Point:

Turns around a point are a logical extension of both the rectangular course and S-turns across a road. The maneuver is a 360° constant radius turn around a single ground-based reference point. These turns are easy in concept and difficult in practice. Before starting the maneuver, the student pilot must be aware of wind and wind drift.

Let's take a look at critical steps:

- Clear the area, find the right prominent, ground-based reference point, Pick the Pivotal Altitude *(600-1000 feet AGL)*
- Determine the wind direction,
- Enter the downwind,

- Fly the circle by varying the bank angle according to the wind drift to maintain the same distance all the way around a point.
- Pay attention primarily altitude, drift and ground track control.
(Altitude Control, slipping and skidding in turns are the Common Errors)

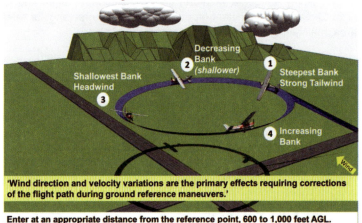

Figure-38 Turns Around A Point

'Wind direction and velocity variations are the primary effects requiring corrections of the flight path during ground reference maneuvers.'

Enter at an appropriate distance from the reference point, 600 to 1,000 feet AGL.

Rectangular Course:

The main purpose of rectangular course is to develop the skills for airport traffic pattern.

Figure-39 Rectangular Course

While performing the course, the altitude and airspeed are held constant. *(Never lover than 600' AGL)*
- Enter a left or right pattern, 1,000 feet above ground level (AGL) at an appropriate distance from the selected reference area, 45° to the downwind leg.
- Apply adequate wind-drift correction during straight and turning flight to maintain a constant ground track around a rectangular reference area, maintain coordinated flight and trim the airplane.

- **"S" Turns:** *(two-constant radius turn across the road)*

S-Turns include a series of 2-180° turns in opposite directions crossing the straight road or reference line as appropriate.

It's a maneuver which improves your ability to correct for wind during all turns, and is especially helpful in developing your ability to compensate for wind while flying in the traffic pattern.
- Perform a downwind entry,
- Resume your first 180° turn,
- Apply the corrections of wind.
- Perform another half circle.
- Rollout and level flight.

Note: Maintain altitude ±100 feet; maintain airspeed ±10 knots.

Figure-40 S-Turns (Half Circles)

Note: Continuously think of the effects of wind on ground track and your relation to a ground reference point.

- **Emergency Procedures:**
 During emergency, the first and the most important responsibility is to maintain control of the aircraft, second is to resolve or respond to the emergency.

  - **In-Flight Emergency Procedures:**
  Engine-Out (Engine failure) Procedures in Flight:
  An engine failure in flight requires a precise and timely reaction. "maintain aircraft control (fly the airplane), analyze the situation, try to restart the engine, land in an appropriate field."
  Apply ABC Checklist *(Figure-41)*
    Steps:
    * **A**- Airspeed establish 65-70 K. glide, *(best gliding speed), turning* into the wind will result in maximum lift and lower trend on the VSI *(less loss of altitude)*
    * **B**- Best place to land *(Look for best suitable landing area with the smoothest and longest landing surface)*
    * **C**- Checklist *(Engine restart sequence, Refer to the POH.)*

Engine Failure During Flight (Restart Sequence)

- Airspeed – 65-70 (best gliding speed).
- Fuel Shutoff Valve -- ON *(push full in)*.
- Fuel Selector Valve -- BOTH.
- Auxiliary Fuel Pump Switch – ON *(if available)*
- Mixture -- RICH (if restart has not occurred) – Primer- In / Locked
- Ignition Switch-- BOTH *(or START if propeller is stopped)*.
- Auxiliary Fuel Pump Switch -- OFF.

Note (1) If the propeller is wind milling, the engine will restart automatically within a few seconds. If the propeller has stopped (possible at low speeds), turn the ignition switch to START, advance the throttle slowly from idle and lean the mixture from full rich as required for smooth operation.
(2) When executing an emergency approach to land in a single-engine airplane, it is important to maintain a constant glide speed because <u>variations in glide speed nullify all attempts at accuracy in judgment of gliding distance and landing spot.</u>
<u>(3)</u> Note: Altitude (Energy) is the most important factor that makes the difference between straight-in landing or turning toward the best spot. In the checkride, DPE will pay close attention your attitudes and attempts in decision making. (ABC, restart, best glide SPEED atc.) The best course of action is to plan and assume a course direct to a suitable and potential

landing spot in according with the location and altitude of the aircraft.

> **Forced Landing to the Best Place:** Refer to the POH/AFM.
> - Seats and Seat Belts-- SECURE.
> - Airspeed -- 70 KIAS (flaps UP). 65 KIAS *(flaps down).*
> - Look for an eligible place to land.
> - Mixture-- IDLE CUT OFF.
> - Fuel Shutoff Valve -- OFF *(Pull Full Out).*
> - Ignition Switch-- OFF.
> - Wing Flaps --AS REQUIRED *(30° recommended).*
> - Master Switch -- OFF *(when landing is assured).*
> - Doors-- Unlatch prior to touchdown.
> - Touchdown-- Slightly tail low.
> - Brakes-- Apply heavily.

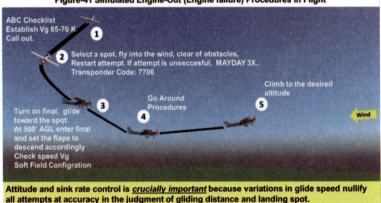

Figure-41 Simulated Engine-Out (Engine failure) Procedures in Flight

Attitude and sink rate control is *crucially important* because variations in glide speed nullify all attempts at accuracy in the judgment of gliding distance and landing spot.

- **Engine-Out** *(Flameout-Engine failure)* **Procedures After Takeoff:**

If your engine fails immediately after takeoff, you won't have time to attempt a restart. Instead, you will need to focus on flying the airplane and picking a safe landing spot.

> **Engine-Out *(Flameout-Engine failure)* After Takeoff:**
> -Airspeed: 65-70 Kt.
> - Mixture: Idle Cutoff *(Pull full back)*
> - Full Shutoff Valve- Off *(Pull full back)*
> - Magneto Switch- OFF
> - Master Switch *(Alternator-Battery)*- OFF
> - Cabin Do**or- Unlatch**
> - Land - Straight ahead.

> *Partial engine failure after take-off:*
> Aircraft may still have some power enabling different options (Decision making) Maintain airspeed/attitude control. *(Coordinated Turns)*

• **Engine Fire In-Flight: (Emergency Descent)**
    (Pitch for maximum structural cruising speed for maximum air to enter the cowling and extinguish the fire)

> **Engine Fire In-Flight: (Emergency Descent- Refer to the POH/AFM)**
> - Mixture-- IDLE CUT OFF.
> - Fuel Shutoff Valve-- Pull Out *(OFF)*.
> - Auxiliary Fuel Pump Switch-- OFF.   – Ignition-OFF
> - Master Switch-- OFF.
> - Cabin Heat and Air-- OFF *(except overhead vents).*
> - Airspeed -- 100 KIAS *(If fire is not extinguished, try a higher glide speed to find an airspeed - within airspeed limitations (Va) - which will provide an incombustible mixture).*
> - Forced Landing -- EXECUTE *(See Pg.66)*
> * Use bank angle between 30° and 45° to maintain positive load factors.

• **System and Equipment Malfunctions: Apply the POH/AFM and be prepared for answering all below emergencies.**

    You are expected to identify the problem and clarify the situation with the best course of action. *(COA)*
    * Partial or complete power loss related to the specific powerplant, including: *See Pg.114.*
    - Engine roughness or overheat. *(focus on the possible reasons including detonation, preignition, carburetor icing, incorrect mixture setting, faulty ignition, magneto, the best COA: If problem persists, look for a place to land ASAP.)*
    - Carburetor or Induction Icing *(See Page 13,159)*

- Loss of oil pressure. *(lack of oil, oil leak, relief valve, best course of action: engine seizure could happen, land ASAP)*
- Fuel starvation. *(rough running engine, fuel vaporization, incorrectly adjusted fuel tank selector. Best COA: Check the fuel selector valve position, fuel pump-ON, increase the mixture.)*

* System and equipment malfunction specific to the airplane, including: *(See Pg.114)*
- Electrical malfunction. *(See Pg.114)*
- Vacuum/pressure and associated flight instrument malfunctions.
- Pitot/static system malfunction *(See Pg.104)*
- Electronic flight deck display malfunction.
- Landing gear or flap malfunction.
- Inoperative Trim.

* Smoke/fire/engine compartment fire. *(See Pg.114)*
* Any other system specific to the airplane (e.g., supplemental oxygen, deicing).
* Inadvertent door or window opening.

Pre-Solo Preparation:
Before first solo flight, there are a number of required maneuvers, these tests are needed before performing the first solo flight. Required maneuvers should be received and logged for flight training for the following maneuvers and procedures. Here are the mandatory titles needed to be done: pre-solo test is presented in the following pages.

Required maneuvers, pre-solo knowledge test, phase check performed by another instructor to ensure.

Required Maneuvers. *Figure-42*
Pre-solo Knowledge Exam/Test.
Pre-solo Flight Review. *Figure-43*

The main objective of pre-solo knowledge test is to evaluate knowledge prior to solo endorsement, but testing can also be used to reinforce and refresh past learning, and serve as a reference for future questions, such as Private Pilot Written/Oral Exam.

The pre-solo written test will also include questions on the flight characteristics and operational limitations of the make and model aircraft to be flown. Your flight instructor will determine that you are familiar with pre-solo knowledge test requirements. See Pg.69-74

PRIVATE PILOT HANDBOOK

Required Maneuvers.

Pre-Solo Requirements:

A student pilot who is receiving training for a single-engine airplane rating or privileges must receive and log flight training for the following maneuvers and procedures:

1. Proper flight preparation procedures, including preflight planning and preparation, powerplant operation, and aircraft systems ○○○○
2. Taxiing or surface operations, including runup ○○○○
3. Takeoffs and landings, including normal and crosswind ○○○○
4. Straight and level flight, and turns in both directions ○○○○
5. Climbs and climbing turns ○○○○
6. Airport traffic patterns, including entry and departure procedures ○○○○
7. Collision avoidance, windshear avoidance, and wake turbulence avoidance ○○○○
8. Descents, with and without turns, using high and low drag configurations ○○○○
9. Flight at various airspeeds from cruise to slow flight ○○○○
10. Stall entries from various flight attitudes and power combinations with recovery initiated at the first indication of a stall, and recovery from a full stall ○○○○
11. Emergency procedures and equipment malfunctions ○○○○
12. Ground reference maneuvers ○○○○
13. Approaches to a landing area with simulated engine malfunctions ○○○○
14. Slips to a landing ○○○○
15. Go-arounds. ○○○○

FAR/AIM: 61.87 Solo requirements for student pilots.

Note: As a course of action, Instructor Pilot should be ranking for the last four flights to ensure.

A-Excellent   B- Good   C- Fair   D- Unsatisfactory

Instructor Pilot   Date of Solo

Figure-42 Pre-Solo Requirements

PRIVATE PILOT HANDBOOK

Pre-Solo Written Exam:

Name:
CFI:
Date:
Grade:

1. Please list and define each of the following speeds in KIAS:

Vso
Vs1
Vx
Vy
Vfe
Va
Vno
Vne
Best Glide/Vg

2. List five (5) items for the pre-landing checklist when on downwind.
   a. _____
   b. _____
   c. _____
   d. _____
   e. _____

3. If voice communications are lost, which transponder code should be squawked? (AIM 6-4-2)

4. What are the "signs of a stall" in probable sequence?

   a. _____

   b. _____

   c. _____

   d. _____

5. Pls, determine the positions of the aircraft in relation to glide path?

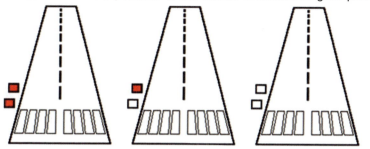

6. What is the minimum fuel requirement for?
   Day VFR flight? (91.151)

   Night VFR flight? (91.151)

7. While on a cross country flight, you see a military aircraft pass you on the left, and maintain a position ahead and to the left of your position. The aircraft then rocks its wings. What does this mean, and what should you do? (AIM 5-6-4)

8. What documents are students required to carry while flying solo?

9. Please draw the runways and traffic patterns at KPMP?

10. What are the Tower, Ground and AWOS frequencies at KPMP?

11. What should you do if you notice your oil temperature rising too high while on the ground? While in the air?
Ground:

Air:

12. When should you execute a go-around?

13. Explain the procedure for executing a go-around.

14. At what time of day must the aircraft's strobe lights be turned on?

15. If there is no altimeter setting available, what setting should be used for a local flight?

16. In the event of a total electrical failure, which of the following items or systems will become inoperative in the aircraft you currently fly?

    a. Alternator.

    b. Attitude Indicator.

    c. Turn Coordinator.

    d. Engine Ignition System.

    e. Suction Gauge.

    f. Beacon.

    g. Fuel Selector.

    h. Fuel Pump.

    i. Tachometer.

j. Flap extension/retraction system.

17. What is the fuel capacity of the aircraft you fly? _____ gals.

18. What is the proper grade of fuel?

19. What is its color?

20. Name the instruments connected to the pitot tube.

21. What is the maximum gross weight of the airplane in the normal category?

22. List the procedures to respond to an in-flight engine fire.

23. During run-up what is the maximum allowable RPM drop between the Magnetos? If the limit exceeded, what action should be taken?

24. What are the basic VFR weather minimums for Class D and Class E,G below 1200 feet?

25. List the day-VFR weather minimums in Class G, E, D airspace.

26. What are you, as a student pilot, required to have before operating in Class B airspace?

27. List the documents that must be aboard the aircraft at all times.

28. When must the aircraft's navigation lights be on?

29. Draw the pavement marking requiring you to stop before entering a runway.

30. Explain the "left turning tendencies of Single-Engine Airplane?

31. Emergency: While on a VFR cross country and not in contact with ATC, what frequency would you use in the event of an emergency?

Figure- 43 Pre-Solo Flight Review		
Rewiew Subject Items		Performance
1	Written Quiz (V speeds and their definitions, emergency procedures, Aircraft Systems, Avionics, Navigation Equipment.) What documents and endorsements are you required to have in your possession to legally operate the airplane as a student pilot? List the documents that must be aboard the aircraft at all times.	
2	Open-Book Exam (Aircraft limitations, Aircraft operation, FARs, Aeronautical Information Manual, Local procedures, Meteorlogy, Aerodynamic etc.)	
3	Performance (What is the distance to clear a 50 foot obstacle on a standard day? , What is the landing distance when landing over a 50 foot obstacle on a standard day?	
4	Weight & Balance (What is the maximum gross weight of the aircraft?, What is the empty weight of the aircraft? , What is the useful load of the aircraft? With full fuel, how much weight can you carry in the aircraft?	
5	Flight Planning (In addition to other preflight actions for a VFR flight away from the vicinity of the departure airport, What actions should be done ? What altitude should you fly when operating in level cruising flight at more than 3,000 feet AGL?	
6	What are the weather minimums, as defined on your solo endorsement? Class G, Class D Airspaces ?	
7	What type and grade of fuel is used in the aircraft?	
8	Will the engine run with the master switch turned off? Why?	
9	During a magneto check, what is the maximum RPM drop?	
10	Draw a runway and a traffic pattern and label each leg.	
11	How do you enter and exit the traffic pattern at an uncontrolled airport? Which turn direction is standard for a traffic pattern?	
12	When are you required to wear a safety belt? Shoulder harness?	
13	What must a pilot do before entering Class D airspace?	
14	What is the minimum altitude you can fly anywhere?	
15	If the altimeter setting is not available at an airport, what setting should you use before departing on a local flight?	
16	List the procedure for a go-around and touch and go.	
17	What is the minimum altitude you can fly anywhere? Over congested areas? Over other than congested areas? Over sparsely populated areas or open water?	
18	Please define in your own words and list the speed for each of the following in the aircraft: Vr, Vx,Vy, Best Glide, Vne,Va, Vfe, Vso..	
Instructor	Date of Review Student Pilot	Logbook Endorsement

• **Weight and Balance (W&B)**

Weight and Balance calculation describes the procedure for establishing the basic empty weight and moment of the airplane. Any calculation mistake made has the potential to cause both the instability and uncontrollability of the aircraft. In conducting a preflight, it is the PIC's responsibility to use *the most current weight and balance data.*

Too much weight and, too forward CG will make it difficult to raise the nose, too far aft CG may make it more difficult to recover from a stall. Improper loading decreases the efficiency and performance of an aircraft from the standpoint of attitude, maneuverability, controllability, rate of climb, and speed.

It should be noted that specific information regarding the weight, arm, moment and installed equipment for the airplane as delivered from the factory can only be found in the plastic envelope carried in the back of this handbook.

Note: Each aircraft's weight and moment are different. Weight and Usable Fuel information will be found in the Pilot's Operating Handbook (POH, Section VI) specific to the aircraft you are flying. W&B is the responsibility of the PIC to ensure that the airplane is loaded properly.

With an aft CG, It is harder to recover from a stall/spin, and there is a risk of striking the tail. It seems like the airplane would be less controllable, but with an aft CG, the flight controls are easier to manipulate and it's easier to overstress the airplane. So, the airplane is more 'controllable' (maneuverable) with an aft CG as long as you are loaded within limits.

Center of lift (CL), the relationship between the CL and the CG locations determine the stability of the airplane. As long as you are within the aircraft's CG limits, CL is always aft of your CG in a stable airplane.

How to calculate and fill weight & balance (CG) sheet out:

- Calculate the moments for the pilot, all passengers, fuel, and baggage. If the pilot and front passenger weighed 360 pounds, you would find 360 on the vertical axes on Figure-45. You then follow that over to where it intersects the line labelled "Pilot and front passenger". You then follow that down to the horizontal axes to get your moment value of about 13.3. Basic Formula is *Weight X Arm: Moment* (360X37:13.300), 13.300/1000: 13.3 Moment.

Center of Gravity (CG): Weight, Arm, Moments.

Forward CG (Nose Heavy)	Aft CG (Rearward):
Increased Longitudinal Stability	*Decreased Longitudinal Stability (Pitch)*
Lower Cruise Speed	Higher Cruise Speed
Higher Stall Speed	Lower Stall Speed
More Stable (Nose Heavy)	Less Stable
Favorable Stall Recovery	*Poor Stall/Spin Recovery*
Stronger Tail Load	Lighter Tail Load
Difficulty in rotating and rounding out (in steering) during landing.	Shorter arm between CG and control surfaces *(more tail down force)*
The CG must always be within limits, however, depending where in the allowable range the C.G. falls will affect performance.	

Figure-44A   Center of Gravity Limitations

Weight & Balance Sheet

Type of Aircraft:	Tail Number:	
	Weight (lb)	Moment/1000
Basic Empty Weight	**1639**	**62.1**
Pilot/Front Pax	360	13.3
Rear Pax	180	13.1
Baggage Area-1	-	-
Baggage Area-2	40	4.9
Zero Fuel Weight (ZFW)	2219	93.4
Fuel (30 Gal)	250	12.8
Ramp Weight	2469	106.2
Taxi/Run-up	-10	-0.5
Takeoff Weight	**2459**	**105.7**

CG Location in Inches of Datum: Locate this point (2459 at 105.7) on the Center of Gravity Moment Envelope Figure-46, and since this point falls within the envelope, the loading is acceptable.
(Maximum Takeoff Weight : 2550 lb. Maximum Useful Load: 911 lb.)
You re safe to go in this example.

Figure-44B Weight & Balance Sheet

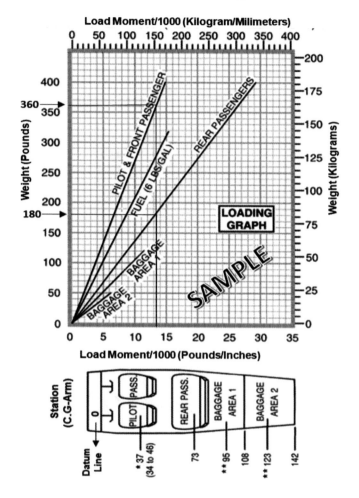

Figure- 45 Moment/Weight Graph

Note: Flying **"inside of the envelope"** is the greatest safety factor. CG must be within limits to maintain _longitudinal stability_ (resistance to pitch). *Case: During your flight you burn 25 gallons of fuel. What effect would this have on the weight and balance of your airplane at destination? <u>As the moment decreases how well</u>, lateral and longitudinal CG change.*

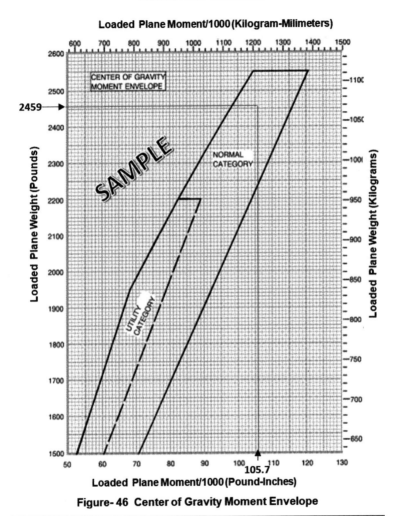

Figure- 46 Center of Gravity Moment Envelope

What we do is place the weight and moment figures from the POH, See Figure-44/45, Check if you are in envelope. Now, the aircraft is safe to fly.
*Case: You determine that your airplane is 90 pounds over maximum certified gross weight. What should you do? You must drain the fuel (AVGAS)?
How much fuel (AVGAS) must be drained to bring it within limits?
15 Gallons: 90 Pounds.*

Performance Charts:
Takeoff Distance Roll (Normal Takeoff / 50' Obstacle)

Example: OAT (Outside Air Temperature): 30°C
Pressure Altitude: Sea Level
Wind: 330°/20 Kt.
Active Runway: 30
From Chart (Figure- 47) Ground Roll: 925 feet, for 50-feet Obstacle Clearance 1570 feet.
Head wind component, go to the Figure-28 and calculate it, 18 Knot.
Takeoff Ground roll: 925-185: 740 feet, for 50-feet Obstacle Clearance 1570-314: 1256 feet. *(Notes says below it would be decreased the distance by 20% due to 18 K. headwind component.)*
Note: High temperatures (less dense air), high relative humidity, high density altitude. <u>These lead to longer takeoff rolls and decreased climb performance.</u>

At 2400 Pounds

Flaps 10°, Full Throttle Prior to Brake Release
Zero Wind, Pawed, Level, Dry Runway
Lift Off Speed: 51 Knots
Speed at 50 feet Obstaqcle: 56 Knots

Press Alt In Feet	0°C		10°C		20°C		30°C		40°C	
	Grnd Roll Ft	Total Ft To Clear 50 Ft Obst	Grnd Roll Ft	Total Ft To Clear 50 Ft Obst	Grnd Roll Ft	Total Ft To Clear 50 Ft Obst	Grnd Roll Ft	Total Ft To Clear 50 Ft Obst	Grnd Roll Ft	Total Ft To Clear 50 Ft Obst
S.L.	745	1275	800	1370	860	1470	925	1570	995	1685
1000	810	1390	875	1495	940	1605	1010	1720	1085	1845
2000	885	1520	955	1635	1030	1760	1110	1890	1190	2030
3000	970	1665	1050	1795	1130	1930	1215	2080	1305	2230
4000	1065	1830	1150	1975	1240	2130	1335	2295	1430	2455
5000	1170	2015	1265	2180	1365	2355	1465	2530	1570	2715
6000	1285	2230	1390	2420	1500	2610	1610	2805	1725	3015
7000	1415	2470	1530	2685	1650	2900	1770	3125	1900	3370
8000	1560	2755	1690	3000	1815	3240	1950	3500	2095	3790

<u>Notes:</u>
- Short Field technique as described in Section 4, POH.
- Increase the distances by 10 % for each 2-knot tailwinds
- Decrease the distances by 10 % for each 9-knot headwind.
- For operations on grass, wet runway, increase the distances by 15 % for ground roll.

Figure- 47 Takeoff Distance Roll

- **Flight Planning and VFR Navigation Log.**

The purpose of flight planning is to become familiar with information pertaining to an intended flight. Filing of a VFR flight plan is recommended, It is good operating practice to accurately complete FAA Form 7233-1, known as a flight plan *(Figure-68)*. The VFR Navigation Log is an essential and useful tool that you use to guide your preflight planning. The navigation log helps you record the known values and compute the unknown values. In order to better understand how to prepare the VFR Navigation Log, we have divided the exercise into 12 steps which explain how to fill it out properly. Before you can go flying on your cross-country flight, you need to know how to file a VFR flight plan. *(Flight Plan provides Search and Rescue with your proposed route of flight and ETA)*

What will you need to complete the VFR Navigation Log? Current VFR Sectional Chart, Navigational Plotter, E6B Mechanical Flight Computer of Electronic Flight Computer, VFR Navigation Log Sheet, Cruise Performance page from POH, Pencil, Winds Aloft Forecast *(Aviationweather.com /Wind -Temps)*, Compass Deviation Table *(attached to the magnetic compass)*. You will find all the sample required forms in the coming pages.
Note: All charts presented are sample and not for operational/actual use.

- **Route: VFR Flight Planning Kissimmee-KISM to Orlando Executive- KORL.** *(Jacksonville Sectional Chart)*

E6B Flight Computer has two sides. Computer side and wind side. It is easier to use without having to remember where everything is. Time, speed, distance problem, fuel consumption, density altitude, true airspeed, and conversion problems are done on the computer side. Wind side of E6B allows you to compute "ground speed (GS) and wind correction angle (WCA)".
Steps for VFR Nav. Log: See all numbers described in the Figure-48.
Nu-1. Plot your course and determine the checkpoints *(spaced landmarks, obstructions, roads, lake, power lines etc.)* and distances *(sectional charts using plotter)*
KISM- Antennas, Antennas- Lake, Lake-Stadium, Stadium-KORL.
Note: Pay attention to the Disney World- TFR (Permanent), Temporary Flight Restriction, Flight Restricted Zone (Red Circle)
Nu-2. Measure **_True Course_** and distance (nautical miles) with plotter: True Course: First Leg: 345°(17 NM), Second Leg: 70°(15 NM).
Nu-3. Select an altitude: **Cruising Altitude:2500 feet.**
VFR altitude, the rule states that "each person operating an aircraft under VFR in level cruising flight more than 3,000 feet above the surface shall

maintain the appropriate altitude explained below;
- There is no cruising **rule below 3000** AGL.
- On a magnetic course of 0° through 179°, *any odd thousand foot MSL altitude+500 feet* (such as 3,500, 5,500, or 7,500); or)
- On a magnetic course of 180 °through 359 °, *any even thousand foot MSL altitude+500 feet* (such as 4,500, 6,500, or 8,500).

Nu-4. Determine winds aloft: MLB-3000 feet, 1515 means wind **150°/15 Kt.** *(Figure-49 Win/Temp Data),* go to the webpage: aviationweather.com /wind -temps Map, pick MLB *(Melbourne, closeby our route, Wind/Temps Forecasts.)*

Nu-5. True airspeed-TAS and fuel consumption: 105 Kt./ 8.6 GPH *(Nu:12)* in POH *(Figure-51, Cruise Performance Chart, 2000 feet, 2300 RPM.)*

Nu-6. Calculate Wind Correction Angle (WCA) and Groundspeed (Nu:10) using E6B. GS and WCA for First Leg:119 Kt./+3, Second Leg:100 Kt /+9

Nu-7. True Heading: Look up Magnetic Variation (on sectional chart), *(Memory Aid for variation: West is best (+), East is least (-))*
* The angular difference between true north and magnetic north is magnetic variation.

Nu-8. Magnetic heading: Look up Magnetic Deviation Chart (on compass card in the plane), (Figure-50, Magnetic Compass Deviation Table)

Nu-9. Calculate the compass heading (CH:Nu.2+Nu.6+Nu.7+Nu.8). First Leg: 356° Second Leg: 002°. *(Figure--51)*

Nu-10. Calculate minutes for each leg that will be flown using E6B: DIST refers to the fact that LEG and REM are distances. LEG is the distance for that leg from KISM to LAKE (first leg- two checkpoints). REM is the total distance remaining.

Nu-11. Calculate ETE/ETA- ATE/ATA. (Actual Takeoff time: 10.00 AM) ETA- Estimated Time of Arrival, ETE-Estimated Time en route (between waypoints or departure/arrival airports), ATE-Actual Time en route. ATA- Actual Time of Arrival. ATA: 10.23
Note: Add in 6 minutes to allow for getting turned on course after takeoff.

Nu-12. Calculate fuel consumption and remaining fuel for each leg and check point using E6B. Total fuel on board: 30 gallons, Total fuel consumption for all route: 3.4 gallons, **Remaining Fuel: 26.6 gallons**.

<u>Reserve Fuel:</u> For day VFR, enough fuel to reach destination plus <u>30 min.</u> For night VFR, enough fuel to reach destination plus <u>45 min.</u>
In order to check your progress when using dead reckoning with no radio instrumentation, <u>make corrections by using pilotage and keep track of your checkpoints.</u>

— PRIVATE PILOT HANDBOOK —

VFR Navigation Planning Kissimnee-KISM to Orlando Executive- KORL

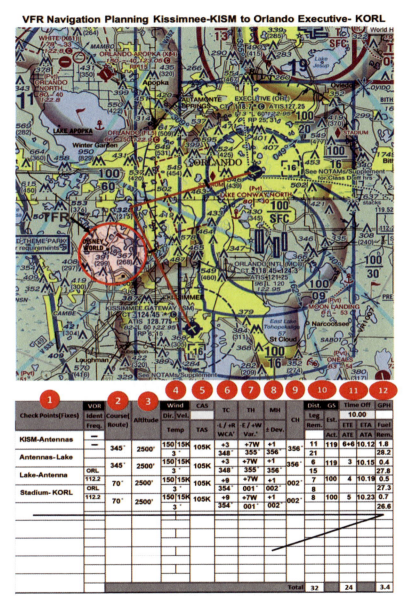

Figure- 48 VFR Navigation Log

Winds/Temps Data
Level (Low) Time 02Z-09Z Southeast (Miami)

```
(Extracted from FBUS31 KWNO 020155)
FD1US1
DATA BASED ON 020000Z
VALID 020600Z    FOR USE 0200-0900Z. TEMPS NEG AB\

FT   3000    6000    9000    12000    18000    24000
EYW  1220  1410+10 2409+07 2721+03  3148-09  2972-19
JAX  2012  2414+07 2418+02 2525-04  2940-19  2860-29
MIA  1217  1310+11 2208+05 2720+00  2938-12  3096-20
MLB  1515  1706+10 2511+03 2623-02  2945-16  3082-25
PFN  1917  2016+07 2222+03 2528-02  2750-17  2981-26
PIE  1622  2016+09 2317+05 2726+00  2943-14  2996-23
TLH  1928  2024+07 2323+02 2624-03  2745-16  2863-30
```

Figure-49 Wind Aloft Data

Note: No info about the temperature at 3000', but temperature is 10 ℃ at 6000 '(1706+10), You need to make interpolation by using the rule of thumb; 'Temp. decreases about 2 ℃, (or 3.5°F) per 1,000 feet of altitude above sea level so <u>the temperature at 2,500 feet is 17 ℃</u>. (6000-2500:3500 feet, 3.5x2:7°C, 10+7: 17°C.)
Question: <u>What wind is forecast for TLH at 6,000 feet?</u>
2024+07 means 200 ℃ True, 24 Kt. +7 ℃.

TO FLY	STEER	TO FLY	STEER
N	001	180	179
15	016	195	194
30	031	210	209
45	046	225	224
60	062	240	238
75	077	255	253
90	092	270	268
105	107	285	283
120	122	300	298
135	135	315	314
150	149	330	330
165	164	345	346

Deviation in a magnetic compass is caused by <u>the magnetic fields within the aircraft distorting the lines of magnetic force. This is caused by certain metals and electrical systems within the aircraft..</u>

Figure-50 Magnetic Compass Deviation Table

Conditions:
2400 Pounds.
Recommended Lean Mixture at All Altitudes
(Refer to POH, Section IV)

PRESS ALT FT	RPM	20°C BELOW STANDARD TEMP			STANDARD TEMPERATURE			20°C ABOVE STANDARD TEMP		
		% BHP	KTAS	GPH	% BHP	KTAS	GPH	% BHP	KTAS	GPH
2000	2550	83	117	11.1	77	118	10.5	72	117	9.9
	2500	78	115	10.6	73	115	9.9	68	115	9.4
	2400	69	111	9.6	64	110	9.0	60	109	8.5
	2300	61	105	8.6	57	104	8.1	53	102	7.7
	2200	53	99	7.7	50	97	7.3	47	95	6.9
	2100	47	92	6.9	44	90	6.6	42	89	6.3
4000	2600	83	120	11.1	77	120	10.4	72	119	9.8
	2550	79	118	10.6	73	117	9.9	68	117	9.4
	2500	74	115	10.1	69	115	9.5	64	114	8.9
	2400	65	110	9.1	61	109	8.5	57	107	8.1
	2300	58	104	8.2	54	103	7.7	51	101	7.3
	2200	51	98	7.4	48	96	7.0	45	94	6.7
	2100	45	91	7.0	42	89	6.4	40	87	6.1
6000	2650	83	122	11.1	77	122	10.4	72	121	9.8
	2600	78	120	10.6	73	119	9.9	68	118	9.4
	2500	70	115	9.6	65	114	9.0	60	112	8.5
	2400	62	109	8.6	57	108	8.2	54	106	7.7
	2300	54	103	7.8	51	101	7.4	48	99	7.0
	2200	48	96	7.1	45	94	6.7	43	92	6.4

Notes:
- Short Field technique as described in Section 4, POH.
- Increase the distances by 10 % for each 2-knot tailwinds
- Decrease the distances by 10 % for each 9-knot headwind.
- For operations on grass, wet runway, increase the distances by 15 % for ground roll.

Figure-51 Cruise Performance

Reminder: What is pressure altitude?
The altitude indicated when <u>the barometric pressure scale is set to 29.92.</u>
Case: How far will an aircraft travel in 7.5 minutes with a True Air Speed of 105 knots? <u>13.1 NM.</u> (105/60:1.75 NM for Per Minute, 1.75x7.5:13.1 NM)

Private Pilot Oral/Written Exam Preperation :

To Be a Private Pilot and Limitations (L)/Privileges (P):
Requirements:
- be at least 17 years old,
- be able to read ,speak ,write and understand English,
- Valid medical certificate.
- Logbook endorsements and IACRA FTN Number.
- Knowledge and practical tests. (70 % to pass Knowledge test)

Private Pilot. Here Limitations (L) / Privileges (P) :

* **L** – You can't carry property for compensation or hire **P**- you may be paid or hired in connection with any business or employment if the flight is only incidental to that business or employment.

* **P**- You may demo an aircraft for sale. * **L**- But You must have at least 200 H. of logged flight time.

* **P**- You may provide airplanes with rides to raise money * **L**- for a charity, including nonprofit and community events.

* **P**- If you fly a passenger on a cross country, **L**- You may equally share the operating expenses of a flight with passengers, only including fuel, oil, airport expenditures, or airplane rental fee. (*pro-rata share of the operating expenses*)

* **P**- You may tow gliders. * **L- 100 H.** PIC time and *3 actual towing flights within 12 Months* and endorsements are required.

* **P**- You may participate in search and rescue operations, (reimbursed for the operating expenses) **L**- provided the expenses involve only fuel, oil, airport expenditures, or rental fees,

Pilot Logbook:
You have to preserve your old log book at least 5 yrs.
The most entries to log in your log book are:
* Biennial flight review (1 H. of flight & 1 H. of ground) and hours required to meet any requirement.
* Check rides.
* *3 T/O and Ldg. in the last 90 days for currency requirements..*

Recent Flight Experience
* To act as PIC of an aircraft carrying a passenger:
You must, within the preceding 90 days, **make three takeoff and landings** during day time, **three takeoff and landings to a full stop** during night time at *the same category and class of aircraft to be flown. (Night, 1 H. after sunset to 1 H before sunrise.)*

PRIVATE PILOT HANDBOOK

ARROW Checklist: Mandatory documents required in order to fly.

* **_Airworthiness certificate_** Does not expire, You have to maintain the same way you have got the aircraft from the manufacture, It's like date of birth certificate. _Owner/operator is responsible for ensuring AD's are OK._

* **_Registration certificate_** It expires every 3 years, It can expire as well, If; Owner dies, Owner loses citizenship, Aircraft crash, Owners sell the aircraft, Pink registration is valid for 60 days _(Temporary registration)_

* **Radio License (FCC)** – Required When crossing ADIZ (air defense identification zone) In order to cross ADIZ, the pilot has to have IFR equipped A/C, IFR rated, IFR flight plan, 2-way communication, ATC Clearance, VFR flight plan (DVFR)

* **_POH_** –Pilot's Operating Handbook (Owner Manual)

* **Weight & Balance** – Documentation that lists the aircrafts Basic empty weight, Standard empty weight, Payloads / useful loads, Gross weight.

Medical Class and Certificate
       Below 40 Above 40
(M-Calendar Month)
* **SPL** 3rd Class 60 M 24 M
* **PPL** 3rd Class 60 M 24 M
* **CPL** 2nd Class 12 M 12 M
* **CFI** 3rd Class 60 M 24 M
* **ATPL**1st Class 12 M   6 M
* BASICMED   _48 M._

Special (Ferry) Flight Permit:
It is issued to an aircraft which doesn't meet the airworthy requirement but SAFE TO FLY.
It is Issued By:
* FAA or LOCAL FSDO (Flight Standards District Office)
* DAR (Designated Airworthiness Representative)
When you need this permit
* Weather Problem
* To do repair back to the base
* Export & Import
* Product Testing

An abbreviated weather briefing should be requested to supplement mass disseminated data.

Minimum Equipment List – (MEL) is a precise listing of instrument, equipment, and procedure that allows the aircraft to be operate under specific condition with inoperative equipment. MEL is prepared by the operator by taking reference of the MMEL. (Master MEL) While the MMEL is for an aircraft type, the MEL is tailored to the operator's specific.
If you have inoperative instrument can you fly? For example (clock) Yes, but you have to call and coordinate with maintenance engineer.

Airworthiness Directives (AD) is issued by the FAA to the owner or the operator saying that the aircraft is not SAFE TO FLY because of maintenance, design, etc.... but it is mandatory to comply with it *by the owner or operator.* There are two types of AD.
1- Urgency – Time Limit is given to rectify the problem.
2- Emergency – Ones you receive the directive you cannot fly the aircraft

Special Use Airspace (SUA):
M - MOA- Military Operations Area **"NO need for permission"** , *exercise extreme caution when military activity is being conducted*.
C- Control firing Area (CFA) **"NO need for permission"** if it's Hot/Cold be cautious.
W - Warning Area **"NO need for permission"** if it's Hot/Cold be cautious, 3NM on domestic and international water.
R- Restricted Area YES ***"Need for permission"*** *from the controlling agency.* Cold be in contact with someone .
A – Alert Area **"NO need for permission"** *All Pilots responsible for collision avoidance and Pilot Position Report PPR"*
P - Prohibited Area ***"NEVER ENTER N/A"***
NSA- National Security Areas " AVOID Flying" through NSA.
Note: Contact with controlling agency to make sure, frequencies of agency are in the IFR/VFR Charts. Pilot should report abnormal activity to the control agency.

Cockpit Resource Management- CRM
Pilot should use all the resources inside and outside the aircraft. CRM includes the concepts of Aeronautical Decision Making (ADM), risk management, task management, automation *(FMS, GPS etc.),* Controlled Flight into Terrain Awareness (CFIT), and Situational awareness.

5P Approach to SRM:
* **Plan** (A/FD, Charts, GPS/FMS, VOR, WX) * **Plane** (Systems, limitations)
* **Pilot** (I M SAFE) * **Passengers** (No distractions) * **Programming** (GPS, FMS, WX, ADS B)

Preflight Planning:
* **I M SAFE ! (GO/No-GO** Check List (Pg.10)
* Weather Briefing (Pg. 140)
   -Flight Visibility, (Figure-19)
   - Cloud Coverage (Overcast, Broken) at departure, en route and destination.
   -Flight School/Institute WX Minimums.
* Performance (W&B, VFR NAV Sheet, T/O and Landing RWYs,)
* Fuel Check and Planning at Destination.

PRIVATE PILOT HANDBOOK

ADM- Aeronautical Decision Making   DECIDE CHECK LIST
D- Detect the fact
E- Estimate the needç
C- Choose the best course of action
I – Identify actions
D – Do the necessary action
E – Evaluate the effect of the action.

Risk Management- PAVE
P- Pilot – IMSAFE (Illness - Medication - Stress - Alcohol 0,04 or 8 hours - Fatigue -Eating or Emotion)
A –Aircraft ARROW (Airworthiness - Registration – Radio license - owner manual book, POH, Weight and balance)
V- Environment – Weather condition
E – External Pressure

Where is the weather information available on the ground?
- FSS (Flight Service Station)
- Call 1-800-WX-BRIEF (request Standard Weather Briefing) See Pg. 139
- Determine the sources of data: Applications and web Pages- aviationweather.gov , fltplan.com, foreflight, sky vector, PIREPs, etc.
- Assess the expected weather hazards including departure, en route, alternate, and destination under VFR Conditions such as: - METAR&TAF, - PIREPs
- Atmospheric composition and stability. Figure-69, Pg. 93,109, 189
- Wind (e.g., crosswind, tailwind, wind shear, mountain wave, etc.)
- Temperature – Dew Point - Moisture/Precipitation – Weather System Information (masses, fronts, etc) – Clouds – Turbulence – Thunderstorms and Microbursts – Icing and Freezing Level Information – Obstruction to visibility (e.g., smoke, haze, volcanic ash, etc.) - Fog/Mist - Frost

How do we keep our pilot certificate current?
Student pilot, with valid medical certificate
PPL: Flight review, every 24 calendar months.

Do you need to have an ELT in the airplane today for traffic pattern? Not needed for training within 50 nm of home airport.

Do you need to take your logbook with you?
* Only as a solo student pilot on a X-C flight

If a flight is made from an area of low pressure into an area of high pressure without the altimeter setting being adjusted, the altimeter will indicate:
- *lower than the actual altitude*.

Day VFR Instrument
ATOMATOFLAME
A – Altimeter
T- Tachometer (RPM gauge)
O - Oil Pressure gauge
M - Magnetic Compass
A – Airspeed Indicator
T- Temperature Gauge
O - Oil Temp Gauge
F - Fuel Gauge
L - Landing gear indicator light
A – Anti collusion
M - Manifold pressure
E – ELT (Emergency locator transmitter)
S – Seat belt

Night VFR Instrument Requirement FLAPS
F – Fuses (3 of each kind or one set)
L- Landing Lights ()
A – Anti- collision Light
P – Position Light
S- Source of Electricity

Mode C Transponder Requirement
1- Class A   2- Class B (within 30 miles)
3- Class C
4- Crossing ADIZ
5- Flying at or above 10000ft.

Maintenance/inspection Requirements: AV1ATE

A – Annual inspection *(refer to the aircraft maintenance records)*
V – VOR (30 Days, performed by any pilot for IFR Flight, Date, Place, Discrepancy (Bearing Error), and Signature required.)
1 – 100 hrs. (Every 100 hrs.)
A – Altimeter /pitot static (24 Calendar Months)
T – Transponder (24 Calendar Months)
E – ELT (12 Calendar Months or half of that battery is used)

In the Maintenance Book –
* Airframe – 100 hrs., annual / ELT
* Engine – 100hrs , annual   * 50 Hours Oil Change
* Propeller – 100 hrs., annual
* Avionic / altimeter / transponder – 100 hrs. , annual.
* AD'S – sheets should be signed ,complied with service bulletins (SB)

Preventive Maintenance – means simple or minor preservation operations and replacement of the small standard parts, not involved complex assembly, PPL and above can do preventive maintenance.
PIC / Determine airworthiness, Owner / Maintain the aircraft in an airworthy condition in accordance with FAR 47.403.

PRIVATE PILOT HANDBOOK

METAR is Observation, TAF is Forecast... The METAR only gives you a small snapshot in time. They are only good for an hour. *The information in a METAR is sequential, following a prescribed format.*
On the other hand, TAF's cover a 24 to 30 H. period and they are published 6 times a day. TAF is specific to an airport. *The most accurate part of a forecast occurs at the beginning of the forecast period.*

METAR - is meteorological aviation routine hourly observation report. Prepared every 55 minutes of an hour. There are two types of METAR:
1- Routine METAR- transmitted every hour
2- SPECI –Special report given any time, It is necessary to update weather report.

TAF– Terminal Aerodrome Forecast is the brief statement of the expected meteorological condition. It is given for specified time period *within 5 SM of the center of the airport.* TAF is valid for 24hrs. and update every 6 hrs.
-If 24 H. updated every 6 H. and issued 4 times a day.
-If 30 H. updated every 6 H. and issued 6 times.
"Cumulonimbus cloud (CB)" is the only cloud shown in the TAF.

Decode the following METAR: *Do practice on Figure-64, Pg.185.*
KTPA 041553Z 26017KT 1SM R01L/3500VP6000FT RA BR FEW011 *BKN020*
OVC050 23/22 A3006 RMK AO2 TWR VIS 2 RAB34 SLP178 T02280217 PNO $
Tampa 4th of the month 1553Z, Wind 17 Kt. from the West (260°- 17), Visibility 1 Status Mile, Runway Visual Range for Runway 01, Variable from 3500 Feet to 6000 Feet, Rain, Mist, Cloud Cover Few (1-2/8) at 1100 Feet, *BKN (5-7/8) at 2000 feet*, OVC (8/8) at 5000 feet, Temperature in degrees Celsius 23° Dew Point 22°, Altimeter Setting 3006 In Hg,
Remarks: Ao2 Type of automated station, TWR VIS 2 Tower Visibility 2 Miles, RAB34 Rain began at 34 past hour, SLP178 Sea Level Pressure 1017.8 Mb, T02280217 Hourly temperature and dew point in tenths degrees C 22.8 to 21.7°C, PNO Precipitation amount not available; $ Maintenance Check Indicator: ASOS (The automated surface observation system) requires maintenance.

Documents must be in your personal possession or readily accessible, while operating in PIC of an aircraft: *An appropriate pilot certificate, picture identification and appropriate current medical certificate if required.*

Decode the following TAF: The report was made on the 4th of the month 1 hour and 19 minutes ago, at 14:50 UTC Time : 11:09 (16:09 UTC)
KTPA 041450Z 0415/0518 21012G22KT P6SM VCTS SCT025CB OVC050 TEMPO 0415/0417 VRB20G30KT 3SM TSRA BKN015CB FM041700 27015G25KT P6SM SCT015 OVC030 TEMPO 0417/0420 4SM RA _BKN015_ FM042200 31014G24KT P6SM BKN120 FM050600 35010G18KT P6SM SCT250
Forecast valid from 04 at 15 UTC to 05 at 18 UTC.
Wind 210 °/ 12 Kt. from the South/Southwest with gusts up to 22 Kt,
Visibility: 6 miles (Status Mile) Vicinity Thunderstorm (VCTS) Scattered clouds at a height of 2500 ft, Cumulonimbus. Overcast at a height of 5000 ft
Temporary from 04 at 15 UTC to 04 at 17 UTC, Wind 20 Kt. from variable directions with gusts up to 30 Kt., Visibility: 3 miles, Broken clouds at a height of 1500 ft, Cumulonimbus. thunderstorm, rain (TSRA)
From 04 at 1700 UTC: Wind 17 Kt. from the West with gusts up to 25 Kt. Visibility: 6 miles, Scattered clouds at a height of 1500 ft, Overcast at a height of 3000 ft, Temporary From 04 at 17 UTC to 04 at 20 UTC, Visibility: 4 miles, _broken cloud layer at a height of 1500 ft_, Rain (RA),
From 04 at 2200 UTC, Wind 14 Kt. from the Northwest with gusts up to 24 Kt., Visibility: 6 miles, Broken clouds at a height of 12000 ft.,
From 05 at 0600 UTC: Wind 12 Kt. from the North with gusts up to 18 Kt., Visibility: P6SM means **_greater than 6 statute miles_**, scattered clouds at a height of 25000 ft. _Do practice on Figure-64, Pg.185._

- **ATIS** (Terminal Information System) automated terminal information service (human to monitor the system) ATIS usually gives Alphabet Letter, wind direction and speed, temperature, dew point, altimeter setting and remarks, hourly at 55 minutes past the hour unless the weather is changing rapidly, broadcasting the time in Zulu. Absence of the sky condition and visibility on an ATIS broadcast indicates that the ceiling is at least **5,000 feet** and visibility is 5 miles or more.
- **AWOS** – Automated weather observation system. AWOS Provides altimeter setting, wind speed, direction and gust, temperature and dew point and visibility.
- **ASOS** – The automated surface observation system which provides information about Variable cloud height, variable visibility, rapid pressure change, precipitation type, intensity, accumulation etc.

NOTE: * ATIS/AWOS/ASOS broadcasts, or any information a controller gives you over the radio, is magnetic. * All charts and textual sources (METAR, TAF, winds aloft, surface analysis charts, etc) use **_true north_** as the reference.

Severe Weather Reports/Forecasts and Charts:
AIRMETs, SIGMETs, Convective SIGMETs,

AIRMET (WAs) is an Airman's Meteorological Information report to *all pilots*. They are valid for 6 H. It is for all the aircraft, *especially small aircraft.* (including the ceilings less than 1,000 feet and/or visibility less than 3 miles)
There are 3 types of AIRMET
* **SIERRA/IFR** - Describe IFR condition and/or extensive mountain obscuration.
* **TANGO/Turbulence** – Describe moderate turbulence, surface wind 30 knots or more, low level wind shear.
* **ZULU/Icing**– Describe moderate icing and provides freezing level heights.

SIGMET (WSs) stands for Significant Weather Observation that is potentially hazardous *to all aircraft.* It is valid for 4 hrs. Unscheduled Forecast.
SIGMET Is issued for
* Severe icing
* Severe or extreme turbulence, CAT
* Extreme rain * Dust storms
* Volcanic ash.

CONVECTIVE SIGMET(WSTs) issued for **thunderstorm activity**, valid for 2 H., implies severe or greater turbulence, severe icing, and low-level wind shear.
WSTs includes tornadoes, lines of thunderstorms, thunderstorms over a wide area, embedded thunderstorms, hail (3/4 Inch), 50 Knots/ Greater Wind Gusts.

Avoid SIGMETs, SIGMETs are serious, change rapidly, but you can work around AIRMETs. **SIGMETs effect the safety of all aircraft.**

PIREP information concerning weather as observed by pilot in route. There are 2 types of PIREP.
1- UA – Routine   2- UUA – Urgent
PIREP include (Pilot Report)
➢ Location ➢ Time in Zulu
➢ Flight level ➢ Type of aircraft
➢ Message (Wind shear, bird hazard, turbulence etc.)
To obtain current information regarding cloud tops, icing, and turbulence check the: PIREPs.

Wind Shear Report – wind shear described as a **sudden, drastic shift in wind speed** and **direction** that may occur at any altitude any flight level. *(at least 25 Kt.)* **Be alert** for a sudden change in airspeed and carry an extra margin of speed if wind shear is reported or forecasted on PIREP, TAF, ATC, METAR. It *occurs at all altitudes, in all directions.*

What are the standard temperature and pressure values for sea level?
15°C or 59°F – 29.92" Hg or 1013.2

What do you do if you become lost in-flight? 5 Cs

Climb-Obtain a better view of your surroundings. (Climb to cope- Ceiling and visibility) Never Fly over overcast layers.

Circle – Don't become more lost; stay in one spot. Orient yourself.

Conserve – Reduce power, lean your mixture to save fuel as much as you can.

Communicate – Make contact with an FSS or an air traffic controller. Confess – Don't be afraid to admit that you are lost. ATC Units are there to help you!

Note: If required, set transponder 7700.

VFR, IFR, SVFR

VFR – Visibility 3 SM, Ceiling greater than 1000 ft. (Sky Clear)
IFR- Visibility 1-3 SM, 1000 Ft
Special VFR-_Visibility 1 SM, Clear of Clouds._

SAFETY (PAX Briefing)

Seat Belts, Shoulder Harnesses, Seating Position

Air Vents, All Environmental Factors, Action *(In the event of passenger discomfort/sickness)*

Fire Extinguisher. (Where is it ? How does it work?)

Exit doors, Emergency Evacuation Plan and Emergency Equipment

Traffic Scanning and Talking for Sterile Cockpit._(to search 10-degree sector, systematically focus on different segments of the sky for short intervals.)_

Your Questions (Any Questions?)

* PIC must brief the passengers on the use of safety belts and notify them to fasten their safety belts _during taxi, takeoff, and landing._

Aircraft Category, Class, and Type:

Category: _Airplane, Rotorcraft, Glider, Lighter-Than-Air_ etc.

Class: _Single Engine Land/Sea, Multi Engine Land/Sea_

Type: Specific to aircraft – only required for aircraft with a max gross weight equal or greater than 12,500lbs, turbojet, or any aircraft specified by the FAA.

A Cessna 172 is in the category of "airplane," and the class of "single-engine, land."

A Skorsky-76 is in the category of "helicopter," and the class of "multi-engine."

PRIVATE PILOT HANDBOOK

Graphic Weather Charts (Computer Based Charts): Surface Analysis Chart, Weather Depiction Chart, Radar Summary Chart, Satellite Weather Pictures. All charts are useful for Flight Planning. It is easy to reach all charts via Internet, All information is gathered by Special Weather Radar Systems.

Surface Analysis Chart This is computer prepared chart. The chart is transmitted every 3 H., It provides information about pressure system and fronts it also provides an overview of wind, temperature and dew point.

Convective Outlook Chart 48-Hour forecast thunderstorm activity. Helps show where to expect thunderstorm activity, Issued 5 times daily,

Radar Summary Chart (Precipitation Chart) indicates _location of precipitation_ along with type_, intensity,_ configuration, coverage, top of echo, _direction of cell movement._ This chart is available hourly. And contours provide an indication of the precipitation intensity and the size.

A TAF includes _Wind, visibility, weather phenomena, obstructions to vision, cloud coverage and cloud ceilings in MSL_

• **Weather Depiction Chart** provides an overview of favorable and adverse weather conditions for the chart time and is an excellent resource to help _you determine general weather conditions during flight planning._ Valid for 3hrs.
Chart shows observed Visibility and Ceiling for Planning; (Primarily Used)
1. IFR   2. MVFR (Marginal VFR)
3. VFR

Significant Weather Prognostic Chart (SIGWX) can give you an idea of general weather condition expected in the next 12 to 24 H. from the surface to 24000 feet MSL. (Low Level), consists of two panels. (Left/Right)
Issued 4 times in a day.
-SFC---FL 240 / left 12 H. / right 24 H.
Chart depicts freezing levels, turbulence, and low cloud ceilings and/or restrictions to visibility (shown as contoured areas of MVFR and IFR conditions).
Significant weather prognostic charts provide an overall forecast for _determining areas to avoid_ (Freezing Level and Turbulence)

What is the definition of a ceiling? The height above the ground of a broken or overcast layer.

FA- Aviation Area Forecast is a forecast of Visual Meteorological Conditions (VMC), clouds, FAs covers ten areas. Issued 3 times in a day Details provided result in a categorical outlook which allow for determining regions experiencing Instrument Flight Rules (IFR), Visual Flight Rules (VFR), and Marginal VFR conditions (MVFR). Pilots should utilize FA in conjunction with Radar/Weather Summary Charts, AIRMET, SIGMET to determine forecast en-route weather.

Wind and temperature aloft chart (FD) A computer prepared forecast of wind direction, wind speed and temperature at specified time, altitude, and location, issued 4 times daily.

What's the difference between METAR and TAF? *Observation, Forecast*

ARTCC, RCO and FSS. what do they do?

ARTCC Air Route Traffic Control Center, controls traffic, generally in larger areas and above FL180 (Class A airspace), broadcasts some weather info and provide advisories, provides flight following.

FSS Flight Service Stations (FSS) are air traffic facilities that communicate directly with pilots to conduct preflight briefings, flight plan processing, inflight advisory services, search and rescue initiation, and assistance to aircraft in emergencies. FSS also relay Air Traffic Control clearances, process Notices to Airmen (NOTAMs) and provide updates on aviation meteorological and aeronautical information

RCO – Remote Communication Outlet, (Extends the range of FSS broadcasting ability) when aircraft is flying into a place where there is no proper coverage then you can contact RCO and they will reply you on tlf.

NOTAMS "NOTICE TO AIRMEN" *Time-critical information* is
provided by NOTAMs, contains information such as runway closures, obstruction in the approach and departure path to airport, etc., NOTAMS are divided into 4 parts.
1- NOTAM D- Domestic: Runway closures etc.
2- NOTAM L – Local: VOR Not working etc.
3- NOTAM FDC – Flight Data center , chart approach plate under maintenance, amendments to instrument procedures.
4- NOTAM M- is for military use.
*FDC NOTAMS contain regulatory information, such as: TFR.

What is BasicMed?
BasicMed allows you to fly with a valid state-issued driver license and pilot certificate. No more medical required, instead complete a free online medical course every 2 years and get a physical from a regular doctor every 4 years.
How to qualify. You must have held at least a 3rd Class Medical or higher during the previous 10 years that was not denied or revoked. *(after July 14,2006)* If not, your first time through the process you will have to pass the FAA Medical that is 3rd Class or higher.
* Aircraft MTOW of not more than 6.000 pounds.
* Aircraft not authorized to carry more than 6 occupants *(5 pax + pilot)*
* *can fly up to 18.000 feet MSL and 250 Kt.* * Pilot can fly IFR, if current.
* can't fly for compensation or hire. * *can only fly in the USA.*

Temporary Flight Restriction (TFR) Due to VIP, Bad Weather, Air Show etc. You can become familiar with TFR through,
1. NOTAMS
2. DUATS
3. FAA Site
4. FSS and Online Application.

If a pilot changes his *permanent mailing address,* how long can the pilot continue to exercise the privileges of their pilot certificate without notifying the FAA? 30 days.

What would you do if you found that the landing light was inoperative? Did you rent the airplane or do you own it?
If you own the airplane, you can take off without an operative landing light. If it was a rental, you can't take off with an inoperative landing light per FAR 91.205. (We adhere to the regulations in 91.205 /91.213 (d))

How is lift created? Simple, the difference in pressure above/below the airfoil produces the lift.
Newton's 3rd law - Airfoils accelerate airflow downward. The equal and opposite reaction as described by Newton forces the airfoil upwards.
Bernoulli's Principle – As the velocity of a fluid or gas increases the pressure decreases. High speed air over the upper surface of wing creates low pressure area while comparatively lower speed air beneath the wing creates high pressure which produces an **upwards force** that contributes to the total lift.

PRIVATE PILOT HANDBOOK

Memory Items for Airspace Classifications:
A = Altitude. 18,000 feet or above (till FL 600)
B = Big. Big jets, big size, etc ()
C = Crowded (approach control, etc)
D = Dialog (Talk to the tower)
E = Everywhere Else (Anywhere not A, B, C or D)
G = Good for you to Go for it! (Very few rules. Just enter!)

CLASS A From FL180 ft to FL600.
Requirement -
ATC Clearance- Must
Mode C Transponder DME-FL 240
IFR flight plan
IFR equipped Aircraft
IFR rated pilot
Two Way Communications

Class B From Surface to 10000 FT.
Requirements (Upside down Wedding Cake, most stringent rules)
ATC Clearance-Must
Mode C Transponder with encoding alt.
Two-way communication (Mostly IFR)
VFR Possible/Weather minimum 3 SM (5 Km.) visibility, clear of clouds (Keep away from cloud formations)
Pilots in class B airspace must have a private pilot's certificate, or have met the requirement of 14 CFR 61.95.
No Special VFR Flight.
Pilots are expected to comply with the 200 knots speed limit.

Class C *from surface to 4000 FT*
Mode C Transponder
Two-way communication
VFR /Weather minimum 1000 above, 500 Below, 2000 Horizontal \ 3SM Visibility(152)
Core Surface Area: 5 NM Circle
Upper Shelf Area: 10 NM Circle.
Outer Area: 20 NM Circle (Before entering Class C, establish two-way communication here.)
No specific pilot certification required. Speed below 200 knots.
Under what condition may an aircraft operate from a satellite airport within Class C airspace?
* contact ATC as soon as practicable after takeoff.

Class D From Surface to 2500 FT
Requirement (Towered Airport)
Two-way communication
Weather minimum 1000 above, 500 below, 2000 horizontal \ 3 SM Visibility (152)
Class D airspace reverts to class E or G during hours when the tower is closed. No transponder is required.

What is the difference between controlled and uncontrolled airspace? Class G is the only uncontrolled airspace. ATC has no jurisdiction.

Class E – From Surface to 17999 and FL 600 and above. (FAR AIM 3-2-6)
Requirement
Controlled – for IFR (Two way communication), Uncontrolled – For VFR
Weather minimum
  Above 10000 ft 1000 above ,1000 below , 1 SM horizontal \ 5 SM visibility
  Below 10000 ft 1000 above , 500 below , 2000 horizontal \ 3 SM visibility
There are 7 types of class E
(1) <u>*Surface area designated for an airport.*</u> See Pg.36
(2) <u>*Extension to a surface area.*</u> See Pg.36
(3) Airspace used for transition.
(4) En Route Domestic Areas.
(5) Federal Airways.
(6) Offshore Airspace Areas.
(7) Unless designated at a lower altitude..."

Class G – From Surface to 1200 AGL
Surface to 700 AGL. See/ Pg.34
Uncontrolled Airspace
Weather minimum:
 Surface to 1200, Day <u>1 SM, and Clear of Cloud</u>
 Night 1000 above, 500 Below, 2000 Horizontal / 3 SM visibility
 1200 to 10000 , Day <u>1SM,</u> 500 below, 1000 above 2000 horizontal
 Night 1000 above ,500 Below, 2000 Horizontal / 3 SM visibility
 ABOVE 10,000   1000 above,1000 below, 1 SM horizontal / 5 SM visibility

How to select altitude
* Airspace
* Terrain
* VFR Checkpoint
* VFR Cruising Altitude
* Weather
* Performance

What is the airspeed where Induced and Parasite drag meet? ***Vg – Best glide speed.*** This is also described as L/D Max or the maximum lift to drag ratio. See Figure-11

Why higher stall speed with Forward CG? More airflow deflection of the elevator required to maintain altitude at slower airspeeds resulting in high AOAs.

ALTITUDES:
Absolute Altitude- The height of an aircraft above the surface.
Indicated Altitude- The altitude read directly from the altimeter
Pressure Altitude – When the altimeter setting is adjusted to 29.92.
True Altitude – The height of the aircraft above the sea level
Density Altitude –Pressure altitude corrected for nonstandard temperature.

AIRSPEEDS:
Indicated Airspeed - The speed of the airplane as observed on the airspeed indicator.
Calibrated Airspeed - The airspeed indicator reading corrected for instrument and position.
True Airspeed - Calibrated airspeed corrected from altitude and nonstandard temperature.

Center of Gravity (CG): Weight, Arm, Moments.
The CG must always be within limits, however, depending where in the allowable range the C.G. falls will effect performance

Forward CG (Nose Heavy)	**Aft CG (Rearward):**
Lower Cruise Speed	Higher Cruise Speed
Higher Stall Speed	Lower Stall Speed
More Stable (Nose Heavy)	Less Stable
Favorable Stall Recovery	Adverse Stall Recovery
Difficulty in rotating and rounding out (in steering) during landing.	Shorter arm between CG and control surfaces, making the tail less effective *(more tail down force)*

What s the main concern about Aft CG (rearward CG)?
Should the aircraft stall or spin, it will be much more difficult to recover and increase airspeed.

Why do you drain a sample of fuel before each flight?
Fuel weighs roughly 6 lbs. and water weighs about 8 lbs. Because water is heavier it always sinks to the bottom of the fuel tanks. Therefore, we drain from the lowest points in the fuel system.

Spin and Stall.

Stall: when you _exceed the critical angle of attack,_ (AOA), usually 15°, and no more lift up wing. Critical AOA is an aerodynamic **constant** for a given airfoil.
Spin: Spin is _an aggravated stall_ resulting in rotation about the center of gravity. TOO MUCH rudder in the direction of the bank at the stall is the main reason of spin. A spin requires full rudder and a stalled wing, which usually means pulling the yoke or stick back a lot. Don't Forget: If there is no yaw there is no spin.

Spin Recovery:
- **P -** Power to idle
- **A -** Neutral Aileron
- **R -** Opposite Rudder
- **E -** Elevator Down and then Pitch Up

FREDA: VFR Navigation Checklist
F – Fuel. What is our current fuel state, and do we have sufficient remaining.
R- Radio. Are we on the correct frequency, with a backup frequency set?
E – Engine. Are all the warning lights out? Are all temperatures and pressures in the green arc and carburetor heat out of the yellow arc (if available).
D- Direction. Are we on the right heading or course? Is our direction indicator aligned correctly with our magnetic compass? Does our current heading correct appropriately for wind drift? Is the moving map on GPS is working correctly?
A – Altitude. Are we flying at the planned altitude and is it appropriate for the area we are flying over?

What factors affect air density?
The air's density depends on its temperature, its pressure and how much water vapor is in the air.
Temperature (Heat) – warm air expands is less dense
Height (Pressure altitude) – air at higher altitudes is less dense
Humidity – A parcel of humid air is less dense because water molecules take up more room and spread out the air molecules. (geometry of air molecules)

Describe the engine of Airplane to be flown:
Engine manufactured by AVCO LYCOMING, Model Number O-235-L2C, Max Power 110 BHP, Max engine speed 2550 RPM, 4- cylinder, 4- Stroke, air cooled, horizontally opposed, direct drive carbureted reciprocating piston engine.

Primary Flight Controls
* **Rudder** – (yaw) controls the movement of airplane about vertical axes.
* **Ailerons** – (roll) controls the movement of airplane about its longitudinal axes.
* **Elevators** – (pitch) control the movement of airplane about its lateral axes.

Secondary Flight Controls
* Trim- Trim tabs are small, adjustable surfaces on the elevators which allow the pilot to relieve pressure on the control.

Flaps – used for increasing the angle of descent without increasing the speed.
1. Single Slotted flap system.
2. It is electrically driven by electric engine on the right wing
3. Provide lift and drag
- 10 degree – Lift
- 20 degree- lift & drag
- 30 degree – drag

4-Process of Piston Engines and how It works.:
- Intake -Compression -Combustion – Exhaust
Compression makes the air-fuel combination more volatile for easier ignition.
C- Carburetor mixes fuel and air in the correct proportion.
H- Horizontally opposed: back and forth movement of the internal engine components. Reliable, simple and easy to maintain.(Flat Engine)
A- Air Cooled- it is cooled by the air (reduce the weight)
N- Normally Aspirated- Ambient air enters the intake manifold. (there is no turbo or supercharger)
D-Direct Driven (convert pressure into a rotational motion.)

Propeller- generates thrust to keep the airplane moving forward.
* manufactured by McAuley or Hartzell
* *Fixed Pitch Propeller*
* Effective for cruise or climb
* 2 blades.

Oil System – Wet oil system. Oil tank capacity is 6 quarts. Oil is used for; (Refer to POH/AFM)
* Cooling
* Sealing
* Cleaning
* Lubricating

The proper adjustment to make on the attitude indicator during level flight is to align the miniature airplane to the horizon bar.

PRIVATE PILOT HANDBOOK

Left Turning Tendencies.
(See Page 32, 171,181)
Torque Effect,
P-Factor,
Gyroscopic Precession,
Spiraling Slipstream.

Hot Spot is the area at the airport where most of the collision, runway incursions take place. You need to be extra caution and to clear the HOT SPOT area, You should stop, make sure and start taxiing again.

Landing Gear Fixed tricycle landing gear
* The main landing gear include brakes which are the hydraulically actuated disk type and can be controlled separately by each rudder pedal.
* The nose gear is equipped with struts and shimmy damper to absorb shock and to protect the propeller and engine.

Fuel System Gravity feed fuel system. The fuel flow from the wing fuel tank to the fuel shutoff valve which is in ON position allows the fuel to flow through fuel strainer and then to the carburetor from there the fuel mix with air and then flows into the cylinder.
As a student pilot, You have to know below to calculate W&B, Check POF or AFM for more information..
If there is, the boost pump is electrically powered and is used as a backup.
(Total tank capacity – 35/45 gal (varied to type of AC), Usable fuel – 30/42
Unusable fuel, Each tank capacity etc.
Type of Fuel and its color: Aviation Gasoline AVGAS 100LL – Blue.
What is the main purpose of Primer - to inject fuel directly to the carburetor.
We drain out fuel to check: Firstly Color, Secondly Water/ moisture for engine performance and Icing, Finally, Dirt (Fuel contamination)

Aircraft Stability: If straight-and-level flight (all the forces acting on the airplane are in equilibrium) is disrupted by a disturbance in the air, such as wake turbulence, the airplane might pitch up or down, yaw left or right, or go into a roll. *Stability is the ability to return to a state of equilibrium.*
Positive Stability – Tendency to return to equilibrium
Neutral Stability – Tendency to stay in new position
Negative Stability – Tendency to continue to move away from equilibrium
Static Stability – Initial tendency Dynamic Stability – Response over time.

Hydraulic Systems
Hydraulically-actuated brake. Disk type brakes on each main gear wheel. The hydraulic line connects each brake to the master cylinder located in each pilot rudder pedals. When applying equal pressure to the top of rudder pedals, the brakes slow and stop the airplane.

Electrical System - Electrical energy is provided by 28-volt direct current system powered by engine driven 60-amp alternator and a 24-volt 14-amp hour battery located on the right forward side of firewall.
Avionics: Radio, GPS, VOR, ADF

What does the mixture control do? (Performance and Protection)
As we gain altitude, the air becomes less dense. (The more you climb up, the less air pressure (due to the oxygen level)) If we do not make any adjustments then we will have an *excessively rich fuel/air mixture. This can result in carbon build up in the cylinders which can foul the spark plugs and reduce engine power.* Leaning the mixture decreases the fuel flow and compensates for this.
Case: As you are climbing to your cruise altitude, you realize you forgot to lean the mixture control. What happens to fuel/air mixture entering the engine? *The fuel-air mixture becomes richer* because the density of air decreases while the amount of fuel remains constant.

Pitot Static System:
Pitot-tube: Airspeed
- If pitot-tube partially blocked and drain hole remains open the *Airspeed* indicator will show "0 "ZERO
- If the pitot-static system is blocked, the *Airspeed* indicator will act as Altimeter.

Static-port: Airspeed, Altimeter, Vertical speed.
- If static-port blocked the *Airspeed* will be over sensitive.

Altimeter freezes at last altitude, *Vertical speed* will show zero "0"

Supplemental Oxygen requirement
* 12500 ft. –if the flight more than 30min for crew (Figure-68, pg. 188)
* 14000 ft. – all time for crew
* 15000ft – all occupant all time

Environmental Systems:
* Air Vents   * Cabin Heat
● Deicing and anti-icing
* Pitot Heat   * Carb Heat

Gyroscopic Instruments:
Vacuum Gyro: Heading, Altitude, Suction gauge.
-If the vacuum pump fails,
* the **Heading Indicator (HI)** will keep moving or turning.
* the **Attitude Indicator (AI)** will be shaking.
* the **Suction Gauge** will be indicating high / low
Why does the aircraft have vacuum Gyro and Electric Gyro?
Because if the vacuum Gyro fails, there will be a back up.
Electric Gyro: Turn coordinator.

Hyperventilation: Lack of carbon dioxide or excess of oxygen in the body. _Results from: emotional tension, anxiety, or fear._
Symptoms:
* _Faster/extra deep_ breathing rate
* Tingling of feet
* Dizziness * Headache
* Drowsiness
Prevention:
* Breath in paper bag
* Speak loudly
* _Breath slowly_

Spatial Disorientation the inability of a pilot to correctly interpret aircraft _attitude, altitude or airspeed in relation to the Earth_
When does it happen?
* Dark Night
* In the Clouds
* No horizon
Symptoms confusion
Prevention
* Rely on your instrument
* Fly the instruments

Hypoxia Lack of oxygen in the body.
Symptoms
* Body change in color (blue finger nail)
* Dizziness * Drowsiness
* Headache * Nausea
Preventions
* Supplementary Oxygen
* Descend to lower altitude
* If symptoms persist, Land as soon as possible.

Middle Ear and Sinus Problem
Atmospheric pressure change associated with ascending and descending can cause pain and discomfort if the air becomes trapped in your ears or sinus cavities.
Prevention (climb or descend slowly) If your or sinuses become blocked. climb or descend as required to help equalize pressure.

Types of Hypoxia :
Hypemic Hypoxia : Occurs when the blood is not able to carry a sufficient amount of oxygen to the body's cells, because of a disease like anemia, CO poisoning or blood loss.
Stagnant Hypoxia : Oxygen deficiency in the body due to poor circulation of the blood caused by excessive G Force and cold temperatures . may cause hyperventilation.
Histotoxic Hypoxia: The cells can't use Oxygen effectively because of drugs, alcohol, or other poisons
Hypoxic Hypoxia: Lack of Oxygen in the atmosphere due to high altitude.
Note: 50% of Earth's atmospheric pressure is lost by 18,000' and 75% by 34,000'.
Although we have the same oxygen, why don't we breathe effectively after 15000 feet? *Because the partial pressure of oxygen decreases.*

Carbon Monoxide Poisoning
Odorless, colorless gas which can comes through a faulty cabin heat pipe if there is any leakage from exhaust, *increases with altitude.*
Symptoms:
* Drowsiness   * Dizziness
* Death   * Headache
* *Fatigue, loss of muscular power*
Prevention: ➢ Close the cabin heat ➢Open window (Let the air in) ➢Land

If the aircraft's radio fails, what is the recommended procedure when landing at a controlled airport?
Observe the traffic flow, enter the pattern, and look for a light signal from the tower.

Prior to takeoff, the altimeter should be set to which altitude or altimeter setting?
The current local altimeter setting, if available, or the departure airport elevation.

Motion sickness is a common disturbance of the inner ear. This is the area of the body that affects your sense of balance and equilibrium. Motion sickness happens when your brain receives conflicting messages about motion and your body's position in space.
Symptoms ➢ Vomiting ➢ Nausea ➢ Dizziness ➢ Uneasiness ➢ Sleep **Prevention** ➢ Focus on a point outside along the horizon ➢ No movement of head

Wake Turbulence Avoidance- Turbulence produced by the wing tip vortex of heavy, clean and slow aircraft. Vortex goes downwards and outwards. When following a larger aircraft on final approach, the key points the FAA recommends to avoid wake turbulence are:
To avoid turbulence *(The greatest vortex strength occurs when the generating aircraft is <u>heavy, clean, and slow.</u>)*
➢ <u>*Stay at or above the larger aircraft's final approach flight path.*</u>
➢ Note liftoff point, and take-off before.
➢ <u>*Note the touchdown point, and land beyond it.*</u>

Power Line/Wires Strike Avoidance: Pilots have to fly away from any antenna and not at low altitude because power lines and wires are hard to be seen.
* Use proper VFR Sectional chart for making flight plan,
* Try to avoid the places where there is chance of wire strike. Especially while flying in valleys.
* Fly over with sufficient distance and safe altitude
* Don't choose a place for an emergence landing where there are power lines.
• **Check List Usage** - Pilots should use the checklist all the time so as not to forget anything by mistake. **"DO and Read or Read and DO "**
<u>*If you fly into or away from the sun, pay more attention to the wires crossing the valleys.*</u>

Collision Avoidance:
1- Right of way. Pg.112
2- See and Avoid.
3- Approach clear, runway clear.
4- Communicate, Readback correctly.
5- Visual scanning in 10˚sector
6- Night focus at a point and feel any movement. <u>*Scan slowly to permit offcenter viewing.*</u>

What is an Alternate?
A second option for landing in case you cannot land at your planned destination.

Positive A/C Control – I have to control the A/C all the time
1- Aviate – Fly You're A/C
2- Navigate - Flight plan / Navigation
3- Communicate – Communicate correctly.
• **Positive Exchange of Flight Control**
1- Your Control –
2- My Control – He takes the control
3- Your control – you leave the control.
4- Make sure he takes the control (visual Check)

LAHSO Land and Hold Short Operations is an air traffic control procedure for aircraft landing and holding short of an intersecting runway or point on a runway, to balance airport capacity and system efficiency with safety.
* As a pilot You have the right to accept or reject LAHSO Clearance.
* to accept LAHSO I have to know / landing distance /weight / temperature .
Requirement:
* *Student pilot cannot participate*
* *Pilot can reject any time*
* Minimum visibility 3 mile and ceiling 1000 feet.

How to avoid Runway Incursion
* Use airport diagram / Progressive taxi / make sure the instructions given are correct
* Maintain situational awareness
* Good communication / read back correctly
* Effective CRM/SRM
* Familiar with airport
* Look outside (heads up while moving)
* When entering a runway or taxiway, check the sign
* NOTAM's
* Check compass before takeoff roll. (Confirm the runway)

CFIT-Control Flight into Terrain occurs when an airworthy aircraft under the complete control of the pilot is inadvertently flown into terrain.
you must fly the aircraft away from and above any obstacle. *(Check Sectional Chart before the flight and determine the height and location of obstacles and mountainous areas)*
In order to avoid: (Maintain Visual Contact with the ground, Don't descent below MSA)
* Congested area 1000 ft above - 2000 ft horizontal from highest obstacle
* Uncongested area 500 ft above
* Always try to fly above the maximum elevation/obstruction
* Familiarize yourself with surrounding terrain and obstacles.
* Maintain Situational Awareness all time
* Maintain safe altitude (MSA), be alert to the Power Lines /Wires
* Wildlife area 2000 ft above.

Where can I Find Runway Lengths? A/FD or VFR Sectional Charts

What type of clouds, visibility and precipitation would you expect from stable/unstable air? *(See Figure-65, Pg.185)*

Stable Air:	**Unstable Air:**
* _High_ barometric pressure	* _Low_ barometric pressure
* _Stratiform clouds,_	* _Cumuliform clouds_
* Fair to _poor visibility,_	* Clouds with vertical _(CB)_
* Smooth air,	*_Turbulence (bumpy)_
* _Continuous rain,_ drizzle	*Showery precipitation
* Shallow lapse rate	*_Good visibility,_
* Good flying conditions	* Steep lapse rate, gusty

**Warming from below _decrease the stability of an air mass._
** Moist, stable air flowing upslope can be expected to _produce **stratus** type (low level, layered) clouds._

What are the general characteristics of low/high pressure areas? *Note: Winds blow towards the low pressure. See Figure.*

Low	**High** (lower altitude on altimeter)
Cyclone	Anti Cyclone
Counterclockwise	Clockwise
Rising air (cooling air) ↑	Descending (Sinking) air ↓
Trough (extended area of LP)	Ridge (extended area of HP)

Factors must be present for a thunderstorm (Moisture, Instability, A lifting force are three necessary conditions.)
Greatest Turbulence and Lightning
A- Sufficient Water vapor.
B- Unstable air.
C- Updraft.
Three Stages of thunderstorm:
* **Cumulus Stage** – _Updraft_ cause raindrop to increase in size
* **Mature stage** – lightning, perhaps roll clouds. _(start of precipitation at surface)_
* **Dissipating Stage** – Downdraft and rain begin to dissipate.
Note: If there is thunderstorm activity in the vicinity of an airport at which you plan to land, _be prepared for wind-shear turbulence_

Isobars (lines of equal air pressure), The closer together the isobars are, the greater the wind speed. See Figure-67

Discuss the types of fog. Evaporation from the rain saturates the cool air and fog forms. (Advection, Radiation, Upslope)
Advection Fog: _Moist warm air moves over colder land or water._ (East Cost/Florida, Gulf of Mexico) _An air mass moving inland from the coast in winter._ Advection fog has a greater impact on aviation. Advection and Upslope fogs depend upon wind in order to exist.
Radiation (Ground-Inland) Fog: Forms on **clear/calm nights** with little or no wind and only over land. (West Cost/California)
Upslope: Moist unstable air is cooled as wind pushes it up a slope
Precipitation Induced: Warm rain falls through cool air.
Low-level turbulence can occur and icing can become hazardous in steam fog.

What does dew point and _temperature/dew point spread_ mean? Dew point is the temperature at which the air becomes saturated. (temperature to which air must be cooled to become saturated) _Fog and low clouds are most likely_ when the temperature/dew point spread is 5°F (2°C) or less and decreasing.
When the dew point is colder than 32°F (0°C), then **_frost_** will form. _Frost will disrupt (spoil) the smooth flow of air over the wing,_ adversely affecting its _lifting capability._ So, Frost on the wing of an airplane must always _be removed before flying._

Changes in weather is are caused by the sun and _unequal heating of the Earth's surface._ Shortly, _weather (winds)_ is a direct result of the Earth spinning.

The atmosphere is a mixture of gases that surround the Earth. The troposphere, up to FL480 (14.5 km) over the equatorial regions. The vast majority of weather, clouds, storms, and temperature variances occurs. The tropopause is t the top of the troposphere. (Jetstream)

How does icing affect airplane performance?
Structural Ice accumulation disrupts the airflow around the aircraft, causing _adverse effects on the aircraft's performance._ For example, ice build-up on the wings increases weight, and reduces lift. Icing on the aircraft's propeller increases drag and reduces thrust. **Discuss the types of icing.** See Pg.168

110

Clouds are divided into four families according ***to their height range***.

Low	Middle	High
Stratus *(Layered Clouds)*	Altostratus	Cirrus
Cumulus	Altocumulus	Cirrocumulus
Stratocumulus	Nimbostratus	Cirrostratus Note:

Clouds with vertical development Cumulonimbus (CB).

What are the hazardous attitudes and their antidotes? **RAIIM**

Hazardous Attitudes	**Antidotes**
- Resignation ⟶	I'm not helpless.
What's the use?	I can make a difference.
- *Anti-Authority* ⟶	*Follow the rules-*
"Don't tell me what to do"	They are usually right.
- *Impulsivity* ⟶	*Not so fast! Think first.*
"Do something quickly"	
- *Invulnerability* ⟶	*It could happen to me*
"It won't happen to me!"	
- *Macho* *"I can do it"* ⟶	*Taking changes is foolish.*

Weather Fronts: The zone between *contrasting air masses* is called a "Front". All fronts create lifting forces. *(Rising air cools, causes condensation and respectively clouds and precipitation that limits the ceiling)* Fronts are usually detectable at the surface by a significant change in air temperature, pressure, *wind speed and direction.* Pg.188
Cold Front A cold front is when a mass of cold air moves to displace warm air. (Cold air is dense) *Fast Moving Cold Front* causes thunderstorm
Warm Front: Warm air mass overtakes and rides over a cold air mass.
Stationary Front: Forces of the two air masses are relatively equal
Occluded Front: Cold front catches up to a slow-moving warm front.
(See Figure-65, Pg.185)

HIWAS-Hazardous Inflight Weather Advisory Service, transmitted over selected VORs, includes AIRMETs, SIGMETs, Convective SIGMETs, Center Weather Advisories (CWAs), Severe Alert Weather Watches (AWWs), and urgent PIREPs.

Upon encountering severe turbulence, what action should be taken?
* *Maintain level flight attitude.*

Types of Aviation Weather Briefings

Standard	Abbreviated	Outlook
- See Page 139.	- _Supplement mass disseminated data_	- Proposed time of departure
- _Easiest way_ to get complete planning.	- Update a previous one	_6-8 H. in advance_

What the right-of-way rules are as applied to the different categories of aircraft?
* Emergency - _Aircraft in distress have priority_.
* Balloon
* Glider
* Aircraft Refueling/_Towing other_
* Airship
* Rotorcraft/ Airplane

What is the definition of ADM? A systematic approach to risk assessment and stress management. The two defining elements of ADM are hazard and risk.

Sea Breezes are cool, dense air masses (High Pressure) _moving inland from over the water_ to replace warm air (Low Pressure) that has risen over the land.

Lens-shaped clouds are known as standing lenticular clouds.

The wind at 5,000 feet AGL is southwesterly while the surface wind is southerly. Tell me the reason.
This difference in direction is primarily _due to friction_ between the wind and the surface.

For severe weather, you need warm, moist air (via evaporation and sublimation). _Moisture_ in the air creates more hazards during flight than any other weather. Humid air means _instability and thunderstorms._
The most hazardous: Squall Line

The basic purpose of adjusting the fuel/air mixture at altitude is to decrease the fuel flow in order to compensate for decreased air density.

You have been running an excessively rich mixture for some time now. As a result: _The spark plugs may become fouled._

While cruising at 9,500 feet MSL, the fuel/air mixture is properly adjusted. What will occur if a descent to 4,500 feet MSL is made without readjusting the mixture?
 * *The fuel/air mixture may become excessively lean.*

What is the purpose of the airplane engine's mixture control, Air/fuel ratio (AFR)?
To regulate the ratio of gasoline to air entering the fuel distribution system.

Detonation may occur at high-power settings when the fuel mixture ignites instantaneously instead of burning progressively and evenly.

If a flight is made from an area of high pressure into an area of lower pressure without the altimeter setting being adjusted, the altimeter will indicate higher than the actual altitude above sea level. *HIGH TO LOW: LOOK OUT BELOW*

If the pitot tube and outside static vents become clogged, which instruments would be affected? *The altimeter, airspeed indicator, and vertical speed indicator*

A constant-speed propeller is more efficient than other propellers because: *It allows selection of the most efficient engine rpm* and permits the pilot to select the blade angle for the most efficient performance. The throttle controls power output as registered on the manifold pressure gauge *and the propeller control* regulates engine RPM.

If a pilot suspects that the engine (with a fixed-pitch propeller) is detonating during climb-out after takeoff, the initial corrective action to take:
It would be to lower the nose slightly to increase airspeed.

Layers of Atmosphere: Troposphere, stratosphere, and mesosphere.

Excessively high engine temperatures, either in the air or on the ground, will cause loss of power, excessive oil consumption, and possible permanent internal engine damage.

Loss of oil pressure: Look for a place to land as soon as possible.

Electrical Malfunctions: Symptom: red low voltage light and/or discharge reading on ammeter. Immediate actions to taken include:
- All non-critical instruments should be turned off immediately.
- Notify ATC of situation and intentions, Squawk 7600
- Land as soon as practical. (No flap landing may be required)

Structural Icing: *(Visible moisture, freezing rain/temperature)*
- Fly the aircraft and Notify ATC.
- Carb. Heat and Pitot Heat ON.
- Descend to the an altitude, above freezing temperature (if possible)
- Land ASAP.

Smoke/Fire In Cabin: (usually caused by electrical, heating system malfunction)
- Eliminate/reduce the fire (after fire extinguished, open windows.)
- Land ASAP. Emergency Descent *(If electrical fire, turning off all electrical equipment to reduce the aggravation of the fire, if some equipment is vital, turn on one at a time, and check for odors or smoke to determine if needed equipment was the cause of the fire)*

Vacuum Malfunction: (air block, pump failure, See Pg.105)
- Terminate the VFR Flight
- Land as soon as practible.

Engine Compartment Fire:
(See POH Procedures.)
-During Start Up: (Continue cranking to keep air moving)
 *If engine starts up,
- Set at high RPM to put out.
- Mix. Idle Cutoff, Throttle- Full, Fuel-Off, Evacuate the plane,
* During flight, (If the fire exists)
- Apply Forced Landing Procedures (See Pg.65)

Asymetrical Flap Deployment:
(Flap actuator motor or corrosion of power connector)
- Ailerons have the authority to overcome the imbalance in lifting (asymetrical chord lines)
- Avoid landing with crosswind to the deployed flaps.
- Increase the approach speed (due to the different stall speeds over the wings.)

Carburetor Icing: Carburetor Heat-On, Monitor RPM. Engine will run rough and loose RPM as ice melts, followed by an increase in RPM and a return to smooth operation. Leave Carb. Heat On until engine smooths out and increases RPM. (If drop and fluctuation persists, descend to the safe altitude, lans as soon as practical)

Private Pilot Written Exam Hints:

When taking a knowledge test, please keep the following points in mind: Figure-52 gives an idea related to the subject matters you should focus on before taking a test.
• Carefully read the instructions provided with the test.
• Answer each question in accordance with the latest regulations and guidance publications.
• Read each question carefully before looking at the answer options. You should clearly understand the problem before trying to solve it.
• After formulating a response, determine which answer option corresponds with your answer. The answer you choose should completely solve the problem.

Subject Title	Numbers
Aircraft Performance	8-10
Airplane Systems	8-12
Aviation Weather	6-8
FAA Regulations	9-10
Flight Operations	8-12
Flight Planning	12-15
Aerodynamics	5-7
Aeronautical Decision Making (ADM)	2-4
Total Number of Questions	60

Figure- 52 Private Pilot Knowledge Test

• Remember that only one answer is complete and correct. The other possible answers are either incomplete or erroneous. If a certain question is difficult for you, mark it for review and return to it after you have answered the less difficult questions. This procedure will enable you to use the available time in the most efficient manner.
• When solving a calculation problem, be sure to read/go over all the associated notes and graphs/tables.
• For questions involving use of a graph, you may request a printed copy that you can mark in computing your answer. This copy and all other notes and paperwork must be given to the testing center upon completion of the test.

How to carry out Private Pilot Certificate Check ride (Oral/Practical Exam):

Let's take a closer look at the sequence of events that constitute the PPL check ride.

You will be asked questions related to the following tasks, mostly including ACS tasks and objectives *(See Figure-2B, Student Pilot Certification Standard Checklist, Pg.6)*. You don't have to impress the DPE, you only need to show a specific level of competency in terms of knowledge and skill. Fly with discipline, be methodical and be rigorous about your answers. utilize the checklist in every stage of flight and brief whoever is flying with you (CFI or DPE). Don't forget aviation is the ultimate **"learn from others"** arena. Don't be rush in answering the questions. Don't assume that you know all. When the DPE is talking, listen, take notes and don't interrupt.

I. Preflight Preparation.

- Task A – Pilot Qualifications. Logbook Endorsements and IACRA. Place and check sticky notes in your logbook to donate XC, night, hood, towered airports etc.

- Task B – Airworthiness Requirements. Documents required to be on you/in the plane, ARROW, instruments required for day/night VFR, T-Check, Ad's, how can you find and What they mean to you as a pilot? Where/how I can make sure AD's have been addressed on a plane I'm renting, Special Flight Permit *(Ferry Flight)*, MEL?

- Task C – Weather Information. VFR Minimums, differences between Marginal VFR, Special VFR and IFR? What information could be obtained with radar charts? *(direction of movement, speed, intensity of precipitation and cloud tops).*, types of fronts? What do they look like on the charts and which direction do they move around high- and low-pressure areas? What ISOBAR? What information can we gather from ISOBARS? *(winds/pressure)*, AIRMETs and SIGMETs, Icing Conditions, effects on carburetor icing? Can you explain METAR/TAF and enroute weather at departure/destination of the XC Route? "Would you fly this cross country as planned today?" What does ADS-B mean? How would you obtain an in-flight update on weather at your destination?

- Task D – Cross-Country Flight. Flight Planning on VFR NAVLOG, Sectional Chart, Minimum Safe Altitude (MSA), Checkpoints, limitations of route, sectional/performance chart readings should be as easy as reading a road map. *(See Figure-70, Pg.190)*

- Task E – National Airspace System (NAS). Symbols on a sectional charts *(airspace, TFR, obstructions, elevation, MOA, Prohibited Areas, Airport Info, Lightning Systems of Runways, LAHSO etc.)*
- Task F – Performance and Limitations. Weight and balance (W&B), the effects of improper balance (aft/forward CG and Stall Speed relation) and/or being overweight, Weight and Moment Envelope Graph, be ready for case questions, stall and spin awareness and recovery, if the runway is wet and/or grass during takeoff and landing, what action should be taken? Procedures for landing over 50-foot obstacle?
- Task G – Operation of System. Axes of airplane, flaps and their effects on performance, why do we use them for short/soft field takeoffs? What type of fuel does the aircraft use and what color is it? (dye color: blue,100LL), How do you handle an emergency? You run into IMC conditions unintentionally, what should you do? *(Emergency Declaration, Squawk, Request Radar Vector, VOR Tracking, etc.),* discuss the microbursts' wind shear and the effects on the airplane's performance.
- Task H – Human Factors. How carbon monoxide (CO) affects you and what you should do if you suspect exposure to it *(faulty cabin heaters and engine exhaust systems)*, Hypoxia, symptoms **of CO** poisoning, headache, dizziness, etc., how to detect, avoid, and recover from hypoxia? Supplemental Oxygen, descend to below 10.000 feet, if you start breathing very quickly, what should you do? Hyperventilation? What causes this? Describe the spatial disorientation? Why can it be fatal?

II – Preflight Procedures

- Task A – Preflight Assessment. Perform the usual preflight of the aircraft using the checklist,
- Task B – Cockpit Management
- Task C – Engine Starting *(Checklist- Cold-start.)*
- Task D – Taxiing *(maintain the proper positioning of flight controls, (Pg.38), talk to ATC with confidence (Pg.140-152))*
- Task F – Before Takeoff Check. *(Pax. Briefing (Pg.94), Engine flameout during takeoff (Pg.66), MCC, SRM, give a brief summary about XC Flight, etc.)*

III – Airport Operations

IV – Takeoffs, Landings, and Go-Arounds. First takeoff/ landing is a normal takeoff/landing and be ready to perform a short field takeoff and landing prior to a soft field takeoff and landing, go-around, during the approach to the airport, *you should fly on or slightly above the glide path, follow PAPI/VASI on final approach.(for safe obstruction clearance in the approach area.)*

V – Performance Maneuvers. Climb to the altitude, perform the clearing turns, steep turns, turn around a point, S-Turns, fly the plane with confidence and use trim (let the plane fly itself)

VII – Slow Flight and Stalls.

VIII – Basic Instrument Maneuvers. Recovery from Unusual Attitudes, turns, descents and climbs under the hood, VOR Orientation and tracking? On Which radial are you flying? What is the bearing to the airport?

Common Mistakes During A Checkride :

During the checkride, You ll be acting as a PIC, *PIC is responsible for determining if an aircraft is in condition for safe flight.*

- Failure to Use Checklists (A checklist provides the structure to flying.)
- Disregarding a Topic Listed as "Airmen Certification Standards"
- Traffic pattern entry procedures, losing the situational awareness while entering the pattern, bad pattern work power settings and failure to initiate checklist result in unstable approach and bad landing. *(causing severe bouncing, porpoising, floating conditions during landing.)*
- Consistently floating during landings. (too fast on final)
- Failure to recover from a "Stall/Initial Spin" correctly.
- Failure to brief spins and "Spin Recoveries" correctly.
- Failure to execute clearing turns.
- Undershooting/Overshooting during a simulated Emergency Approach.
- Deficiencies in planning the Short/Soft Field Takeoffs and Landings.
- Forgetting calculating the takeoff, cruise, and landing performance.
- Failure to stay ahead of the airplane.
- **Safety of Flight Operations:** Maintaining the safety of flight is your number one priority as a pilot. You must be aware of collision avoidance, runway incursion, maintaining minimum safe altitude, wind correction during taxi, LAHSO, flight into MOA, prohibited, restricted, etc., exchange of flight controls with instructor/examiner.

ATC Glossary and VFR Communications

Pilots who operate in the Air Traffic Control (ATC) system need to communicate effectively with controllers. Aviation phraseology combines brevity with the transfer of complete and correct information. This section will help pilots to do so easily and confidently.

A

Abeam An aircraft is "abeam" a fix, point, or object when that fix, point, or object is approximately 90° to the right or left of the aircraft track. Abeam indicates a general position rather than a precise point. While flying in the traffic pattern, "ABEAM the numbers" means 90° to the right or left of the runway numbers.

Acknowledge Let me know that you have received and understood this message.

Active Runway The runways to which you'll be cleared for takeoffs and landings by ATC. Active runways are the runways most closely aligned with the wind.

Advisory (Frequency) similar to common traffic advisory frequency *(CTAF). Pilots use the advisory frequency at nontowered airports to let other air traffic know they are on approach or taking off.*

Aeronautical Beacon A visual NAVAID displaying flashes of white and/or colored light to indicate the location of an airport, a heliport, a landmark, a certain point of a Federal airway in mountainous terrain, or an obstruction.,

Airborne An aircraft is considered airborne when all parts of the aircraft are off the ground.

Airborne Collision Avoidance System (ACAS/TCAS) A system that operates independently of ground-based equipment and air traffic control in warning pilots of the presence of other aircraft that may present a threat of collision.

Aircraft Approach Category A grouping of aircraft based on a speed of 1.3 times the stall speed in the landing configuration at maximum gross

landing weight. An aircraft must fit in only one category. If it is necessary to maneuver at speeds in excess of the upper limit of a speed range for a category, the minimums for the category for that speed must be used. The categories are as follows:
Category A- Speed less than 91 knots.
Category B- Speed 91 knots or more but less than 121 knots.
Category C- Speed 121 knots or more but less than 141 knots.
Category D- Speed 141 knots or more but less than 166 knots.
Category E- Speed 166 knots or more.

Airport/Facility Directory (AFD) A United States government publication that provides information about airports, seaplane bases, heliports and navigation facilities. Use the A/FD to obtain information about communications data, runways, instrument approaches, layout of airports, and other details. _The most complete and up-to-date information regarding an airport can be found in the chart supplements publication (formerly The Airport/Facility Directory A/FD)_

Airspace Designated volumes of space that determine whether and by which controlling agency a particular area is controlled.

Air Traffic Control (ATC) A service operated by appropriate authority to promote the safe, orderly and expeditious flow of air traffic. This service provided for the purpose of: Preventing collisions between aircraft and between aircraft, obstruction clearance in the coverage area, expediting and maintaining an orderly flow of air traffic. _Air Traffic Control and General Operations are issued under Advisory Circular-90._

Affirmative simply answering "Yes" to a question.

Altitude Readout An aircraft's altitude, transmitted via the Mode C transponder feature, that is visually displayed in 100-foot increments on an ATC radar scope having readout capability.

Altimeter Setting The local barometric pressure reading and setting into the Kollsman window of an altimeter to adjust a pressure altimeter for variations in existing atmospheric pressure or to the standard altimeter setting (29.92). _If an altimeter setting is not available before flight, the pilot adjusts the altimeter to the elevation of the departure airport._

Approach Control An air traffic controller that directs aircraft in and out of congested areas. Approach usually handles traffic between the tower-controlled and center-controlled phase of flight. Approach controllers frequently handle departing as well as arriving flights.

ARTCC The Air Route Traffic Control Centers direct aircraft between the phases of IFR flight controlled by departure and arrival controllers. They may also handle VFR traffic on Flight Following.

ASOS (Automated Surface Observation System) A continuously updated (minute-by-minute) automated weather briefing system used at some United States airports.

ATIS (Automated Terminal Information System) The continuous broadcast of recorded aeronautical *information concerning noncontrol information in selected high-activity and busier terminal areas.* Its purpose is to improve controller effectiveness and to relieve frequency congestion by automating the repetitive transmission of essential but routine information; e.g., *Stuart Witham Field Airport Information X-Ray, 1454 zulu. Wind zero-0ne-zero at eight*
Visibility 7 miles, light rain, Ceiling 2200 Few, 3800 broken, and 5500 overcast, temperature four, dew point one, altimeter three-zero-zero-one, Landing and Departing Runway 12, RNAV GPS Runway 12 approaches are in use, Clearance Delivery is 121.025, Ground control 121.7, Advise on initial contact you have information X-Ray.

AWOS (Automated Weather Observation System) A continuously updated (minute-by-minute), automated airport weather briefing system used at some United States airports.

B

Base A pattern leg at right angles to the landing runway. Base leg connects the downwind leg to the extended runway centerline in airport traffic pattern.

Blocked Phraseology used to indicate that a radio transmission has been distorted or interrupted due to multiple simultaneous radio transmissions. You will probably hear this when the frequency is busy.

Broadcast Transmission of information for which an acknowledgement is not expected.

C

Call Sign The identification that ATC and pilots use for a particular flight or aircraft. Call signs are generally a combination of the aircraft type or manufacturer and the aircraft registration for civilian planes, a combination of the airline and flight number for airline flights, and a combination of branch of service and flight number for military flights. Call signs should always be included in any communication with ATC to avoid confusion about who's talking.

Circle-To-Land Maneuver A maneuver initiated by the pilot to align the aircraft with a runway for landing when a straight-in landing from an instrument approach is not possible or is not desirable. At tower-controlled airports, this maneuver is made only after ATC authorization has been obtained and the pilot has established required visual reference to the airport; e.g., N172SP Pompano Tower "Cleared LOC Runway one Five Approach circle to Land Runway One Zero,"

Climb to VFR ATC authorization for an aircraft to climb to VFR conditions within Class B, C, D, and E surface areas when the only weather limitation is restricted visibility. The aircraft must remain clear of clouds while climbing to VFR.

Clearance Delivery Clearance delivery issues IFR clearances. A clearance is necessary before departing on an instrument flight plan.

Cleared for Takeoff ATC authorization for an aircraft to depart. It is predicated on known traffic and known physical airport conditions.

Cleared for the Option ATC authorization for an aircraft to make a touch and go, low approach, missed approach, go around, stop and go, or full-stop landing at the discretion of the pilot.
It is mostly used in training flight so that an instructor can assess a student's performance under changing situations.

Cleared to Land ATC authorization for an aircraft to land. It is predicated on known traffic and known physical airport conditions.

Closed Traffic Operations including mostly takeoffs, landings (touch-and-goes), go around, power off 180's or low approaches where the aircraft does not exit the traffic pattern. A landing during which the pilot doesn't let the airplane come to a complete stop before adding power and taking off again. This is often done to practice takeoffs and landings. This is called a "touch and go".

Common Traffic Advisory Frequency (CTAF) A VHF radio frequency designed for the purpose of carrying out airport advisory practices while operating to or from an airport without an operating control tower. The CTAF may be a UNICOM, Multicom, FSS, or tower frequency and is identified in appropriate aeronautical publications. *CTAF is used at non-towered airport* or when the tower is not in service.

Correction An error has been made in the transmission and the correct version follows.

Crosswind A pattern leg at a right angle to the landing runway off the departure end in airport traffic pattern.

D

Departure Control Departure control directs aircraft out of congested traffic areas. Departure usually handles traffic between the tower-controlled and center-controlled phase of flight. Departure controllers frequently handle arriving as well as departing flights.

Downwind The direction the wind is blowing. In airport traffic pattern, downwind refers to the pattern leg flown parallel to the runway in the direction the wind is blowing (opposite to the direction of landing).

DPs (Departure Procedures) DPs are published procedures for departing a particular airport on an instrument flight plan.

Expedite Used by ATC when prompt compliance is required to avoid the development of an imminent situation and convey the need to comply quickly with an instruction. In other words-**HURRY UP!** For taxiing faster than usual *(Expedite vacating for taxiway B, cleared for expedited take-off, expedite exit on taxiway C, etc.)*

F

Final Leg In airport traffic patterns, the pattern leg directly along the extended runway centerline on the approach path/course.

Flight Following A radar service for VFR flight that provides traffic advisories. This can include vectors, traffic alerts and weather information. This is very helpful service when pilots are flying X-C and may have to transition through multiple controllers' airspaces (Class B, C and D); e.g., *Miami Control N172SP, Cessna 172, 7 miles northwest of Boca Raton, 3000 feet, requesting VFR Flight Following to TAMPA Executive (KVDF)*

Fly Heading (Degrees) The specific heading ATC wants the pilot to fly. The pilot may have to turn to, or continue on, a specific compass direction in order to comply with the instructions.
The pilot is expected to turn in the shortest direction to the heading unless otherwise instructed by ATC.

Flight Plan Flight plans are documents filed by a pilot or flight dispatcher in accordance with VFR and IFR Flights, and ATC will clear you along that route.

Flight Level In the United States, pilots flying above 18,000 (FL180) feet are required to set the digits in the altimeter's Kollsman window to 29.92 Inch/Hg. The resulting altimeter reading is called a flight level. When the Kollsman window is set to 29.92 (1013.2 millibars) and the altimeter reads 28,000 feet, the altitude is stated as, "Flight Level 280 (two eight zero)."

Flight Service Station (FSS) Air traffic facilities which provide pilot briefings, en route communications, VFR search and rescue services to assist lost aircraft and aircraft in distress situations, relay ATC clearances, originate Notices to Airmen, broadcast aviation weather and NAS information, receive and process IFR flight plans, and monitor NAVAIDs. In addition, at selected locations, FSSs provide En Route Flight Advisory Service (Flight Watch), take weather observations, issue airport advisories, and advise Customs and Immigration of transborder flights. During an emergency which has caused the pilot to deviate from an ATC clearance, the pilot must submit a detailed report of an emergency <u>within 48 hours if requested by ATC, to the administrator only upon request.</u>

Fuel Remaining A phrase used by either pilots or controllers when relating to the fuel remaining on board until actual fuel exhaustion.
When transmitting such information in response to either a controller's question or a pilot initiated cautionary advisory to air traffic control, pilots will state the ***Approximate Number Of Minutes*** the flight can continue with the fuel remaining.
All reserve fuel **should be included** in the time stated, as should an allowance for established fuel gauge system error.

Full-Stop Landing A landing that includes a complete stop on the runway, or when the aircraft vacates the runway on the ground before taxiing back for another takeoff.

G

Go Ahead Proceed with your message. Not to be used for any other purpose.

Go Around Instructions for a pilot to abandon their approach to landing. Additional instructions may follow. Procedures vary for VFR and IFR traffic. Unless otherwise advised by ATC, a VFR aircraft or an aircraft conducting visual approach should overfly the runway while climbing to traffic pattern altitude and enter the traffic pattern via the crosswind leg.
A pilot on an IFR flight plan performing an instrument approach should execute the published *"Missed Approach Procedure (MAP)"* or proceed as instructed by ATC; e.g., *"N172SP Stuart Tower Go around due to the traffic on the runway"(additional instructions if required).*

Ground Control Ground control commands aircraft traffic between parking and the runway. This generally includes all taxiways, inactive runways, holding areas, and some transitional aprons or intersections where aircraft arrive, having vacated the runway or departure gate. In Class B, C and D airspaces, the last point of contact with Ground Control is, <u>*"Hold Short Runway XX"*</u> before switching to the Tower Frequency.

H

Handoff (Handover) An action taken to transfer the radar identification of an aircraft from one controller to another if the aircraft will enter the receiving controller's airspace and radio communications with the aircraft will be transferred.
As an aircraft reaches the boundary of a center's control area it is "handed off" or "handed over" to the next area control center; "e.g., N172SP Miami Center, contact Jacksonville Center 127.25"

Have Numbers Used by pilots to inform ATC/Controller that they have received runway, wind, and altimeter setting information.

Hold Short Lines *This is the most critical marking on the runway. If the pilot is facing the two solid lines, be absolutely sure you have to have a clearance to cross.* If the pilot is facing the two dashed lines, taxi across without a clearance. Otherwise, you may inadvertently become involved in runway incursions. The entire instruction is, *"Hold short of RWY 12L on taxiway Alpha"* See Figures-59-61-62.

Hold Short Points on Taxiways When a ground or tower controller requests an aircraft to stop at a certain location while taxiing, the controller will tell the pilot to "hold short." This is usually in reference to a runway. The entire instruction is, *"Hold short of Delta on Taxiway Mike,"* where the hold short point is the Delta taxiway sign. See Pg.141 (A Point, Nu.5)

How do you hear me? A question concerning the quality of the transmission or to determine how well the transmission is being received mutually.

I

I Say Again The message will be repeated.

Ident A request for a pilot to activate the aircraft transponder identification feature. This will help the controller to confirm an aircraft identity or to

identify an aircraft.
Do not confuse this with the term **"squawk"**, which means to tune the 4-digit transponder code or transponder operating mode, such as Mode C, altitude reporting.

IFR (Instrument Flight Rules) A set of rules governing the conduct of flight under instrument meteorological conditions.

Immediately Used by ATC when such action compliance is required to avoid an imminent situation.
In other words-**DO IT NOW!** *(e.g., cleared for immediate departure)*

Indicated Airspeed (IAS) The speed shown on the aircraft's airspeed indicator. This is the speed used in pilot/controller communications under the general term "airspeed."

IFR clearance An IFR clearance is issued by clearance delivery prior to departure. The clearance includes information regarding the route of flight, altitude to be flown, radio frequency and the transponder code for the departure controller.

ILS (Instrument Landing System) A precision approach system that includes a glide slope (vertical guidance), localizer (horizontal guidance), marker beacons, and airport lighting systems.

Instrument Rated Pilots who have received the required IFR training and have passed both written and practical exams are awarded an instrument rating. They can then fly in weather conditions during which they *fly solely by reference to the cockpit instruments.*

Intersecting Runways Two or more runways which cross or meet within their lengths.

Intersection Departure A departure from any runway intersection except the end of the runway.

Known Traffic With respect to ATC clearances, means aircraft whose altitude, position, and intentions are known to ATC.

L

Land and Hold Short Operations (LAHSO) Operations which include simultaneous takeoffs and landings and/or simultaneous landings when a landing aircraft is able to hold short of the intersecting runway/taxiway or designated hold-short point when instructed by ATC. Pilots are expected to promptly inform the controller if the hold short clearance cannot be accepted.

Landing Roll The distance from the point of touchdown to the point where the aircraft can be brought to a stop or exit the runway.

Local Traffic Aircraft operating in the traffic pattern or within sight of the tower, aircraft known to be departing or arriving from flight in local practice areas, or aircraft executing practice instrument approaches at the airport.

Low Approach Maneuver executed when an aircraft intends to overfly the runway, maintaining runway heading but not landing. This is commonly used by aircraft flying practice instrument approaches.

M

Maintain Concerning altitude or flight level, the term means to remain at the altitude or flight level specified.
The phrase "climb and" or "descend and" normally precedes "maintain" and the altitude assignment; e.g., "descend and maintain 5,000."
Concerning other ATC instructions, the term is used in it's literal sense; e.g., maintain VFR, descend and maintain six thousand."

Make Short Approach is a request used by ATC to inform a pilot to alter/make abbreviated traffic pattern (downwind and final approach legs); e.g., make a short final approach. It simply means that Controller wants you to cut your downwind short and turn early for your base leg.

MAYDAY The international radio distress signal.
When repeated three times, it indicates imminent and grave danger and that immediate assistance is requested. Mayday signals a life-threatening

emergency"; e.g., *"MAYDAY, MAYDAY, MAYDAY N172SP, 10 Miles West of Pompano Beach Airport, 2500 feet, Cessna 172, Engine Flame-out, 2 people on board, forced landing imminent."*

Missed Approach (MAP) Declaration by a pilot on an instrument approach that he has reached the point designated as a missed approach point without seeing the runway or airport lighting. Declaring a missed approach also signals the pilot's intent to execute the published missed approach procedure.

Minimum Fuel Indicates that an aircraft's fuel supply has reached a state where, upon reaching the destination, it can accept little or no delay. This is not an emergency situation but merely indicates an emergency situation may arise if any undue delay occurs.

Mode C transponder A transponder is a transmitter/receiver that returns a signal when interrogated by a signal from the ground. When a pilot dials a particular code into the transponder, that code shows up on controllers' radar screens next to the aircraft's radar image. Mode C provides the aircraft's altitude to the controller as well.

Movement Area The runways, taxiways, and other areas of an airport/heliport that are used for taxiing/hover taxiing, air taxiing, takeoff and landing of aircraft. See Figure-61.

N

Negative "No," or "permission not granted," or "that is not correct."

Negative Contact/ No Visual Contact used by pilots to inform ATC that traffic is not in sight. It may be followed by the pilot's request for the controller to provide assistance in avoiding the traffic.
Also used by pilots to inform ATC they were unable to contact ATC on a particular frequency.

Non-Movement Area is defined as ramps and aprons and is not controlled by ATC, which means you may move or taxi the airplane without clearance or communications with the control tower. See Figure 61 (Pg.156)

Notice to Airmen (NOTAM) A notice containing information *(not known sufficiently in advance to publicize by other means)* concerning the establishment, condition, or change in any component *(facility, service, procedure, or hazard in the National Airspace System)* the timely knowledge of which is essential to personnel concerned with flight operations.

O

On Course Used to indicate that an aircraft is established on the route centerline. Used by ATC to advise a pilot making a radar approach that his/her aircraft is lined up on the final approach course. *Tower N172SP Cessna 172, 3000 feet, 6 miles North, on course Orlando VOR, request VFR flight following.*

Out The conversation is ended and no response is expected.

Over My transmission is ended; I expect a response.

Overhead Approach is normally performed by aerobatic or high-performance aircraft and involves a quick 180° turn and descent at the approach end of the runway before turning to land

P

PAN-PAN The international radio-telephony urgency signal. When repeated three times, indicates uncertainty or alert followed by the nature of the urgency. *PAN-PAN, PAN PAN, PAN PAN, Orlando Approach, N172SP, 10 nm West of Kissimmee Airport, passenger with suspected heart attack, diverting to Kissimmee, Altitude 13000, request paramedic and ambulance on arrival.*

Parking Gate Parking areas that attached to airport terminal buildings.

Parking Spot The airport apron, flight line, or ramp is the area of an airport where aircraft are parked. See Figure-61.

Pilot's Discretion When used in conjunction with altitude assignments, means that ATC has offered the pilots the option of starting climb or descent whenever they wish and conducting the climb or descent at any rate they wish. They may temporarily level off at any intermediate altitude. However, once They have vacated an altitude, they may not return to that altitude.

Progressive Taxi Precise taxi instructions given to a pilot unfamiliar with the airport or issued in stages as the aircraft proceeds along the taxi route. Progressive directions from a ground controller to a pilot assist the pilot in navigating between parking and the runway. But this is rare as it is very labor intensive for ATC. Before it's used, controllers should send 'Expect Progressive Taxi Instructions' to the aircraft in question (although this may not always be possible), once this is done the following commands are available: – Cross runway 10, – Turn left/right next taxiway B, – Continue straight ahead via Taxiway B, – Make a 180° turn on the taxiway B. Once the Progressive Taxi Instructions are no longer required, the controller must send "Continue Taxi at your discretion"
There are also vehicles with "Follow Me" signs and lights which can be sent as well, especially in Europe and Asia. ("Follow Me" vehicles need clearances too).

Pushback The act of being pushed back from an airport terminal gate. This is usually done by hooking a small tug to the nose wheel of a large aircraft and pushing it backwards into the taxi lane.

R

Radar Contact Used by ATC to notify an aircraft that it has been identified on the radar display and "Radar Flight Following" will be provided until radar identification is terminated. After requesting "Flight Following" from ATC, a transponder code is issued to the pilot, and the pilot sets the code into the transponder. When the controller views the image of that aircraft on the radar screen, Controller advises the pilot he/she has "radar contact"; e.g., "N172SP Palm Beach Approach, 6 miles west bound of Boca Raton, 3100 feet, Radar Contact, Proceed on course."

Radar Service Terminated Used by ATC to inform a pilot that he will no longer be provided any of the services that would normally be received while in positive radar contact.

Radar service is automatically terminated, and the pilot is not advised in the following cases:

An aircraft cancels its IFR flight plan, except within Class B airspace, Class C airspace, a TRSA, or where Basic Radar service is provided.

An aircraft conducting an instrument, visual, or contact approach has landed or has been instructed to change to advisory frequency.

An arriving VFR aircraft, receiving radar service to a tower controlled airport within Class B airspace, Class C airspace, a TRSA, or where sequencing service is provided, has landed; or to all other airports, is instructed to change to tower or advisory frequency.

An aircraft completing a radar approach (ASR or SRA).

Read Back repeating the message that ATC has relayed to you, absolutely essential for clearances and hold-short instructions, when it's critical that ATC knows you understood them: e.g., *"Maintain at or below 1,300 traffic, turn left 30° for traffic, make 360° turns to the right/left due to the traffic on short final."* With each of these ATC instructions, you have to readback the entire instruction and comply as directed (14 CFR 91.123). Note: A controller is supposed to give you the reason for a vector or altitude restriction.

Report Used to instruct pilots to advise ATC of specified information; e.g., "Report passing PBI VOR."

Roger I have received all and understand of your last transmission. It should not be used to answer a question requiring a yes or a no answer. Shortly, "Roger" is saying you'll comply with a request or command.

Runway Incursion An incident where <u>an unauthorized aircraft, vehicle or person is on a runway.</u> This adversely affects aviation and runway safety and may cause an accident.

S

Say Again Used to request a repeat of the last transmission. Usually specifies a transmission or a portion not understood or received; e.g., *"Say again all after PBI VOR."*

Say Altitude Used by ATC to ascertain an aircraft's specific altitude/flight level. When the aircraft is climbing or descending, the pilot should state the indicated altitude rounded to the nearest 100 feet.

Say Heading Used by ATC to request an aircraft's heading. The pilot should state the actual heading of the aircraft.

Self-Announce Position and/or Intentions. "Self-announce" is a procedure whereby pilots broadcast their aircraft call sign, position, altitude, and intended flight activity or ground operation on the designated CTAF. This procedure is used almost exclusively at airports that do not have an operative control tower or an FSS on the airport. If an airport has a control tower that is either temporarily closed or operated on a part-time basis, and there is no operating FSS on the airport, pilots should use the published CTAF to self-announce position and/or intentions when operating within 10 miles of the airport. *["Self-announce" includes Aircraft Type, distance, intention (inbound full-stop, touch and go etc.)]*

Short Approach A maneuver in which the pilot makes an *abbreviated downwind*, base, and final legs turning inside of the standard 45-degree base turn. This can be requested at a towered airport for aircraft spacing, but is more commonly used at a non-towered airport or a part-time-towered airport when the control tower is not in operation, when landing with a simulated engine out, or completing a power-off 180° accuracy approach commercial-rating maneuver.

Speak Slower Used in verbal communications as a request to reduce the rate at which a pilot or controller is speaking. When a message is transmitted to an aircraft and its contents may need to be written down, the speaking rate should be slightly slower than normal.

Squawk Terminology used by air traffic controllers to request a pilot to key a specific code into the transponder; e.g., *"Squawk four one zero one"*.

Squawk Ident A phrase used by ATC to ask a pilot to activate the identification feature on the aircraft transponder. Once the feature is activated, the ground controller can immediately determine the aircraft's identity. <u>Aircraft not equipped with a Mode C transponder are unable to transmit altitude information to the ATC secondary surveillance radar,</u> and thus <u>the controller will not know their</u> <u>altitude, only position and track.</u>

Stand by means the controller or pilot must pause for a few seconds, usually to attend to other duties of a higher priority. This can also mean to wait as in *"stand by for additional clearance."* The pilot should reestablish contact if a delay is lengthy. "Stand by" is not an approval or denial.

Straight-in Approach VFR Entry into the traffic pattern by interception of the extended runway centerline (final approach course) without flying any other portion of the traffic pattern. See Pg.148.

STARs (Standard Terminal Arrival Routes) Published procedures for particular airports to get a flight from the enroute to the approach phase of flight. See Pg.19

Standard Rate Turn A standard rate turn is defined <u>as a 3° per second turn</u>, which completes a 360° turn in 2 minutes. This is also known as a 2-minute turn.

Stop and Go A procedure wherein an aircraft will land, make a complete stop on the runway, and then commence a takeoff roll and take off from that point.

T

Tailwind Any wind more than 90° to the longitudinal axes of the runway. The magnetic direction of the runway shall be used as the basis for determining the longitudinal axes. See Pg.49.

Takeoff Roll The process whereby an aircraft is aligned with the runway centerline and the aircraft is moving with the intent to take off. For helicopters, this pertains to the act of becoming airborne after departing a takeoff area.

Taxi The movement of an airplane under its own power on the surface of an airport. Also, it describes the surface movement of helicopters equipped with wheels. See Pg.141, Figure-53.

Taxiway A *taxiway* is a path on which *aircraft* travel at an airport connecting runways with aprons, hangars, terminals and other facilities. By using a taxiway, the pilot avoids conflicts with other aircraft on the runway. See Pg.154-156

Taxi-Back (Back-Taxi) A term used by air traffic controllers to taxi an aircraft on the runway opposite to the traffic flow. The aircraft may be instructed to taxi-back to the beginning of the runway *(active runway)* or at some point before reaching the runway end for the purpose of departure or to exit the runway; e.g., *"Ground Control N172SP on taxiway C, Request taxi-back for Runway 12 via Taxiway A."*

Temporary Flight Restriction (TFR) A TFR is a regulatory action issued by the FAA via the U.S. NOTAM System, under the authority of United States Code, Title 49. TFRs are issued within the sovereign airspace of the United States and its territories to restrict certain aircraft from operating within a defined area on a temporary basis to protect persons or property in the air or on the ground. While not all inclusive, TFRs may be issued for disaster or hazard situations such as: toxic gas leaks or spills, fumes from flammable agents, aircraft accident/incident sites, aviation or ground resources engaged in wildlife suppression, or aircraft relief activities following a disaster. TFRs may also be issued in support of VIP movements; for reasons of national security; or when determined necessary for the management of air traffic in the vicinity of aerial demonstrations or major sporting events. NAS users or other interested parties should contact a FSS for TFR information. Additionally, TFR information can be found in automated briefings, NOTAM publications, and on the internet at http://www.faa.gov. The FAA also distributes TFR information to aviation user groups for further dissemination.

Terminal The building through which arriving and departing passengers pass when getting onto or off of aircraft at an airport. Parking positions of all commercial aircraft are attached to terminals.

Tetrahedron A device normally located on uncontrolled airports and used as a landing direction indicator. The small end of a tetrahedron points in the direction of landing. At controlled airports, the tetrahedron, if installed, should be disregarded because tower instructions supersede the indicator.

Touchdown The point at which an aircraft first makes contact with the landing surface. See Pg.155, Figure-60-61

Touch and Go A landing during which the pilot doesn't let the aircraft come to a complete stop before applying power and taking off again. This is often done to practice takeoffs and landings. Also known as closed traffic. Make sure if the runway is eligible for touch and go by checking A/FD.

Tower Control A terminal facility that uses air/ground communications, visual signaling, and other devices to provide ATC services to aircraft operating in the vicinity of an airport or on the movement area. *See Pg.155/156.* Authorizes aircraft to land or takeoff at the airport controlled by the tower or to transit the Class B/C/D airspace area regardless of flight plan or weather conditions *(IFR or VFR)*. A tower may also provide approach control services *(radar or nonradar)*.

That is correct the understanding you have is right.

Threshold The beginning of that portion of the runway usable for landing. See Figure-60' Pg. 155.

Traffic Alert and Collision Avoidance System An airborne collision avoidance system based on radar beacon signals which operates independent of ground-based equipment. TCAS-I generates traffic advisories only. <u>TCAS-II generates traffic advisories, and resolution (collision avoidance)</u> advisories in the vertical plane.

Traffic In Sight Used by pilots to inform a controller that previously issued traffic is in sight.

Traffic No Factor When traffic is no longer in conflict with your flight path, you will hear ATC say, *"Traffic No Factor"*

Traffic Pattern The traffic flow that is prescribed for aircraft landing at, taxiing on, or taking off from an airport. The components of a typical traffic

pattern are upwind leg (departure), crosswind leg, downwind leg, base leg, and final approach leg.
An aircraft making a straight-in approach under VFR is also considered to be on final approach. See Figure-15,53,54. Pg.31, 146,150.

Traffic Pattern Radio Communications Phraseology and Techniques:
The single, most important thought in pilot-controller proper communications is understanding. Aviation phraseology combines brevity with the transfer of complete and correct information. Communication should be kept as brief as possible, but controllers must know absolutely what you want to do before they can properly perform their control duties. See Pg.141.

Transition To cross through controlled airspace. You can request clearance from ATC to transition through controlled airspace; e.g.; *Boca Tower N172SP 6 miles North, Cessna 172 Skyhawk, 2000 feet, request transition at 3 miles, on shore.*
N172SP Boca Tower transition approved, report over white house.

Transponder An electronic device that produces a response when it receives a radio-frequency interrogation. Aircrafts have transponders to assist in identifying them on air traffic control radar. A transponder code *(often called a squawk code)* is assigned by air traffic controllers. For VFR Flight, the squawk code is 1200. This code allows air traffic controllers to identify specific aircraft in VFR Conditions moving across their radar screens. *When making routine transponder code changes, pilots should avoid inadvertent selection of 7500, 7600, 7700.*

U

UNICOM *(Universal Communications Frequency)* A non-government air/ground radio communication station that may provide airport information at public-use airports. This frequency is an air-ground communication facility operated by a non-air traffic control private agency to provide advisory service at uncontrolled aerodromes and airports and to provide various non-flight services, such as requesting a taxi, even at towered airports.

Upwind/Departure/Takeoff Leg A pattern leg parallel to the landing runway in the direction opposite the wind In airport traffic pattern.

V

Vectors Directions given by a controller to pilots to position them for an approach or to avoid other aircraft. The directions include the direction in which pilots should turn *(left or right)* and the new compass heading they should fly. *"N172SP Palm beach Approach, left heading 090, 2500 feet, report visual contact for Lantana Airport.*

Verify Request confirmation of information; e.g., "verify assigned altitude."

Visual Flight Rules (VFR) and Flight Visibility Rules that govern the procedures for conducting flight under visual conditions. The term "VFR" indicates weather conditions that are equal to or greater than minimum VFR requirements. *(Basic VFR Weather Minimums; cloud ceiling at least 1,000 feet AGL; ground visibility at least 3 statute miles)* In addition, it is used by pilots and controllers to imply a type of flight plan. *(VFR minimums FAR 91.155)* The term may be used, during the practice instrument approach during the Instrument training. See Figure- 19B, Pg.37, 94.

VFR Not Recommended An advisory provided by a flight service station to a pilot during a preflight or inflight weather briefing that flight under visual flight rules is not recommended. To be given when the current and/or forecast weather conditions are at or below VFR minimums. It does not abrogate the pilot's authority to make his/her own decision.

VHF Radio Very high frequency radio range used for aircraft communication and navigation. *(between118.000 to137.000 MHz)*

Victor Airway An airway system based on the use of VOR facilities. The north-south Victor Airways have Numbers *(V7, V159 etc.)*

Visibility The ability to see and identify prominent unlighted objects by day and prominent lighted objects by night. Visibility is reported by weather services as statute miles, hundreds of feet as Runway Visual Range, or meters in some ICAO Countries.

Visual approach An IFR approach that authorizes the pilot to continue visually and clear of clouds to the airport. The pilot must, at all times, have either the airport or the preceding aircraft in sight. The approach must be authorized by and under the control of the appropriate air traffic control facility. Weather at the airport must include a reported ceiling at or above 1,000 feet and visibility of three miles or greater.

W

Weather Briefing *(3 Types: Standard, Outlook, Abbreviated Briefing)* Pilots/Student Pilots can receive a complete preflight briefing from a Flight Service Station (1-800-WXBRIEF). The FAA has established a universal toll-free telephone number for FSSs: 1–800–WX–BRIEF (1–800–992–7433). Before contacting Flight Service, *you should have the general route of flight and destination.* When you reach Flight Service Station, It is the easiest way to request "Standard Weather Briefing, when departing within the hour, if no preliminary weather information has been received, including Adverse Conditions, Synopsis, Current Conditions, En-route Forecast, Destination Forecast, Winds Aloft, Notice to Airmen (NOTAMs),
For your pre-flight weather briefing, give the briefer the following background information:
Type of flight VFR, IFR or DVFR, Aircraft identification or pilot's name, Aircraft type, Departure point, Route-of-flight, Destination, Altitude(s), Estimated time of departure, Estimated time en-route or time of arrival.
If you feel that the weather conditions are *beyond your capabilities or that of your aircraft or equipment*, you should consider terminating the briefing, and your flight.
An outlook briefing is another type of weather briefing that is provided when the information requested is *6 or more hours in advance* of the proposed departure time. *(for the following morning)*

Wind-check A call to the tower to request the latest wind direction and strength.

WILCO I have received your message, understand it, and will comply with it.

Word Twice As a request: "Communication is difficult. Please say every phrase twice." As information: "Since communications are difficult, every phrase in this message will be spoken twice."

- **Traffic Pattern Communication Procedures.**

It is recommended that single engine (SE) aircraft observe a 1000-feet above ground level (AGL) traffic pattern altitude. Unless otherwise indicated, all turns in the traffic pattern should be made to the left. *(Check VFR Sectional Chart and AFD)*

> **Basic Terminology:**
> - **Who are you calling?** The station that we are making a call. To Pompano Tower/ Pompano Ground / Miami Approach/ Traffic in this frequency (for uncontrolled airports)
> - **Who are you?** Registration Number of Aircraft- Each Aircraft has to have a call sign. Our Call sign is N172SP
> - **Where are you** (with information?) Current ATIS letter in airport (Information C), 8 miles south of Space Coast with Information Charlie.
> - **What we want to do** *(Intention)*? (touch and go, full stop) Inbound, Full-stop.
> Call Sign will be announced as **"N172SP"**
> Follow and study the below procedures over Runway Layout Chart, Current Sectional Chart. Figure-53, Pg.144
> **Report Points and Way of Communication:** The main purpose of this example is to give you information, self-confidence and an idea how the procedures are conducted. Please keep in mind every situation is different. So, be ready for different instructions that may arise.

- **Controlled Airspace, Traffic Pattern Procedures:** Class D Airspace.(KPMP-Pompano Beach Airpark). *See Figure-53, 54A.*

> **A Point (Obtain ATIS and Taxi Clearance Rwy.10):**
> After conducting preflight and engine start checklist, set ATIS, listen and take notes about active rwy., wind components and pressure altitude, set the radio to ground frequency.
> **PILOT:** "Pompano Ground – N172SP at the east of spot 3, with information X-Ray *(ATIS)* requesting taxi to the rwy. 10 -one zero-., closed traffic or North/West/South departure"
> **GROUND:** N172SP Pompano Ground, cleared taxi Rwy. 10, via taxiway L, cross rwy. 06. *(Figure-53, Nu.1-2-3) Normally, Prior to taxi, complete the pre-takeoff checklist.*
> **PILOT:** Pompano Ground – N172SP, taxi via L, cross Rwy. 06. *(begin taxiing to the Run-Up area (Nu.2)*

B Point (Complete Run-up and Obtain Departure Clearance):
After completing the run-up checks (Nu.2) and then taxi to the holding point RWY 10. To Nu.3, Figure-53.
Before Departure/Take off. Complete pre-takeoff checklist.
Switch to the tower frequency 125.4, Position Nu.3, holding point.
PILOT: Pompano Tower N172SP holding short runway 10, ready for departure"
TOWER: "N172SP Pompano Tower: Clear for take-off. (Left traffic ...or proceed on course -*if you leave the pattern.*)
Note: Be alert when listening to the tower instructions, e.g., make left/right close traffic, report midfield on downwind/abeam the numbers, proceed on course, make short approach, short turn to crosswind.

A Point (Obtain Taxi and Takeoff Clearance), Taxi and Run up Check Rwy. 15:
Departure For Runway 15: (See Figure-53, Numbers 1, 4,5,6,7)
PILOT: Pompano Ground – N172SP at the east of spot 3, with information X-Ray (ATIS) requesting taxi to rwy. 15, closed traffic or North/West/South bound departure"
GROUND: N172SP Pompano Ground, cleared to taxi for rwy.15 run-up area, via taxiway L-C, cross rwy. 10, taxiway M, **hold short Delta on Mike.** *(Take notes for readback all taxiway instructions to Ground.)*
PILOT: Pompano Ground – N172SP, cleared taxi rwy.15 run- up area, via taxiway L-C, cross rwy. 10, Taxiway M, hold short Delta on Mike.
PILOT: Pompano Ground – N172SP, holding short Delta on Mike. (Nu.5)
GROUND: N172SP POMPANO Ground, Cross rwy. 6, Taxiway Delta, Advise Run-Up Check Completed.
PILOT: Pompano Ground – Cross rwy. 6 Taxiway Delta. Advise Run Up Completed.
PILOT: Pompano Ground – N172SP, run-up completed. (Nu.6)
GROUND: N172SP POMPANO Ground, cleared taxi on G, hold short for rwy. 15.
PILOT: Pompano Ground – N172SP, cleared taxi on G, hold short rwy. 15.
Switch to tower frequency at Nu.7, Contact Tower. 125.4
PILOT: Pompano Tower N172SP, holding short runway 15 on taxiway G1, ready for departure, left closed traffic"
TOWER: "N172SP Pompano Tower: Cleared for take-off.

G Point: (Prelanding Clearance/Reporting Point)
PILOT: Pompano tower N172SP, Midpoint Rwy. 10, full stop.
TOWER: N172SP Pompano tower, cleared to land rwy. 10.
PILOT: N172SP Pompano tower, Cleared to land.
Note: Be prepared for additional instructions: "Extend downwind, make right/left 360, -traffic 11 o'clock 2 mile final 1000' (unable to see/traffic insight) (follow the traffic/ maintain visual separation)

K Point: (Final/Landing Clearance)
Don't make any other call to the tower, because you have already got the clearance to land. Tower may call you to advise the last wind and gust.
TOWER: N172SP Pompano Tower, Cleared to land rwy. 10, Wind 090°/12 Knots, Gusting 17 Knots.
PILOT: Pompano Tower N172SP Cleared to land, wind copied.
TOWER: N172SP Pompano Tower, Exit taxiway C, contact ground point niner/monitor 121.9/remain in this frequency. Because we report on downwind for full-stop, after landing, tower will instruct you about the taxiway to vacate the rwy. 10.
Note: Don't stop in front of the hold short line when exiting the runway! If you are facing the two dashed lines, taxi across and stop for taxi clearance. After the entire aircraft has cleared the solid double lines. Otherwise, you may inadvertently become involved in runway incursion. (See Figure-62)

D Point (Taxi clearance after landing)
After stopping beyond the "hold short line", switch to the ground frequency.
PILOT: Pompano Ground N172SP, On taxiway C, request taxi to east of spot 3. *See Pg.145*
GROUND: N172SP Pompano Ground, cleared to taxi via C and L.

Leaving Procedures:(Departing from Airport)
E Point (Upwind Leg Departing Procedure- Straight Out Departure)
* E Point allows the pilots to leave the pattern Straight-out, left/right turns to pre-determined heading by Tower.
* This procedure is given to pilots before takeoff. N172SP Pompano Tower "Cleared for takeoff Rwy.15, straight-out departure or Fly Rwy. Heading."

Departing from a runway intersection. (Figure-53, Nu.8) Pilots should state their position on the airport when calling the tower for departure from a runway intersection.
Pompano Tower N172SP at the intersection of taxiway Golf three (G3) and runway one five, ready for departure.

F Point (Departing Procedure)
Crosswind leg is another way of leaving the traffic pattern. Departure on the depending on the volume of traffic, ATC may instruct the pilot to leave the pattern in the direction of Crosswind Leg.
N172SP Pompano Tower extend crosswind leg heading 270°, traffic on downwind.

R Point (Departing Procedure)
If you request west bound departure at the first clearance, Flying to R (out side of pattern) point from downwind is the best track to leave the pattern.
At the S point, 4 miles out, Tower will give you another instruction.
TOWER: N172SP Pompano Tower 'You are clear of the Class Delta Airspace, Miami Approach 119.7, frequency change approved.'

General Approaching Procedures:
Rule: An ATC clearance must be obtained *prior* to operating within a Class B (Mode C Circle, 30 miles out), Class C (20 miles out, before reaching outer circle), Class D (10 miles out), (See Pg.34) or you have to report your position and intention to the Class G Airspace/E surface area traffics on CTAF, (8-10 miles out). *See Figure-54A*
Steps:
- Tune in the ATIS to determine which runway is in use to plan your entry before your arrival.
- How far out you switch over to the tower/approach control is likely to depend on what direction you are approaching from and what type of aircraft you are flying. *(Check the directions coming through L-M-N points arrival to the pattern. See Pg. 146)*
- Since the Class D airspace begins 5 NM from the airport, you are required to contact the tower before you are 5 miles out. Use good ADM / airmen judgment to determine when you should contact the tower.

N Point (Approach Clearance- Entry Point to Downwind)
See Figure-54A
- Tune in the ATIS to find out which runway is active (10-12 miles out). Contact with Tower at 8-10 miles out. (O)

PILOT: Pompano tower N172SP approximately 10 miles North with information Romeo, inbound full stop.

TOWER: N172SP Pompano Tower, proceed on course, report over Light House (Significant Reference Points should be determined on chart in advance; e.g., Turnpike, I-95, Landfill, blue town house.

PILOT: Pompano tower N172SP over Light House,

TOWER: N172SP Pompano Tower cleared to left downwind entry for rwy. 10.

PILOT: Pompano tower N172SP Cleared left downwind rwy. 10.

PILOT: *(at the midfield of downwind)* Pompano Tower N172SP midfield downwind, rwy 10.

If there is not any other traffic in the Pattern,
Simply:

TOWER: N172SP Pompano Tower Cleared to land for Rwy. 10 or
If there is traffic, Tower may give you other instructions such as,
"extend downwind traffic on base", or
"make a right 360 due to the traffic entering base leg", or
"cleared to land Number 2, traffic 10 o'clock 2 miles final 1000'."

Figure-53 Airport Taxiway Diagram

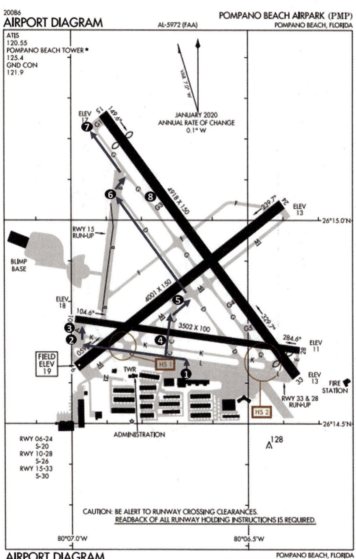

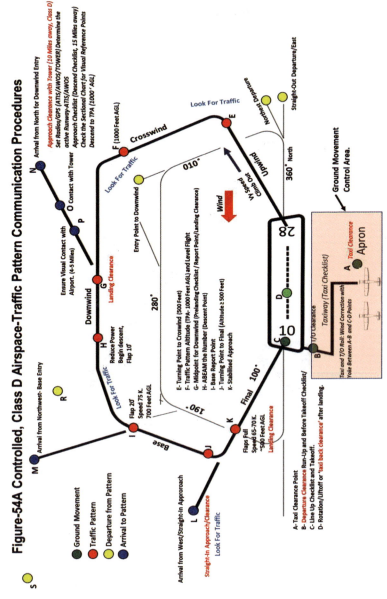

M Point (Approach Clearance- Entry Point to Base Leg)

* M point provides you with a direct entry to base leg. The tower may give you this instruction when the airport is not busy.
- Tune to the ATIS to determine which runway is active (10-12 miles out). Contact Tower 8-10 miles out.

PILOT: Pompano Tower N172SP 10 miles North West with information Romeo, inbound full stop / touch and go/ stop and go.
TOWER: N172SP Pompano Tower, proceed on course, report 4 miles out.
PILOT: Pompano Tower N172SP 4 miles out.
TOWER: N172SP Pompano Tower "make left base for rwy. 10.
PILOT: Left base rwy. 10, 2SP.
PILOT: (Over I) Pompano Tower 2SP "base rwy. 10."
TOWER: 2SP Pompano Tower cleared to land.
Note: In the even that a high-speed airplane is in the pattern, Tower Control will not allow the traffic to enter the traffic pattern on base, as you will cut off a fast-moving aircraft flying a larger traffic pattern.

L Point (Approach Clearance- Straight-In Approach)
What is "Straight- in Approach?"
- Any approach where the final course is with 30° of runway heading is considered *straight in.*
- Aircraft on final and flying in the pattern have the right of way.
- An approach after a turn to final five or six miles out (not 2-3 miles out) would be considered a straight-in approach.
- You can fly a straight in approach as long as you don't interfere with someone flying a standard pattern. *The FAA encourages pilots to use the standard traffic pattern.* However, for those pilots who choose to execute a straight-in approach, maneuvering for and execution of the approach should be completed so as not to disrupt the flow of arriving and departing traffic.
* L Point provides you with direct entry to final leg. If there is no other traffic in the pattern, Control Tower may instruct you to execute a ***"straight-in approach"***

> **L Point (Straight-in Approach Procedure)**
> * Tune to the ATIS to determine which runway is active *(10-12 miles out).* Contact Tower at 8-10 miles out. Let's use Rwy. 15 in this example.
> **PILOT:** Pompano tower N172SP approximately 10 miles West with information Romeo, inbound full stop / touch and go/ stop and go.
> **TOWER:** N172SP Pompano Tower, proceed on course, cleared to straight-in approach Rwy. 15, report 4 miles out.
> **PILOT:** Pompano tower N172SP 4 miles out, Straight-in Rwy.15, 2SP.
> **TOWER:** N172SP Pompano Tower cleared to land Rwy. 15.
> **PILOT:** Cleared to land Rwy. 15., 2SP

- **Untowered Airports: Traffic Pattern Communication Procedures.** *See Figure-54B*

For use during operation at or in the vicinity of an airport without a control tower or an airport with a control tower that operates only part time (non-towered or part-time-towered airports).

> Recommended Pilot Actions to achieve the greatest degree of safety:
> * The observance of a standard traffic pattern,
> * The use of CTAF procedures in detail,
> * Remain alert and look for other traffic,
> * Review all appropriate publications (e.g., Chart Supplements, AFD, AIM, and NOTAMs), for pertinent information regarding obstacles, hazards, procedures, etc. at the departure and arrival airports.
> **Note:** A visual flight rules (VFR) aircraft on a long, straight-in approach for landing never enters the traffic pattern unless performing a go-around or touch and go after landing.

Recommended Traffic Advisory Practices. All traffic within a 10-mile radius of a non-towered airport or a part-time-towered airport when the control tower is not operating should continuously ***monitor and communicate, as appropriate, on the designated CTAF*** until leaving the area or until clear of the movement area.

Departing aircraft should continuously monitor/ communicate on the appropriate frequency from startup, through taxi, and until 10 miles from the airport.

After first monitoring the frequency for other traffic present within 10 miles of the airport, self-announcing of your position and intentions should occur between 8 and 10 miles from the airport.

Prior to entering the traffic pattern at an airport without an operating control tower, aircraft should avoid the flow of traffic until established on the entry leg. For example, the pilot can check wind and landing direction indicators while at an altitude above the traffic pattern, or by monitoring the communications of other traffics that communicate the runway in use, especially at airports with more than one runway. When the runway in use and proper traffic pattern direction has been determined, *(If you are not sure, ask for the other traffics)* the pilot should then proceed to a point well clear of the pattern before descending to and entering at pattern altitude. *See Figure-55/56*

Arriving aircraft should be at traffic pattern altitude and allow for sufficient time to view the entire traffic pattern before entering. Entries into traffic patterns while descending may create collision hazards and should be avoided. Entry to the downwind leg should be at a 45° angle abeam the midpoint of the runway to be used for landing. (G Point.) *See Figure-54B.*

The pilot may use discretion to choose an alternate type of entry, depending on the current traffic flow *(See Figure-55-56, Pg.51 compatible with FAA, ICAO JAA, EASA Standards, depending on what direction you are approaching from, either direct entry or teardrop entry to downwind.)* especially when intending to cross over midfield, based upon the traffic and communication at the time of arrival. (when the pattern is congested)

Note: (1) Helicopters operating in the traffic pattern when landing on the runway may fly a pattern similar to the fixed-wing aircraft traffic pattern but at a lower altitude (500 feet AGL) and closer to the runway.

*(2) Remember, there is no such thing as **"position and hold"** at a non-towered airport and it is one of the most dangerous things a pilot could do. Runways are just for taking off or landing, not for holding and positioning.*

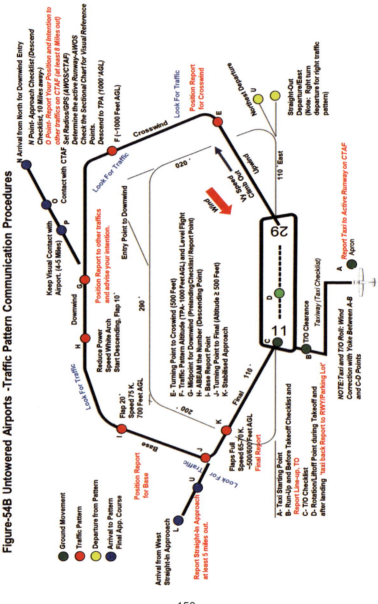

Figure-54B Untowered Airports - Traffic Pattern Communication Procedures

• **Overflying the Airport**

According to the AIM, you are supposed to monitor the airport's ASOS/AWOS and CTAF when You are 10 miles out, make the first radio call, position your airplane for either a downwind entry or teardrop entry.

If you're crossing over midfield and turning directly into downwind, you're not flying a standard pattern. If you're flying over midfield and continuing out (at least 20-30 seconds, Figure-55, Nu.4) until you can complete the teardrop maneuver, or turn around and enter on a 45, then that would be considered a standard entry.

Note: Standard traffic pattern (TP) turns are always to the left, unless the airport specifies it otherwise. *(Check out A/FD or VFR Sectional Chart)*

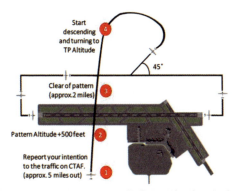

Figure- 55 Preferred Entry to the Traffic Pattern When Crossing Over Midfield

Figure- 56 Alternate Downwind Entry to the Traffic Pattern

PRIVATE PILOT HANDBOOK

Untowered Airports: Traffic Pattern Communication Procedures
Entering the Traffic Pattern:
Position L- Merritt Island traffic, N172SP 8 miles west of the airport inbound, straight-in approach for runway 11. Merritt Island.
Position U to J - Merritt Island traffic, N172SP is long final Rwy 11. Merritt Island.
Taking off:
Position C- Merritt Island traffic, N172SP departing Rwy.11, closed traffic or N/S/W/E bound. Merritt Island.
In the Traffic Pattern:
Position E- Merritt Island traffic, N172SP departure leg Rwy.11 Merritt Island.
Position F- Merritt Island traffic, N2SP crosswind runway 29.
Position G- Merritt Island traffic, N172SP downwind Rwy. 11, full stop,
Position I- Merritt Island traffic, N172SP base Rwy.11., Full Stop Merritt Island.
Position K- Merritt Island traffic, N172SP final Rwy. 11., Full Stop Merritt Island.
Position U- Merritt Island traffic, N172SP departure leg Rwy. 11, departing northeast bound. Merritt Island.

- **Requesting Flight Following: FSS Communication**

After taking off, contact with Radar/Approach Control *(Check Sectional Chart for App. Frequency in the sector flown.)*

PILOT: Miami Approach N172SP
MIAMI App: N172SP Go ahead.
PILOT: Miami App N172SP- C172 Skyhawk, 10 M NW Pompano Airport (KPMP), climbing 2000 Feet, requesting Flight Following to STUART (KSUA)
MIAMI App: N172SP Miami App: Squawk 3456.
PILOT: Squawk 3456, 2SP(10 or 30 seconds later expect new position information)
MIAMI App: N172SP Miami App 2000 feet, 11 Miles NW Pompano Airport, West Bound Heading, Radar Contact.
Note: To determine the position precisely. ATC may ask the pilot to activate the identification feature by saying.
MIAMI App: N172SP Ident
PILOT: Ident, 2SP.
* The ATC unit where you can request flight following (radar control) during ground operations is *the Ground control, on initial contact.*

PAPI/VASI: Are you on glide path!

The VASI *(Visual approach slope indicator)* glide path <u>provides safe obstruction clearance and visual descent information to the runway</u> within 10° of the extended runway center line out to 4 nautical miles from the threshold. During the approach to the airport, you should fly on or slightly above the glide path.

The PAPI (Precision Approach Path Indicator) is normally located on the left side of the runway and allows up to 5 miles visual identification during the day and up to 20 miles at night.

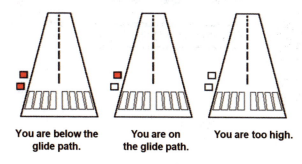

Figure- 57 VASI-Visual Approach Slope Indicator

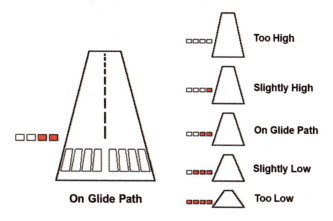

Figure- 58 PAPI- Precision Approach Path Indicator

Airport Signs and Runway Markings:

The links between the airport parking areas and the runways are the taxiways. Taxiways have yellow markings that may include centerline, runway holding position, edge, shoulder, holding position, and taxiway intersection markings.

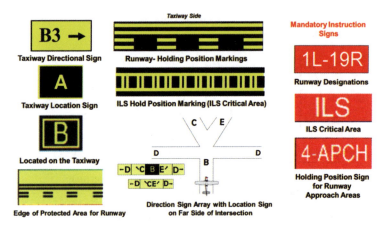

Figure-59 Airport Signs: Taxiway and Runway Markings

Taxiways normally have yellow centerline markings, and hold lines wherever they intersect with a runway.

Taxiway directional sign (B3) indicates designation and direction of taxiway leading out of an intersection.

The numbers 1L-19R on runway designation sign indicate that the runway is oriented approximately 10° and 190°; magnetic heading.

When exiting the runway, do not stop until you have cleared the hold line.

When ILS approaches are in progress, you may be asked by the controller to "... hold short of the ILS critical area."

A runway hold position sign *indicates an entrance to a runway from a taxiway.*

Runway Lights:

- Runway centerline lights (white-red) are located along the runway centerline and are spaced at 50-foot intervals to improve visibility. When viewed from the landing threshold, the runway centerline lights are white until the last 3,000 feet of the runway. The white lights begin to

alternate with red for the next 2,000 feet, and for the last 1,000 feet of the runway, all centerline lights are red.
- The runway edge lights are white.
- Runway Edge Lights on the edges of instrument runways (HIRLs/MIRLs/LIRLs) are steady lights starting out white and change to yellow during the last 2,000 feet, or half the runway length, whichever is less. Then they change to red as the aircraft reaches the end of the runway. They can be high intensity (HIRLs), medium intensity (MIRLs), or low intensity (LIRLs).
- Taxiway edge lights are always blue.
- Taxiway Centerline lights are always green.
- **Touchdown Zone Lights (TDZL).** They consist of two rows of transverse light bars disposed symmetrically about the runway centerline. The system consists of *steady-burning white lights* which start 100 feet beyond the landing threshold and extend to 3,000 feet beyond the landing threshold or to the midpoint of the runway, whichever is less.
- **Taxiway Centerline Lead-Off/Lead-On Lights.** Taxiway centerline lead-off lights provide visual guidance to persons exiting/entering the runway.
Note: To set the high intensity *runway lights on low/medium/high intensity*, the pilot should click the microphone *three/five/seven times* five times within three/five/seven seconds.

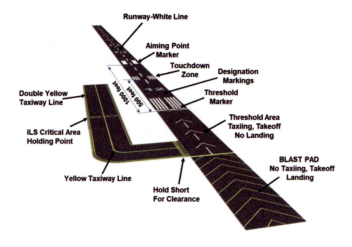

Figure- 60 Airport Signs: Taxiway and Runway Markings

Figure-61 Airport Operations Airport Markings and Signs

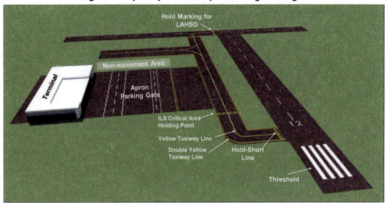

Figure- 62 Runway Holding Position Markings

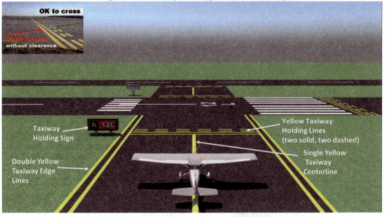

If the pilot is facing the two solid lines, *be absolutely sure you have a clearance to cross.* The entire instruction is, *"Hold short of RWY 12L on taxiway Alfa"*

If the pilot is facing the two dashed lines, taxi across without a clearance, *(OK to cross)* after completely passing the whole yellow lines, stop for taxi clearance from Ground Control. Otherwise, you may inadvertently become involved in runway incursion.

The entire instruction is, *"Exit the RWY. via taxiway Alfa, contact ground point niner/monitor 121.9/ remain this frequency. "*

Private Pilot Dictionary

Aerobatic flight An intentional maneuver involving an abrupt change in an aircraft's attitude, an abnormal attitude, or abnormal acceleration. No person may operate an aircraft in acrobatic flight when the flight visibility is *less than 3 miles* and over any congested area of a city, town, or settlement, below an altitude of 1,500 feet above the surface

ADIZ (Air Defense Identification Zone) The area of airspace over land or water, extending upward from the surface, within which the ready identification, the location, and the control of aircraft are required in **the interest of national security.**

ADS-B Automatic Dependent Surveillance A surveillance technology in which an aircraft determines its position via satellite navigation and periodically broadcasts it, enabling it to be tracked.

Advisory circular (AC) refers to a type of publication offered by the Federal Aviation Administration (FAA) to provide guidance for compliance with airworthiness regulations, pilot certification, operational standards, training standards, and any other rules within the 14 CFR Aeronautics and Space Title. *Advisory Circulars (ACs) are issued to inform the public of nonregulatory material and are not binding.*

Aerodynamics The science of the action of air on an object, and with the motion of air on other gases. Aerodynamics deals with the production of lift by the aircraft, the changing air masses in atmosphere, and the forces acting on bodies moving relative to the air.

Aeronautical Chart. A map used in air navigation including all or part of the following: topographic features, hazards and obstructions, navigation aids, navigation routes, designated airspace, airspace information and airports. Commonly used aeronautical charts are: VFR Sectional Aeronautical Charts, VFR Terminal Area Charts, World Aeronautical Charts (WAC), IFR En Route Low/High Altitude Charts, Instrument Approach Procedures (IAP) Charts, Instrument Departure Procedure (DP) Charts, Standard Terminal Arrival (STAR), Airport Taxi Charts.

Aeronautical Information Manual (AIM) A primary FAA publication whose purpose is to instruct airmen about operating in the National Airspace System (NAS) of the U.S. It provides basic flight information, ATC Procedures and general instructional information concerning health, medical facts, factors affecting flight safety, accident and hazard reporting, and types of aeronautical charts and their use.

A/FD See Airport/Facility Directory.

Ailerons. Primary flight control surfaces mounted on the trailing edge of an airplane wing, near the tip. Ailerons control roll about the longitudinal axes.

Airfoil An airfoil is any surface, such as a wing, propeller, rudder, or even a trim tab, which provides aerodynamic force when it interacts with a moving stream of air.

Airmanship Skills The skills of coordination, timing, decision making, time management, control touch, and speed sense in addition to the motor skills required to fly an aircraft.

Airplane Flight Manual (AFM) A document developed by the airplane manufacturer and approved by the Federal Aviation Administration (FAA). It is specific to a particular make and model airplane by serial number and it contains operating procedures and limitations. AFM is a certification document whose content (procedures, limitations, and performance data) is fundamental to the airplane's certification requirements. Flight Crew Operating Manual (FCOM) is just a company publication. The FCOM contains the systems, the procedures, the performance. The FCOM is the "guide" to know how to use the plane: it's the main reference for pilots.

Airport/Facility Directory (A/FD) A publication designed primarily as a pilot's operational manual containing all airports, seaplane bases, and heliports open to the public including communications data, navigational facilities, and certain special notices and procedures. This publication is issued in seven volumes according to geographic area.

Airport Rotating Beacon A visual NAVAID operated at many airports. At civil airports, alternating white and green flashes indicate the location of the airport. At military airports, the beacons flash alternately white and green, but are differentiated from civil beacons by dual peaked (two quick) white flashes between the green flashes. _An airport's rotating beacon operated during daylight hours indicates that_ _weather at the airport located in Class D airspace is below basic VFR weather minimums._

Approach Light System (ALS) An airport lighting facility which provides visual guidance to landing aircraft by radiating light beams in a directional pattern by which the pilot aligns the aircraft with the extended centerline of the runway on his/her final approach for landing.

Airworthiness A condition in which the aircraft conforms to its type certificated design including supplemental type certificates (STC), and field approved alterations. _The aircraft must also be in a condition for safe flight as determined by annual, 100 hours,_ **preflight** _and any other required inspections._ See Pg.87.

Airworthiness Certificate A certificate issued by the FAA to all aircraft that have been proven to meet the minimum standards set down by the Code of Federal Regulations.

Airworthiness Directive (AD) A regulatory notice sent out by the FAA to the registered owner of an aircraft informing the owner of a condition that prevents the aircraft from continuing to meet its conditions for airworthiness. Airworthiness Directives (AD notes) must be complied with within the required time limit, and the fact of compliance, the date of compliance, and the method of compliance *must be recorded in the aircraft's maintenance records.*

Air Taxi (Hover Taxi). Used to describe a helicopter/VTOL aircraft movement conducted above the surface but normally not above 100 feet AGL. The aircraft may proceed either via hover taxi or flight at speeds more than 20 knots. The pilot is solely responsible for selecting a safe airspeed/altitude for the operation being conducted.

Alternator/Generator A device that uses engine power to generate electrical power.

Altimeter A flight instrument that indicates altitude by sensing pressure changes.

Altitude (AGL) The actual height above ground level (AGL) at which the aircraft is flying.

Altitude (MSL) The actual height above mean sea level (MSL) at which the aircraft is flying.

Angle of Attack (AOA) The acute angle between the chord line of the airfoil and the direction of the relative wind.

Annual Inspection A complete inspection of an aircraft and engine, required by the Code of Federal Regulations, to be accomplished every 12 calendar months on all certificated aircraft. Only an A&P (Airframe & Powerplant) technician holding an Inspection Authorization can conduct an annual inspection.

Attitude and Heading Reference System (AHRS) A device that provides pilots accurate and reliable heading and attitude information, consists of sensors on three axes including roll, pitch and yaw.

Attitude Indicator An instrument which uses an artificial horizon and miniature airplane to depict the position of the airplane in relation to the true horizon. The attitude indicator senses roll as well as pitch, which is the up and down movement of the airplane's nose.

Autokinesis This is caused by staring at a single point of light against a dark background for more than a few seconds. After a few moments, the light appears to move on its own.

Automatic Direction Finder (ADF) An aircraft radio navigation system which senses and indicates the direction to a L/MF nondirectional radio beacon (NDB) ground transmitter. Direction is indicated to the pilot as a magnetic bearing or as a relative bearing to the longitudinal axes of the aircraft depending on the type of indicator installed in the aircraft.

Axes of an Aircraft Three imaginary lines that pass through an aircraft's center of gravity. The axes can be considered as imaginary axles around which the aircraft turns. The three axes pass through the center of gravity at 90° angles to each other. The axes from nose to tail is the longitudinal axes, the axes that passes from wingtip to wingtip is the lateral axes, and the axes that passes vertically through the center of gravity is the vertical axes.

B

Balked Landing A go-around.

Bearing The horizontal angle to or from any point, usually measured clockwise from true north, magnetic north, or some other reference point through 360 degrees.

Best Angle of Climb (VX) Vx is used to clear an obstacle, the speed which the aircraft <u>will produce the most gain in altitude in a given distance.</u>

Best Glide (Vg). The airspeed in which the aircraft glides the furthest for the least altitude lost when in non-powered flight.

Best Rate of Climb (VY) Vy is used to <u>gain the most altitude in the shortest amount of time</u>, the speed which the aircraft will produce the most gain in altitude in the least amount of time.

Blind Spot The term is also used to describe portions of the airport not visible from the control tower.

Bouncing A behavior of the landing aircraft developing after touching the runway, and defined as all wheels or floats briefly and repeatedly losing contact with the runway during landing. If you've bounced well above the runway, go around.

Braking Action (Good, Fair, Poor, Or Nil) A report of conditions on the airport movement area providing a pilot with a degree/ quality of braking that he/she might expect. Braking action is reported in terms of good, fair, poor, or nil. Braking action advisories are in effect on the ATIS broadcast.

Buffeting The beating of an aerodynamic structure or surface by unsteady flow, gusts, etc.; the irregular shaking or oscillation of a vehicle component owing to turbulent air or separated flow.

C

Calibrated Airspeed (CAS) Indicated airspeed corrected for installation error and instrument error. This error is generally greatest at low airspeeds. In the cruising and higher airspeed ranges, indicated airspeed and calibrated airspeed are approximately the same.

Carburetor Ice Ice that forms inside the carburetor due to the temperature drop caused by the vaporization of the fuel. Induction system icing is an operational hazard because it can cut off the flow of the fuel/air charge or vary the fuel/air ratio. Two Types. **Pressure Type:** A hydromechanical device employing a closed feed system from the fuel pump to the discharge nozzle. It meters fuel through fixed jets according to the mass airflow through the throttle body and discharges it under a positive pressure. Pressure carburetors are distinctly different from float-type carburetors, as they do not incorporate a vented float chamber or suction pickup from a discharge nozzle located in the venturi tube. **Float-type Carburetor:** Consists essentially of a main air passage through which the engine draws its supply of air, a mechanism to control the quantity of fuel discharged in relation to the flow of air, and a means of regulating the quantity of fuel/air mixture delivered to the engine cylinders. Float-type carburetor systems in comparison to fuel injection systems are generally _considered to be more susceptible to icing._

Ceiling The height above the earth's surface of the ***lowest layer*** that is reported as broken (5/8 - 7/8) or _overcast (8/8)_. _Clear skies shall be coded in the format, SKC or CLR._ (indicates No layers are present)

Center of gravity (CG) The point at which an airplane would balance if it were possible to suspend it at that point. It is the mass center of the airplane, or the theoretical point at which the entire weight of the airplane is assumed to be concentrated. It may be expressed in inches from the reference datum, or in percent of mean aerodynamic chord (MAC). The location depends on the distribution of weight in the airplane.

Chord Line An imaginary straight line drawn through an airfoil from the leading edge to the trailing edge.

Circuit Breaker A circuit-protecting device that opens the circuit in case of excess current flow. A circuit breaker differs from a fuse in that it can be reset without having to be replaced.

Clear Air Turbulence Turbulence not associated with any visible moisture.

Cockpit Resource Management (CRM) Techniques designed to reduce pilot errors and manage errors that do occur utilizing cockpit human resources. The assumption is that errors are going to happen in a complex

system with error-prone humans.
Coefficient of Lift See lift coefficient.
Coffin Corner The flight regime where any increase in airspeed will induce high speed Mach buffet and any decrease in airspeed will induce low speed Mach buffet.
Combustion Chamber The section of the engine into which fuel is injected and burned.
Common Traffic Advisory Frequency (CTAF) The common frequency used by airport traffic to announce position reports in the vicinity of the airport. (See Page-123,133)
Complex Aircraft An aircraft with retractable landing gear, flaps, and a controllable-pitch propeller, or is turbine powered.
Compression Ratio 1. In a reciprocating engine, the ratio of the volume of an engine cylinder with the piston at the bottom center to the volume with the piston at top center. 2. In a turbine engine, the ratio of the pressure of the air at the discharge to the pressure of air at the inlet.
Constant Speed Propeller. A controllable pitch propeller whose pitch is automatically varied in flight by a governor to maintain a constant rpm in spite of varying air loads. *Power output is controlled by the throttle and indicated by a manifold pressure gauge.*
Control Touch The ability to sense the action of the airplane and its probable actions in the immediate future, with regard to attitude and speed variations, by sensing and evaluation of varying pressures and resistance of the control surfaces transmitted through the cockpit flight controls.
Convective SIGMET A weather advisory concerning convective weather significant to the safety of all aircraft. Convective SIGMETs are issued for *tornadoes, lines of thunderstorms, embedded thunderstorms of any intensity level,* areas of thunderstorms greater than or equal to VIP level 4 (Heavy Rain) with an area coverage of 4/10 (40%) or more, and hail 3/4 inch or greater.
Coordinated Flight Application of all appropriate flight and power controls to prevent slipping or skidding in any flight condition.
Coordination The ability to use the hands and feet together subconsciously and in the proper relationship to produce desired results in the airplane.
Coriolis Force affects the paths of aircraft, caused by the rotation of the Earth.
Cowl Flaps Devices arranged around certain air-cooled engine cowlings which may be opened or closed to regulate the flow of air around the

engine.

Crab A flight condition in which the nose of the airplane is pointed into the wind a sufficient amount to counteract a crosswind and maintain a desired track over the ground.

Critical Angle of Attack The angle of attack at which a wing stalls regardless of airspeed, flight attitude, or weight.

Crosswind Component The wind component, measured in knots, at 90° to the longitudinal axes of the runway.

Cumulonimbus Clouds the most hazardous clouds a plane can get in. If an aircraft penetrates a CB cloud, pilot should be ready for _severe turbulence, icing, wind shear, loss of radio instruments, lightning strike and overstressing of aircraft. Stay away by at least 20 miles from the cell._

D

Datum (Reference Datum) An imaginary vertical plane or line from which all measurements of moment arm are taken. The datum is established by the manufacturer. Once the datum has been selected, all moment arms and the location of CG range are measured from this point.

Dead Reckoning A method navigation of an airplane solely by means of computations based on airspeed, course, heading, wind direction, and speed, groundspeed, and elapsed time. A VFR Sectional Aeronautical Chart is the road map to follow the route for a pilot flying under VFR.

Decompression Sickness A condition where the low pressure at high altitudes allows bubbles of nitrogen to form in the blood and joints causing severe pain. Symptoms can include fatigue and pain in muscles and joints. This condition is called the bends.

Density Altitude This altitude is pressure altitude corrected for variations from standard temperature. _When conditions are standard, pressure altitude and density altitude are the same._ If the temperature is above standard, the density altitude is higher than pressure altitude. If the temperature is below standard, the density altitude is lower than pressure altitude. This is an important altitude because it is directly related to the airplane's performance.

Designated Pilot Examiner (DPE) An individual designated by the FAA to administer practical tests to pilot applicants.

Detonation The sudden release of heat energy from fuel in an aircraft engine caused by the fuel-air mixture reaching its critical pressure and temperature. Detonation occurs as a _violent explosion_ rather than a smooth burning process.

Descent at Minimum Safe Airspeed A minimum safe airspeed descent is a nose-high, power assisted descent condition principally used for clearing obstacles during a landing approach to a short runway. *See Pg.51.*

Dewpoint. The temperature at which air can hold no more water or the *temperature to which air must be cooled to become saturated.*

Directional Stability Stability about the vertical axes of an aircraft, whereby an aircraft tends to return, on its own, to flight aligned with the relative wind when disturbed from that equilibrium state. The vertical tail is the primary contributor to directional stability, causing an airplane in flight to align with the relative wind. *See Pg.25*

Distress A condition of being threatened by serious and/or imminent danger and of requiring immediate assistance. The distress message is the absolute top priority call. It has priority over all others, and the word Mayday should force everyone else into immediate radio silence. Some examples of MAYDAY calls are; flame-out, engine fire, emergency descent, pilot incapacitation, being lost, (very) uncertain of your position, very low on fuel, darkness, when you are not qualified to fly at night and/or the aircraft is not suitably equipped. *See. Page.129*

Downwash Air deflected perpendicular to the motion of the airfoil.

Drag An aerodynamic force on a body acting parallel and opposite to the relative wind. The resistance of the atmosphere to the relative motion of an aircraft. Drag opposes thrust and limits the speed of the airplane.

Dynamic Stability The property of an aircraft that causes it, when disturbed from straight-and-level flight, to develop forces or moments that restore the original condition of straight and level. *See Pg.25*

E

Elevator The horizontal, movable *primary control surface* in the tail section, or empennage, of an airplane. The elevator is hinged to the trailing edge of the fixed horizontal stabilizer.

Emergency Locator Transmitter (ELT) A radio transmitter attached to the aircraft structure which operates from its own power source on 121.5 MHz and 243.0 MHz. It aids in locating downed aircraft by radiating a downward sweeping audio tone, 2-4 times per second. It is designed to function without human action after an accident. *The best action taken to determine if your emergency locator transmitter (ELT) hasn't been activated is to monitor 121.5 before engine shutdown.*

Empennage The section of the airplane that consists of the vertical stabilizer, the horizontal stabilizer, and the associated control surfaces.

Equilibrium A condition that exists within a body when the sum of the moments of all of the forces acting on the body is equal to zero. In aerodynamics, equilibrium is when all opposing forces acting on an aircraft are balanced (steady, unaccelerated flight conditions).

F

Ferry Flight A flight for the purpose of: a. Returning an aircraft to base. b. Delivering an aircraft from one location to another. c. Moving an aircraft to and from a maintenance base. Ferry flights, under certain conditions, may be conducted under terms of a special flight permit. *See Pg.87*

Fixation A psychological condition where the pilot fixes attention on a single source of information and ignores all other sources.

Fixed-Pitch Propeller Propellers with fixed blade angles. Fixed-pitch propellers are designed as climb propellers, cruise propellers, or standard propellers. *(Cessna 172/152 etc.)*

Flaps Hinged portion of the trailing edge between the ailerons and fuselage. In some aircraft, ailerons and flaps are interconnected to produce full-span "flaperons." In either case, flaps change the lift and drag on the wing.

Flameout (Engine-Out) An emergency condition caused by a loss of engine power. See Pg.65

Flight Management Systems (FMS) A computer system that uses a large data base to allow routes to be preprogrammed and fed into the system by means of a data loader. The system is constantly updated with respect to position accuracy by reference to conventional navigation aids. The sophisticated program and its associated data base ensures that the most appropriate aids are automatically selected during the information update cycle.

Flight Plan Specified information relating to the intended flight of an aircraft that is filed orally or in writing with an FSS or an ATC facility. *See Pg.187*

Flight Standards District Office (FSDO) An FAA field office serving an assigned geographical area and staffed with Flight Standards personnel who serve the aviation industry and the general public on matters relating to the certification and operation of air carrier and general aviation aircraft. Activities include general surveillance of operational safety, certification of airmen and aircraft, accident prevention, investigation, enforcement, etc.

Fly Heading (Degrees) Informs the pilot of the heading he/she should fly. The pilot may have to turn to, or continue on, a specific compass direction in order to comply with the instructions. The pilot is expected to turn in the shorter direction to the heading unless otherwise instructed by ATC.

Floating A condition when landing where the airplane does not settle to the runway due to excessive airspeed. See Pg.43. *Floating caused by the phenomenon of ground effect will be most realized during an approach to land when at less than the length of the wingspan above the surface.*

Force (F) The energy applied to an object that attempts to cause the object to change its direction, speed, or motion. In aerodynamics, it is expressed as F, T (thrust), L (lift), W (weight), or D (drag), usually in pounds.

Form Drag The part of parasite drag on a body resulting from the integrated effect of the static pressure acting normal to its surface resolved in the drag direction. *See Pg.24*

Forward Slip A slip in which the airplane's direction of motion continues the same as before the slip was begun. In a forward slip, the airplane's longitudinal axes is at an angle to its flightpath. *See.Pg.44*

Fuel Injection A fuel metering system used on some aircraft reciprocating engines in which a constant flow of fuel is fed to injection nozzles in the heads of all cylinders just outside of the intake valve. It differs from sequential fuel injection in which a timed charge of high-pressure fuel is sprayed directly into the combustion chamber of the cylinder.

Fuel Tank Sump A sampling port in the lowest part of the fuel tank that the pilot can utilize to check for contaminants in the fuel.

Fuselage The section of the airplane that consists of the cabin and/or cockpit, containing seats for the occupants and the controls for the airplane.

G

General Aviation That portion of civil aviation that does not include scheduled or unscheduled air carriers or commercial space operations.

Glide Ratio. The ratio between distance traveled and altitude lost during non-powered flight. ICAO defines that all civil aviation operations other than scheduled air services and nonscheduled air transport operations for remuneration or hire.

Glidepath The path of an aircraft relative to the ground while approaching a landing.

Global Position System (GPS) A satellite-based radio positioning, navigation, and time-transfer system.

Go-around Terminating a landing approach. *See Pg. 45*

Gross Weight The total weight of a fully loaded aircraft including the fuel, oil, crew, passengers, and cargo.

Ground Effect A condition of improved performance encountered when an airplane is operating very close to the ground. When an airplane's wing is under the influence of ground effect, there is a reduction in upwash, downwash, and wingtip vortices. As a result of the reduced wingtip vortices, induced drag is reduced.

Groundspeed (GS) The actual speed of the airplane over the ground. It is true airspeed corrected for wind. Groundspeed decreases with a headwind, and increases with a tailwind.

Gyroscopic Precession An inherent quality of rotating bodies, which causes an applied force to be manifested 90° in the direction of rotation from the point where the force is applied. During a descent the tail rises and causes a force to felt on the top of the propeller. The resultant force is therefore 90 degrees ahead in the direction of the rotation (RIGHT SIDE of propeller) causing a left yawing tendency. See Pg. 32, 171,181

International Civil Aviation Organization (ICAO) A specialized agency of the United Nations whose objective is to develop the principles and techniques of international air navigation and to foster planning and development of international civil air transport.

H

Hand Propping The person pulling the propeller blades through directs all activity and is in charge of the procedure. The other person must be seated in the airplane with the brakes set. it is extremely important that <u>a competent pilot be at the controls in the cockpit.</u>

Heading The direction in which the nose of the aircraft is pointing during flight.

Heading Bug A marker on the heading indicator that can be rotated to a specific heading for reference purposes, or to command an autopilot to fly that heading. *See Figure-7, Pg.19*

Heading Indicator An instrument that senses airplane movement and displays heading based on a 360° azimuth, with the final zero omitted. The heading indicator, also called a directional gyro (*gyroscopic instrument),* is fundamentally a mechanical instrument designed to facilitate the use of the magnetic compass. <u>(It should keep aligned with the magnetic compass)</u>

Headwind Component The component of atmospheric winds that acts opposite to the aircraft's flightpath. *See Pg.48*

Horizon The line of sight boundary between the earth and the sky.

Hot Start In gas turbine engines, A start which occurs with normal engine rotation, but exhaust temperature exceeds prescribed limits. This is usually caused by an excessively rich mixture in the combustor. The fuel flow to the engine must be terminated immediately to prevent engine damage.

Hydroplaning A condition that exists when landing on a surface with standing water deeper than the tread depth of the tires. When the brakes are applied, there is a possibility that the brake will lock up and the tire will ride on the surface of the water, much like a water ski. When the tires are hydroplaning, directional control and braking action are virtually impossible. An effective anti-skid system can minimize the effects of hydroplaning.

Hypoxia A lack of sufficient oxygen reaching the body tissues. *See Pg.105-106*

I

Icing Ice formation on aircraft. Types of icing affecting the performance of aircraft are: *See Pg.110,113,114*

a. Rime Ice- Rough, milky, opaque ice formed by the instantaneous freezing of small supercooled water droplets. It accumulates on the leading edges of wings and on antennas, pitot tubes, etc. The intensity and type of icing reported by a pilot *is light to moderate rime.*

Case: If you are on approach and picking up ½ in. of rime ice on the leading edge of your wings, you should consider: *A faster than normal approach* and *landing speed.*

b. Clear Ice- A glossy, clear, or translucent ice formed by the relatively slow freezing or large supercooled water droplets.

c. Mixed- A mixture of clear ice and rime ice.

Intensity of icing can be reported: Trace, Light, Moderate and Severe.

Induction (air intake), Carburetor and Instrument Icing (Pitot and Static Ports) are the other type of icing. *Page 13*

Instrument Landing System (ILS) is a highly accurate radio signal including vertical (glide path) and horizontal guidance (localizer), by sending radio waves downrange from the runway end when landing in low-visibility and low-ceiling weather conditions. ILS consists of three Categories.

CAT I ILS with minimums down to 200 ft and 1/2 mile (2600 Feet)
CAT II ILS with minimums down to 100 ft and 1/4 mile (1200 feet)
CAT III ILS with zero-zero minimums.

Inclinometer An instrument consisting of a curved glass tube, housing a glass ball, and damped with a fluid similar to kerosene. It may be used to indicate inclination, as a level, or, as used in the turn indicators, to show the relationship between gravity and centrifugal force in a turn. *See Pg. 19.*

Indicated Airspeed (IAS) The direct instrument reading obtained from the airspeed indicator in the cockpit, uncorrected for variations in atmospheric density, installation error, or instrument error. Manufacturers use this airspeed as the basis for determining airplane performance. Takeoff, landing, and stall speeds listed in the AFM or POH are indicated airspeeds and do not normally vary with altitude or temperature.

Indicated Altitude The altitude read directly from the altimeter (uncorrected) when it is set to the current altimeter setting.

Induced Drag That part of total drag which is created by the production of lift. Induced drag increases with a decrease in airspeed. *See Pg.24*

Instrument Flight Rules (IFR) Rules that govern the procedure for conducting flight in weather conditions below VFR weather minimums. The term "IFR" also is used to define weather conditions and the type of flight plan under which an aircraft is operating.

International Standard Atmosphere (ISA) Standard atmospheric conditions consisting of a temperature of 59 °F (15 °C), and a barometric pressure of 29.92 "Hg. (1013.2 mb) at sea level.

Inversion or "temperature inversion" A layer within the atmosphere in which temperature increases with altitude. *(This is opposite or inverted of what is "normal")* A temperature inversion is highly **_stable layer of air_ and has very little turbulence**. If the air is very humid within an inversion, fog or very low clouds are likely to develop and *expect a windshear zone, gusting more than 25 Kt.* Low level inversions may cause **smoke and dust** to be trapped close to the surface. *If the relative humidity is high, you may expect smoot air, poor visibility, fog, haze, or low clouds.* The presence of ice pellets at the surface is evidence that there is a *temperature inversion with freezing rain at a higher altitude.*

L

Land as Soon as _POSSIBLE vs. PRACTICAL_. "Possible" is generally understood to be off-airport while "practical" is understood to be at the next suitable airport. However, AIM 91.3 gives the pilot the ultimate authority and responsibility *(The pilot in command of an aircraft is directly responsible for, and is the final authority as to, the operation of that aircraft.)* for the safety of that flight and to allow the pilot to make the decision and to do what is necessary to have an in-flight event conclude successfully. If the event was self-caused, there might be repercussions.

Lateral Axes An imaginary line passing through the center of gravity of an airplane and extending across the airplane from wingtip to wingtip. *Pg.26*

Lateral stability (Resistance to rolling) The stability about the longitudinal axes of an aircraft. Rolling stability or the ability of an airplane to return to level flight due to a disturbance that causes one of the wings to drop. *See Pg.25*

PRIVATE PILOT HANDBOOK

Leading Edge The part of an airfoil that meets the airflow first.
Lift One of the four main forces acting on an aircraft. On a fixed-wing aircraft, an upward force created by the effect of airflow as it passes over and under the wing. *Pg. 23*
Lift Coefficient A coefficient representing the lift of a given airfoil. Lift coefficient is obtained by dividing the lift by the free-stream dynamic pressure and the representative area under consideration. *Pg.24*
Lift/Drag Ratio (L/D) The efficiency of an airfoil section. It is the ratio of the coefficient of lift to the coefficient of drag for any given angle of attack.
Lift-off The act of becoming airborne as a result of the wings lifting the airplane off the ground, or the pilot rotating the nose up, increasing the angle of attack to start a climb. *Pg.24*
Load Factor (G-Load). Amount of stress, or load factor, that an aircraft can withstand before structural damage or failure occurs. *The ratio of the load supported by the airplane's wings to the actual weight of the aircraft and its contents.* Also referred to as G-loading. *See Pg.30,56*
Logbooks Journals containing a record of total operating time, repairs, alterations or inspections performed, and all Airworthiness Directive (AD) notes complied with. A maintenance logbook should be kept for the airframe, each engine, and each propeller.
Longitudinal Axes An imaginary line through an aircraft from nose to tail, passing through its center of gravity. The longitudinal axes is also called the roll axes of the aircraft. Movement of the ailerons rotates an airplane about its longitudinal axes.
Longitudinal Stability *(Resisting to Pitching)* Stability about the lateral axes. A desirable characteristic of an airplane whereby it tends to return to its trimmed angle of attack after displacement. *See Pg.25*
M
Mach Speed relative to the speed of sound. Mach 1 is the speed of sound.
Magnetic Compass A device for determining direction measured from magnetic north. There is no acceleration/deceleration error on a heading of North or south. *See Pg.14*
Main Gear The wheels of an aircraft's landing gear that supports the major part of the aircraft's weight. *See Figure-4, Pg.12*
Maneuverability Ability of an aircraft to change directions along a flightpath and withstand the stresses imposed upon it. *See Pg.25*
Maneuvering Speed (VA) *The maximum speed at which you may apply full and abrupt input movement without the possibility of causing structural damage. It changes with weight,* increasing weight increases the Va

Speed. *(Weight and Va 2300 lb 96 Knots, 1950 lb 88 Knots, 1600 lb 80 Knots.)*

Manifold Pressure (MP) The absolute pressure of the fuel/ air mixture within the intake manifold, usually indicated in inches of mercury.

Maximum Takeoff Weight (MTOW) The maximum allowable weight for takeoff.

Microburst A downdraft (sinking air) in a thunderstorm that extends 2.5 miles or less. In spite of its small horizontal scale, an intense microburst could induce wind speeds as high as 150 knots. Microburst poses a significant threat to traffics to land/take off.

Minimum Controllable Airspeed. *An airspeed at which any further increase in angle of attack, increase in load factor, or reduction in power, would result in an immediate stall.* See Pg.24,99

Minimum Drag Speed (L/DMAX). The point on the total drag curve where the lift-to-drag ratio is the greatest. At this speed, total drag is minimized.

Mixture. The ratio of fuel to air entering the engine's cylinders.

Moment Arm. The distance from a datum to the applied force. Pg.76.

Moment Index (or Index) A moment divided by a constant such as 100, 1,000, or 10,000. The purpose of using a moment index is to simplify weight and balance computations of airplanes where heavy items and long arms result in large, unmanageable numbers.

Moment *The product of the weight of an item multiplied by its arm.* Moments are expressed in pound-inches (lb-in). Total moment is the weight of the airplane multiplied by the distance between the datum and the CG. See Pg.77

N

National Airspace System (NAS) The common network of U.S. airspace; air navigation facilities, equipment and services, airports or landing areas; aeronautical charts, information and services; rules, regulations and procedures, technical information, and manpower and material. Included are system components shared jointly with the military.

National Transportation Safety Board (NTSB) An independent U.S. government investigative agency responsible for civil transportation accident investigation. You must notify the NTSB if there has been substantial damage *which adversely affects structural strength or flight characteristics.* NTSB defines *the "serious injury" that requires hospitalization for more than 48 hours. In the case of an aircraft accident, the aircraft operator must immediately notify NTSB. (Part 830)*

Night The time between the end of evening civil twilight *(when the sun is*

less than 6° below the horizon.) and the beginning of morning civil twilight.
Negative Static Stability The initial tendency of an aircraft to continue away from the original state of equilibrium after being disturbed.
Neutral Static Stability The initial tendency of an aircraft to remain in a new condition after its equilibrium has been disturbed.
Normal Category An airplane that has a seating configuration, excluding pilot seats, of nine or less, a maximum certificated takeoff weight of 12,500 pounds or less, and intended for nonacrobatic operation.
Notice to Airmen (NOTAM) A notice containing information (not known sufficiently in advance to publicize by other means) concerning the establishment, condition, or change in any component *(facility, service, or procedure of, or hazard in the National Airspace System)* the timely knowledge of which is essential to personnel concerned with flight operations.
- NOTAM(D)- A NOTAM given (in addition to local dissemination) distant dissemination beyond the area of responsibility of the Flight Service Station. These NOTAMs will be stored and available until canceled.
- FDC NOTAM- A NOTAM regulatory in nature, transmitted by USNOF and given system wide dissemination.

P
Parasite Drag That part of total drag created by the design or shape of airplane parts. Parasite drag increases with an increase in airspeed.
Precision Approach Path Indicator (PAPI) An airport lighting facility, similar to VASI, providing vertical approach slope guidance to aircraft during approach to landing. PAPIs consist of a single row of either two or four lights, normally installed on the left side of the runway, and have an effective visual range of about 5 miles during the day and up to 20 miles at night. PAPIs radiate a directional pattern of high intensity red and white focused light beams which indicate that the pilot is **"on path"** if the pilot sees an equal number of white lights and red lights, with white to the left of the red; "above path" if the pilot sees more white than red lights; and "below path" if the pilot sees more red than white lights. *See Pg.151*
Preventive Maintenance Simple or minor preservation operations and replacement of the small standard parts, not involved complex assembly, *servicing landing gear wheel bearings, replenishing hydraulic fluid.* Pilots can perform the preventive maintenance. *Paperwork is required including signature, certificate number, and kind of certificate held by the person approving the work and a description of the work must be entered in the aircraft maintenance records. See Pg.90*

Payload (GAMA) The weight of occupants, cargo, and baggage.

P-factor A tendency for an aircraft to yaw to the left due to the descending propeller blade on the right producing more thrust than the ascending blade on the left. *(Gyroscopic precession)* This occurs when the aircraft's longitudinal axes is in a climbing attitude in relation to the relative wind.

Pilot's Operating Handbook (POH) A document developed by the airplane manufacturer and contains the FAA approved Airplane Flight Manual (AFM) information.

Piston Engine A reciprocating engine. *See Pg.101-102.*

Pitch The rotation of an airplane about its lateral axes, or on a propeller, the blade angle as measured from plane of rotation. *Figure-12, Pg.26*

Pivotal Altitude A specific altitude at which, when an airplane turns at a given groundspeed, a projecting of the sighting reference line to a selected point on the ground will appear to pivot on that point. *See Pg.62*

Pneumatic Systems The power system in an aircraft used for operating such items as landing gear, brakes, and wing flaps with compressed air as the operating fluid.

Position Lights (Navigation Lights) Lights on an aircraft consisting of *a red light on the left wing, a green light on the right wing*, and *a white light on the tail*. CFRs require that *these lights be displayed in flight from sunset to sunrise. Figure-4, Pg.12*

Positive Static Stability The initial tendency to return to a state of equilibrium when disturbed from that state.

Powerplant A complete engine and propeller combination with accessories.

Precipitation Any or all forms of water particles *(rain, sleet, hail, or snow)* that fall from the atmosphere and reach the surface.

Preignition Ignition occurring in the cylinder before the time of normal ignition. Preignition is often caused by a local hot spot in the combustion chamber igniting the fuel/air mixture. *See Pg.13.*

Pressure Altitude The altitude indicated when the altimeter setting window *(Kollsman window-barometric scale)* is adjusted to 29.92. This is the altitude above the standard datum plane, which is a theoretical plane where air pressure (corrected to 15 °C) equals 29.92 "Hg. Pressure altitude is used to compute density altitude, true altitude, true airspeed, and other performance data.

Profile Drag The total of the skin friction drag and form drag for a two-dimensional airfoil section.

Prohibited Area An airspace of defined dimensions, above the land areas

or territorial waters of a State, within which the flight of aircraft is prohibited. Airspace designated under 14 CFR Part 73 within which no person may operate an aircraft without the permission of the using agency. See Pg.35
Propeller. A device for propelling an aircraft that, when rotated, produces by its action on the air, a thrust approximately perpendicular to its plane of rotation. It includes the control components normally supplied by its manufacturer.
QNE The barometric pressure used for the standard altimeter setting (29.92 inches Hg.).
QNH The barometric pressure as reported by a particular station
R
Rate of Turn The rate in degrees/second of a turn.
Receiver Autonomous Integrity Monitoring (RAIM) A software which alerts the pilot if the signal is not precise enough *(at least 5 satellites required)* for IFR or VFR Navigation (LOI). If a LOI *(Loss of Integrity)* indication is displayed or RAIM Capability is lost in-flight, the usage of GPS should be discontinued. *The pilot has no assurance of the accuracy of the GPS position.*
Reciprocating Engine See Piston Engine.
Registration Certificate A State and Federal certificate that documents aircraft ownership.
Relative Wind The direction of the airflow with respect to the wing. If a wing moves forward horizontally, the relative wind moves backward horizontally. Relative wind is parallel to and opposite the flightpath of the airplane.
Roundout A pitch-up during landing approach to reduce rate of descent and forward speed prior to touchdown. Although the FAA uses the terms roundout and flare interchangeably, some instructors see these as distinct parts of the landing sequence. *See Pg.43*
Rudder The movable primary control surface mounted on the trailing edge of the vertical fin of an airplane. Movement of the rudder rotates the airplane about its vertical axes.
Runway A defined rectangular area on a land airport prepared for the landing and takeoff run of aircraft along its length. Runways are normally numbered in relation to their magnetic direction rounded off to the nearest 10 degrees; e.g., Runway 1, Runway 25.
Runway Centerline Lights Runway centerline lights are installed on some precision approach runways to facilitate landing under adverse visibility conditions. They are located along the runway centerline and are spaced

at 50-foot intervals. When viewed from the landing threshold, the runway centerline lights are white until the last 3,000 feet of the runway. The white lights begin to alternate with red for the next 2,000 feet, and for the last 1,000 feet of the runway, all centerline lights are red.

Runway Centerline Markings The runway centerline identifies the center of the runway and provides alignment guidance during takeoff and landings. The centerline consists of a line of uniformly spaced stripes and gaps.

Runway Edge Lights Runway edge lights are used to outline the edges of runways during periods of darkness or restricted visibility conditions. These light systems are classified according to the intensity or brightness they are capable of producing: they are the High Intensity Runway Lights (HIRL), Medium Intensity Runway Lights (MIRL), and the Low Intensity Runway Lights (LIRL). The HIRL and MIRL systems have variable intensity controls, whereas the LIRLs normally have one intensity setting.

Runway End Identifier Lights (REIL) One component of the runway lighting system. These lights are installed at many airfields to provide rapid and positive identification of the approach end of a particular runway.

Runway Incursion Any occurrence at an airport involving an aircraft, vehicle, person, or object on the ground that creates a collision hazard or results in loss of separation with an aircraft taking off, intending to takeoff, landing, or intending to land.

Runway Threshold Markings Runway threshold markings come in two configurations. They either consist of eight longitudinal stripes of uniform dimensions disposed symmetrically about the runway centerline, or the number of stripes is related to the runway width. A threshold marking helps identify the beginning of the runway that is available for landing. In some instances, the landing threshold may be displaced. *See Pg.155*

Runway Visual Range (RVR). It is based on what a pilot in a flying aircraft should see when looking down the runway. If included in a METAR, RVR will be reported following prevailing visibility. *See Pg.91*

S

Search and Rescue A service which seeks missing aircraft and assists those found to be in need of assistance. It is a cooperative effort using the facilities and services of available Federal, state and local agencies. The U.S. Coast Guard is responsible for coordination of search and rescue for the Maritime Region, and the U.S. Air Force is responsible for search and rescue for the Inland Region. Information pertinent to search and rescue should be passed through any air traffic facility or be transmitted directly to the Rescue Coordination Center by telephone.

Service Ceiling The maximum density altitude where the best rate-of-climb airspeed (Vy) will produce a 100 feet-per-minute climb at maximum weight while in a clean configuration with maximum continuous power.

Separation In air traffic control, the spacing of aircraft to achieve their safe and orderly movement in flight and while landing and taking off.

Sideslip A slip in which the airplane's longitudinal axes remains parallel to the original flightpath, but the airplane no longer flies straight ahead. Instead, the horizontal component of wing lift forces the airplane to move sideways toward the low wing. *See Pg.47*

Sidestep Maneuver A visual maneuver accomplished by a pilot at the completion of an instrument approach to permit a straight-in landing on a parallel runway not more than 1,200 feet to either side of the runway to which the instrument approach was conducted.

SIGMET A weather advisory issued concerning weather significant to the safety of all aircraft. SIGMET covers severe and extreme turbulence, severe icing, and widespread dust or sandstorms that reduce visibility to less than 3 miles. *See Pg.93*

Skid A condition where the tail of the airplane follows a path outside the path of the nose during a turn. *Figure-13B, Pg. 27*

Slip An intentional maneuver to decrease airspeed or increase rate of descent, and to compensate for a crosswind on landing. A slip can also be unintentional when the pilot fails to maintain the aircraft in coordinated flight. *Figure-13B, Pg. 27*

Spatial Disorientation The inability of a pilot to correctly interpret aircraft attitude, altitude or airspeed in relation to the Earth or other points of reference. *See Pg.105*

Special Use Airspace (SUA) Airspace of defined dimensions identified by an area on the surface of the earth wherein activities must be confined because of their nature and/or wherein limitations may be imposed upon aircraft operations that are not a part of those activities. *Types of special use airspace are: Alert Area, Controlled Firing Area, Military Operations Area (MOA), Prohibited Area, Restricted Area, Warning Area. See Pg. 35*

Special VFR Operations (SVFR) Aircraft operating in accordance with clearances within Class B, C, D, and E surface areas in weather conditions less than the basic VFR weather minimums. Such operations must be requested by the pilot and approved by ATC.*See.Pg.33, 94*

Spin An *aggravated stall* that results in what is termed an **"autorotation"** wherein the airplane follows a downward corkscrew path. As the airplane rotates around the vertical axes, the rising wing is less stalled than the descending wing creating a rolling, yawing, and pitching motion. *Pg.101*

Spiraling Slipstream The slipstream of a propeller-driven airplane rotates around the airplane. This slipstream strikes the left side of the vertical fin, causing the airplane to yaw slightly. Vertical stabilizer offset is sometimes used by aircraft designers to counteract this left turn tendency. An airplane (except a T-tail) pitching nosedown when power is reduced and controls are not adjusted <u>causes the downwash on the elevators from the propeller slipstream is reduced and elevator effectiveness is reduced.</u>

Stability The inherent quality of an airplane to correct for conditions that may disturb its equilibrium, and to return or to continue on the original flightpath. It is primarily an airplane design characteristic. *Pg.25,75,103*

Stabilized Approach A landing approach in which the pilot establishes and maintains a constant angle glidepath towards a predetermined point on the landing runway. It is based on the pilot's judgment of certain visual cues, and depends on the maintenance of a constant final descent airspeed and configuration.

Stall A rapid decrease in lift caused by the separation of airflow from the wing's surface brought on by exceeding the critical angle of attack. A stall can occur at any pitch attitude or airspeed. *See Pg.57*

Standard Atmosphere At sea level, the standard atmosphere consists of a barometric pressure of 29.92 inches of mercury ("Hg) or 1013.2 millibars, and a temperature of 15 °C (59 °F). Pressure and temperature normally decrease as altitude increases. <u>The standard lapse rate in the lower atmosphere for each 1,000 feet of altitude is approximately 1 "Hg and 2 °C (3.5 °F).</u> For example, the standard pressure and temperature at 2,000 feet mean sea level (MSL) is 27.92 "Hg (29.92 – 2) and 11 °C (15 °C – 4 °C). <u>Actual lapse rate can be used to determine the stability of the atmosphere.</u>

Standard Empty Weight This weight consists of the airframe, engines, and all items of operating equipment that have fixed locations and are permanently installed in the airplane; including fixed ballast, hydraulic fluid, <u>unusable fuel, and full engine oil.</u> *(Basic empty weight includes the standard empty weight plus optional and special equipment that has been installed.) Pg.77*

Standard-Rate Turn A turn <u>at the rate of 3° per second</u> which enables the airplane to complete a 360° turn in 2 minutes.

Static Stability The initial tendency an aircraft displays when disturbed from a state of equilibrium.

Station A location in the airplane that is identified by a number designating its distance in inches from the datum. The datum is, therefore, identified as station zero. An item located at station +50 would have an arm of 50 inches. *See Pg.78*

Sterile Cockpit Federal Aviation Administration (FAA), EASA and ICAO regulation states that during critical phases of flight *(normally below 10,000 feet (3,050 m))*, only activities required for the safe operation of the aircraft may be carried out, and all non-essential activities in the cockpit are forbidden.

Supplemental Oxygen Pilots must use supplemental oxygen when they're above 12,500 feet MSL cabin pressure altitude for more than 30 minutes, and anytime you're above 14,000 feet MSL. Above 15,000 feet MSL, you have to provide it to your passengers. *See Pg.188*

Swept Wing Swept wings are mostly suitable for high speeds, like supersonic. A wing planform in which the tips of the wing are farther back than the wing root to reduce turbulence. Therefore, Modern commercial jet airliners mostly use swept wings.

T

Takeoff Roll (Ground Roll) The total distance required for an aircraft to become airborne. Takeoff roll increases as density altitude increase. (FAA-Written Exam/Calculation on Chart-POH) *See Pg.80, Figure-47*

Taxiway Lights Omnidirectional lights that outline the edges of the taxiway and are blue in color.

Taxiway Turnoff Lights Flush lights which emit a steady green color.

Tetrahedron A large, triangular-shaped, kite-like object installed near the runway. Tetrahedrons are mounted on a pivot and are free to swing with the wind to show the pilot the direction of the wind as an aid in takeoffs and landings.

Throttle The valve in a carburetor or fuel control unit that determines the amount of fuel-air mixture that is fed to the engine.

Thrust A forward force which propels the airplane through the air. The force which imparts a change in the velocity of a mass. This force is measured in pounds but has no element of time or rate. The term, thrust required, is generally associated with jet engines. *See Pg.23', Figure-10.*

Total Drag The sum of the parasite and induced drag.

Touchdown Zone Lights Two rows of transverse light bars disposed symmetrically about the runway centerline in the runway touchdown zone.

Track. The actual path made over the ground in flight.

Trailing Edge The portion of the airfoil where the airflow over the upper surface rejoins the lower surface airflow. *Figure-9, Pg.22*

Transponder The airborne portion of the secondary surveillance radar system. The transponder emits a reply when queried by a radar facility. When squawking the VFR code (1200) on your transponder, <u>the minimum mode the</u> <u>transponder must be is in Mode A. (identification)</u>

Tricycle Gear Landing gear employing a third wheel located on the nose of the aircraft. *(Cessna 152/172 etc.) Figure-4, Pg.23*

Trim Tab A small auxiliary hinged portion of a movable control surface that can be adjusted during flight to a position resulting in a balance of control forces.

True airspeed (TAS) Calibrated airspeed corrected for altitude and nonstandard temperature. Because air density decreases with an increase in altitude, an airplane has to be flown faster at higher altitudes to cause the same pressure difference between pitot impact pressure and static pressure. Therefore, for a given calibrated airspeed, true airspeed increases as altitude increases; or for a given true airspeed, calibrated airspeed decreases as altitude increases. *See Pg.18, 85*

True Altitude The vertical distance of the airplane above sea level—the actual altitude. It is often expressed as feet above mean sea level (MSL). Airport, terrain, and obstacle elevations on aeronautical charts are true altitudes.

T-Tail An aircraft with the horizontal stabilizer mounted on the top of the vertical stabilizer, forming a T., e.g.; Beechcraft 76, 90,200.

Turbocharger An air compressor driven by exhaust gases, which increases the pressure of the air going into the engine through the carburetor or fuel injection system.

Turbofan Engine A turbojet engine in which additional propulsive thrust is gained by extending a portion of the compressor or turbine blades outside the inner engine case. The extended blades propel bypass air along the engine axes but between the inner and outer casing. The air is not combusted but does provide additional thrust.

Turbojet Engine A jet engine incorporating a turbine-driven air compressor to take in and compress air for the combustion of fuel, the gases of combustion being used both to rotate the turbine and create a thrust producing jet.

Turboprop Engine A turbine engine that drives a propeller through a reduction gearing arrangement. Most of the energy in the exhaust gases is converted into torque, rather than its acceleration being used to propel the aircraft.

Turbulence An occurrence caused by the relative movement of disturbed air *(changing to the unstable)* through which an aircraft is flying. <u>Mountain waves are associated with strong winds (> 40 Kt.) down a mountain valley,</u> severe turbulence, strong vertical currents, and icing. Avoid flying below <u>rotor clouds producing dangerous turbulence</u> in mountain waves.

Turn Coordinator A rate gyro that senses both <u>roll and yaw axis</u> due to the gimbal being canted. Has largely replaced the turn-and-slip indicator in modern aircraft. *See Pg.19, Figure-7*

Turn-and-Slip Indicator A flight instrument consisting of a rate gyro to indicate the rate of yaw and a curved glass inclinometer to indicate the relationship between gravity and centrifugal force. The turn-and-slip indicator indicates the relationship between angle of bank and rate of yaw. Also called a turn-and-bank indicator. *See Pg.19, Figure-7*

Turning Error. One of the errors inherent in a magnetic compass caused by the dip compensating weight. It shows up only on turns to or from northerly headings in the Northern Hemisphere and southerly headings in the Southern Hemisphere. Turning Error Memory Aids: ***UNOS*** for Northern Hemisphere. <u>Undershot North, Overshoot South</u>. *See Pg.15*

U

Under the Hood A condition in Instrument training indicating that the pilot is using a hood to restrict visibility outside the cockpit while simulating instrument flight. An appropriately rated pilot is required in the other control seat while this operation is being conducted.

UNICOM A nongovernment air/ground radio communication station which may provide airport information at public use airports where there is no tower or FSS. *See Pg.137*

Unusable Fuel Fuel that cannot be consumed by the engine. This fuel is considered part of the empty weight of the aircraft.

Urgency A condition of being concerned about safety and of requiring timely but not immediate assistance; a potential distress condition.

Useful Load The weight of the pilot, copilot, passengers, baggage, usable fuel, and drainable oil. It is the basic empty weight subtracted from the maximum allowable gross weight. This term applies to general aviation aircraft only.

Utility Category An airplane that has a seating configuration, excluding pilot seats, of nine or less, a maximum certificated takeoff weight of 12,500 pounds or less, and intended for limited acrobatic operation.

V

Va The Design Maneuvering Speed This is the "rough air" speed and the

maximum speed for abrupt maneuvers. If during flight, rough air or severe turbulence is encountered, reduce the airspeed to maneuvering speed or less to minimize stress on the airplane structure. It is important to consider weight when referencing this speed. For example, VA may be 100 knots when an airplane is heavily loaded, but only 90 knots when the load is light.
Velocity. The speed or rate of movement in a certain direction.
Vertical Axes (Yaw Axes) An imaginary line passing vertically through the center of gravity of an aircraft. The vertical axes is called the Z-axes or the yaw axes.
Vertical Speed Indicator (VSI) An instrument that uses static pressure to display a rate of climb or descent in feet per minute. The VSI can also sometimes be called a vertical velocity indicator. *See Pg.19*
Vertical Stability (Resistance to Yawing) Stability about an aircraft's vertical axes. Also called yawing or directional stability. The size of the vertical stabilizer and the area of the fuselage aft of the CG contribute to vertical stability. The bigger and further aft the vertical stabilizer is, the greater the stability. (think of the arm and moment)
VFE The maximum speed with the flaps extended. The upper limit of the white arc.
VFO The maximum speed that the flaps can be extended or retracted.
Vg Diagram A chart that relates velocity to load factor (G-load). It is valid only for a specific weight, configuration, and altitude and shows the maximum amount of positive or negative lift the airplane is capable of generating at a given speed. Also shows the safe load factor limits and the load factor that the aircraft can sustain at various speeds.
Visual Approach Slope Indicator (VASI) The most common visual glidepath system in use. The VASI provides obstruction clearance within 10° of the extended runway centerline, and to 4 nautical miles (NM) from the runway threshold. *Figure-57, Pg. 153*
Visual Flight Rules (VFR) Code of Federal Regulations that govern the procedures for conducting flight under visual conditions.
VLOF (Lift-off Speed) The speed at which the aircraft departs the runway during takeoff.
VMO Maximum operating limit speed for turboprops or jets.
VNE-Never-Exceed Speed Operating above this speed is prohibited since it may result in damage or structural failure. The <u>red radial line</u> on the airspeed indicator. *See Pg.19, Figure-7.*
VOR Very High Frequency Omni Directional Range. A ground-based electronic navigation aid transmitting very high frequency navigation

signals, *360 degrees radial in all directions,* oriented from magnetic north. Used as the basis for navigation in the National Airspace System. The VOR periodically identifies itself by Morse Code and may have an additional voice identification feature. Voice features may be used by ATC or FSS for transmitting instructions/ information to pilots, known as HIWAS. *Pg. 111*

Vr Rotation Speed The speed that the pilot begins rotating the aircraft prior to lift-off. That requires to apply control inputs to cause the aircraft nose to pitch up. *(Refer to the POH)*

Vso Stalling Speed or the minimum steady flight speed in the landing configuration. In small airplanes, this is the power-off stall speed at the maximum landing weight in the landing configuration *(gear and flaps down)*. The lower limit of the white arc. *See Pg.19, Figure-7.*

Vx. Best angle-of-climb speed It allows A/C to climb to altitude within the shortest horizontal distance. It is used during a short-field takeoff to clear an obstacle. *(Refer to the POH) See Pg. 50,52, 58,60*

Vy. Best rate-of-climb speed This airspeed provides the most altitude gain in a given period of time. It allows A/C to climb to altitude in the shortest time. Vy is slightly faster than Vx. *(Refer to the POH)*

W

Wake Turbulence Avoidance *Counter rotating vortices off wingtips of an airplane generating lift.* When an airplane generates lift, air spills over the wingtips from the high-pressure areas below the wings to the low-pressure areas above them. This flow causes rapidly rotating whirlpools of air called wingtip vortices or wake turbulence. *The wind condition that requires maximum caution when avoiding wake turbulence on landing is a light, quartering tailwind.* Under certain conditions, airport traffic controllers apply procedures for separating, sequencing the VFR/IFR aircraft to make the traffics informed and provide the safe distance for wake turbulence.

Wide-Area Augmentation System (WAAS) A satellite navigation system consisting of the equipment and software which augments the GPS Standard Positioning Service (SPS). The WAAS provides *enhanced integrity, accuracy, availability, and continuity over and above GPS SPS.* The differential correction function provides improved accuracy required for precision approach. *If your GPS receiver is equipped with WAAS—* Wide Area Augmentation System—*your position accuracy is less than three meters.*

Weight A measure of the heaviness of an object. The force by which a body is attracted toward the center of the Earth by gravity. Weight is equal to the mass of the body times the local value of gravitational acceleration.

(F=mxA) One of the four main forces acting on an aircraft. Equivalent to the actual weight of the aircraft. It acts downward through the aircraft's center of gravity toward the center of the Earth. Weight opposes lift.

Weight and Balance The aircraft is said to be in weight and balance when the gross weight of the aircraft is under the max gross weight, and the center of gravity is within limits and will remain in limits for the duration of the flight. *See Pg. 76,100,*

Wind Correction Angle (WCA) Correction applied to the course to establish a heading so that track will coincide with course. *See Pg. 82*

Windmilling A typical process to start an engine in case it stops working mid-air. When the air moving through a propeller/turbine vane creates the rotational energy. *See Pg. 66*

Wind Shear A sudden change in wind speed or direction over a relatively short distance in the atmosphere. Wind shear has significant effects on control of an aircraft, and it has been a sole or contributing cause of many aircraft accidents. *See Pg. 93*

Windsock A truncated cloth cone open at both ends and mounted on a freewheeling pivot that indicates the direction from which the wind is blowing.

Wing Airfoil attached to each side of the fuselage and are the main lifting surfaces that support the airplane in flight.

Wing Area The total surface of the wing *(square feet),* which includes control surfaces and may include wing area covered by the fuselage *(main body of the airplane),* and engine nacelles. *See Pg. 12*

Wing Span The maximum distance from wingtip to wingtip.

Wingtip Vortices The rapidly rotating air that spills over an airplane's wings during flight. The intensity of the turbulence depends on the airplane's weight, speed, and configuration. It is also referred to as **_wake turbulence_**. Vortices from heavy aircraft may be extremely hazardous to small aircraft. *(mostly wingtip vortices tend to sink into the flight path of aircraft operating below the aircraft generating the turbulence.) See Pg.107*

Wing Twist A design feature incorporated into some wings to improve aileron control effectiveness at high angles of attack during an approach to a stall.

X-C Flight See Cross Country Flight. *Figure-70, Page.81,189*

X-Wind Component See Cross Wind Component.

Yaw Rotation about the vertical axes of an aircraft. *Rudders control yaw.*

Zero Fuel Weight The weight of the aircraft to include all useful load except fuel.

Figure-63 Pilot Aviation Alphabet and Practice

Letter	Pronunciation
A	Alpha (AL fah)
B	Bravo (BRAH VOH)
C	Charlie (CHAR lee)
D	Delta (DELL tah)
E	Echo (ECK oh)
F	Foxtrot (FOKS trot)
G	Golf (GOLF)
H	Hotel (hoh TELL)
I	India (IN dee ah)
J	Juliet (JEW lee ETT)
K	Kilo (KEY loh)
L	Lima (LEE mah)
M	Mike (MIKE)
N	November (no VEM ber)
O	Oscar (OSS cah)
P	Papa (pah PAH)
Q	Quebec (keh BECK)
R	Romeo (ROW me oh)
S	Sierra (see AIR rah)
T	Tango (TANG go)
U	Uniform (YOU nee form)
V	Victor (VIK tah)
W	Whiskey (WISS key)
X	X Ray (ECKS RAY)
Y	Yankee (YANG key)
Z	Zulu (ZOO loo)

Nu	Pronunciation
0	ZEE row
1	WUN
2	TOO
3	TREE
4	FOW er
5	FIFE
6	SIX
7	SEVEN
8	AIT
9	NINE er

N172SP (November wun Seven too see airrah pah pah)
FL 190 (Flight level wun nine er zee row)
HDG 210˙ (Heading Too wun zee row)
ALT 110 (Altitude wun wun tou-sand)
270˙/12 kt (Wind wun seven zee row degrees / wun too knots)
FL 240 (Flight level too fow er zee row)
ALT 2500 (Altitude too thousand fife hundred)
QNH 1013 (wun zee row wun tree)
FRQ 119.3 (wun wun nine er day-see-mal tree)

Practice I:
ARKES, ATONE, NOVAE, JUMAR, SECOR.
9   0   7.9   9000   4   5.3   129.145   170   800
FL 240
Altitude 1700
QNH 2991
FL 180
Wind 110˙/16 kt
Heading 190˙
ALTITUDE 10000 feet

Practice II:
DOLPHIN, SAXXN, JUNUR, BONNS, MNATE
5   0   9.1   8000   6   3.4   122.175   140   900
FL 330
Altitude 3700 feet
QNH 3019
FL 180
Wind 320˙/ 16 kt
Heading 090˙
ALTITUDE 14500 feet

Practice III:
SNAPE, LAWNN, COPRA, AGLER, BIRDO.
4   7   9.2   6000   0   5.1   122.125   130   700
FL 300
Altitude 6500 feet
QNH 1004
FL 180
Wind 080˙/ 22 kt
Heading 210˙, Speed 210, Report AVSAR at 6000
ALTITUDE 16000 feet

Doing practice is incredibly helpful to read the letters out loud while doing above practice. Do this several times a day for a week.

Figure-64 TAF/METAR Abreviations

Abbreviation	Meaning	Abbreviation	Meaning
-, +, Blank	Light/Heavy/Moderate Intensity	FU	Smoke
SKC FEW SCT BKN OVC	Sky Clear Few Clouds 1-2/3 Scattered 4-5 Broken 6/ 7-8 /9 Overcast 10	TEMPO PROB BECMG OCNL INTMT	Temporary Probability Becoming Occasional Intermittent
MI	Shallow	PR	Partial
BC	Patches	DR	Low drifting
BL	Blowing	SH	Showers
TS	Thunderstorm	FZ	Freezing
RA (Precipitation)	Rain	DZ	Drizzle
SN (Precipitation)	Snow	SG	Snow Grains
IC	Ice Crystals	PL	Ice Pellets
GR (Precipitation)	Hail	GS	Snow Pellets and/or Small Hail
UP (Precipitation)	Unknown Precipitation	VC	In the vicinity (5-10 Miles from RWY)
FG (Obscuration)	Fog	VA	Volcanic Ash
BR (Obscuration)	Mist	HZ	Haze
DU (Obscuration)	Widespread Dust	FU	Smoke
SA (Obscuration)	Sand	PY	Spray
SQ	Squall	PO	Dust or Sand Whirls
DS	Duststorm	SS	Sandstorm
FC	Funnel Cloud	E	Ended At Time
B (Time)	Began At Time	2 digits (Time) 4 digits	Minutes of current H. H/M Zulu Time
A01/A02 RMK RVR SLP SM CAVOK	Station Type Remark Runway Visual Range Sea Level Pressure Status Miles Ceiling/Visiblity OK	VRB G CB FM P6SM NO	Variable Gusting Cumulonimbus From Visibility greater than 6SM Not Available

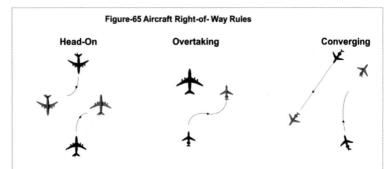

Figure-65 Aircraft Right-of-Way Rules

When two aircraft are flying head on, Each must move to their right.
The faster-moving aircraft must overtake on the right-hand side, or starboard side, of the slower aircraft.
If two aircraft are at the same height and on converging courses, the aircraft with the other on its right-hand side (starboard side) has to give way.

1.Type VFR / IFR / DVFR	2.Aircraft ID	3.Aircraft Type Special Equip.	4.True Airspeed	5.Departure Point	6.Departure Time (Proposed / Actual)	7.Cruising Altitude
8. Route of Flight							

9. Destination(Airport/City)	10. Est Time Enroute (Hours / Minutes)	11.Remarks
12. Fuel on Board (Hours / Minutes)	13. Alternative Airport	14. Pilot's Name/Address/Phone/Aircraft Home Base
		17. Destination Contact Phone(optional)
15.Number Onboard	16. Aircraft Color	CLOSE VFR FLIGHT PLAN WITH _____ FSS ON ARRIVAL /U = Transponder w/Mode C /G = GPS with Enroute & Terminal Capability /A = DME &

Figure- 66 Flight Plan Form

ATC Light Gun Signals

If radio fails, the transponder should be set to 7600 and light signals should be received from the tower.

COLOR & TYPE	ON THE GROUND	IN FLIGHT
STEADY GREEN	**Cleared for takeoff**	**Cleared to land**
FLASHING GREEN	Cleared for taxi	Return for landing (to be followed by steady green)
STEADY RED	**STOP!**	Give way to other aircraft and continue circling
FLASHING RED	Taxi clear of the runway	Airport unsafe, **Do not land**
FLASHING WHITE	Return to starting point	Not Applicable (N/A)
ALTERNATING RED/GREEN	**Exercise extreme caution**	

Figure- 67 ATC Tower Light Gun Signals

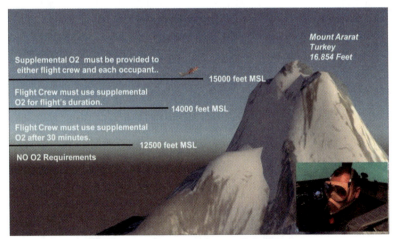

Figure-66 Supplemental Oxygen Requirements

L- Low Pressure (cyclone), counterclockwise, rising warm (less dense, light air), moist air and possibly, converging winds, bad- cloudy weather: severe storms, Cumuluform clouds, vertical development clouds (CB), turbulence (bumpy), showery precipitation, unstable weather. H- High Pressure (anticyclone), clockwise, sinking, dense cold air (air molecules close together), diverging winds, approaching fair, good weather.

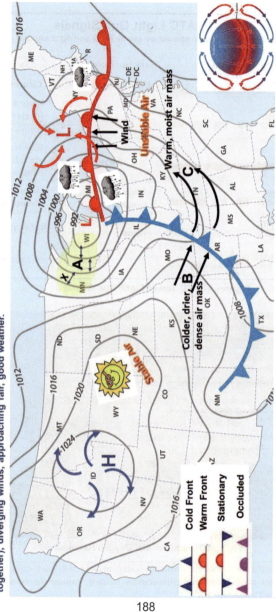

A- Stronger winds, MN/WI, where isobars are close (X), indicating a large pressure change in the region. B-C Air moves from High to Low. Winter Fronts are the strongest, developing over Asia and North America, forming the oceanic air masses.

Figure- 69 ATC Weather Fronts, Lifting Forces, Isobars, High/Low Pressure Systems

Figure-70 VFR Cross Country Flight Planning Checklist

Subject Title	Task / Objective	Performance/ Comments
14 CFR: 61.93 - Solo X-C flight requirements.	Are you familiar with all requirements? (3X50 NM, full-stop landings at three point in the Traffic Pattern)	
Verify you have current charts before X-C.	AF/D, Sectional Charts, NAV Sheet,	
X-C Planning (One day and one at night) See Pg.81	Review course, distance, heading, TAS, GS, Fuel requirements one night before. Be prepared for a detailed review with CFI.	
What will you do if you become lost in-flight?	Determine the actions to be taken respectively. Pg.94	
If the aircraft's radio fails, what is the recommended procedure when landing at a controlled airport?	Determine the actions to be taken respectively. Pg.106	
Have you flown to 2 different airports during X-C Flight Training?	Keep all records related to the X-C flights. (at least one of them a controlled airport.)	
Route airspace regulations, weather briefing and completing certain emergency maneuvers.	Review all subject titles. See Pages 33, 37, 65, 114, 139,	
Equipment malfunction: what's your backup plan?	See. Page.66,113,114. Refer to POH/AFM.	

Instructor   Date of Review   Student Pilot   Logbook Endorsement

Note: Evaluate the student's performance: E- Excellent G-Good F- Fair U-Unsatisfactory. If the applicant needs additional cross-country training, explain the reasons for the training that will be performed.

Abbreviations

AAS Airport Advisory Service
ABM Abeam
ABN Aerodrome Beacon
AC Advisory Circular
ACAS Airborne Collision Avoidance System
ACC Area Control Center
ACFT/AC Aircraft
AD Aerodrome/Airworthiness Directive
ADF Automatic Direction Finding
ADIZ Air Defense Identification Zone
ADM Aeronautical Decision Making
ADS-B Automatic Dependent Surveillance
AFB Air Force Base
A/FD Airport/Facility Directory
AFM Airplane Flying Handbook
AFIS Aerodrome Flight Information Service
AGL Above Ground Level
AIREP Air-Report
AIM Airman's Information Manual
AIRMET Airman's Meteorological Information
AIS Aeronautical Information Services
ALS Approach Lighting System
ALS Low Intensity Approach Lights
ALT Altitude or Alternate
AME Airman's Medical Examiner
AMSL Above Mean Sea Level
AMT Aviation Maintenance Technician
AOA Angle of Attack
AOC Air Operator Certificate
AOPA Aircraft Owners and Pilots Association
AOR Area of Responsibility
A/P Autopilot
APP Approach Control
APT Airport
APU Auxillary Power Unit
ASDA Accelerate Stop Distance Available
ASI Airspeed Indicator
ASOS Automated Surface Observing System
ASR Airport Surveillance Radar
ATC Air Traffic Control
ATCO Air Traffic Control Officer
ATIS Automatic Terminal Information Service
AVGAS Aviation Gasoline
AWOS Automated Weather Observing System
BCN Beacon
BKN Broken
BRG Bearing
CAA Civil Aviation Authority/Mostly ICAO Countries
CAT Category or Clear Air Turbulence
CAVOK Ceiling and Visibility are OK
CB Cumulonimbus / heavy-dense vertical cloud.
CDI Course Deviation Indicator
CDU Control Display Unit (Pilot's Interface to the FMS)
CFI Certificated Flight Instructor
CFII Certificated Flight Instructor, instrument
CFIT Controlled Flight Into Terrain
CG Center of Gravity
CRM Crew Resource Management
CRS Course
CTA/FIR Control Area/Flight Information Region
CTAF Common Traffic Advisory Frequency
CTR Control Zone
CVR Cockpit Voice Recorder
DA (H) Decision Altitude (Height)
D-ATIS Digital ATIS
DCT Direct
DEG Degree

DEP Departure Control/Departure Procedures
DER Departure End of Runway
DEV Deviation
DBA Decibel
DF Direction Finder
DIST Distance
DME Distance-Measuring Equipment
DOD Department of Defense
DP Obstacle Departure Procedure
DZ Drizzle
EAT Expected Approach Time
EET Estimated Elapsed Time
EFAS Enroute Flight Advisory Service
EFB Electronic Flight Bag
EFC Expect Further Clearance
EFIS Electronic Flight Information Systems
ELEV Elevation
ELT Emergency Locator Transmitter
EMERG Emergency
ENG Engine
EOBT Estimated Off Block Time
ETA Estimated Time of Arrival
ETD Estimated Time of Departure
ETE Estimated Time Enroute
ETOPS Extended Range Operation with Twin Engines
FAA Federal Aviation Administration
FADEC Full Authority Digital Engine Control
FAF Final Approach Fix
FAIL Failure
FAP Final Approach Point
FAR Federal Aviation Regulation
FDR Flight Data Recorder
FG Fog
FIR Flight Information Region
FIS Flight Information Service
FL Flight Level (Altitude/Feet)
FLD Field
FMS Flight Management System
FOD Foreign Object Damage
FPM Feet Per Minute
FREQ Frequency
FNPT Flight and Navigation Procedures Trainer
FSDO Flight Standards District Office
FSS Flight Service Station
FIX Fixpoint, Position
FZ Freezing
GA General Aviation or Go Around
GND Ground Control
GP Glidepath
GPS Global Positioning System
GPU Ground Power Unit
GPWS Ground Proximity Warning System
GRADU Gradual or Gradually
GRASS Grass Landing Area
GS Glide Slope
G/S Ground Speed
GWT Gross Weight
H24 24 Hour Service (Day and Night)
HAA Height Above Airport
HAT Height Above Touchdown
HAZMAT Hazardous materials
HDG Heading
HELO Helicopter
HLS Helicopter Landing Site
HF High Frequency (3-30 MHz)
HIALS High Intensity Approach Light System
HIRL High Intensity Runway Edge Lights

Abbreviations

HIWAS Hazardous Inflight Weather Advisory Ser.
hPa Hectopascal (one hectopascal =one millibar)
HR Hours (period of time)
HUD Head-up Display
IACRA FAA Integrated Airman Certification and Rating Application
IAF Initial Approach Fix
IAP Instrument Approach Procedure
IAS Indicated Airspeed
IATA International Air Transport Association
ICAO International Civil Aviation Organization
IDENT Identification
IFF Identification Friend/Foe
ILS Instrument Landing System
IM Inner Marker
IMC Instrument Meteorological Conditions
INFO Information
INOP Inoperative
INS Inertial Navigation
ITT Interstage Turbine Temperature
RNAV Area IR Instrument Restricted Controlled Airspace
JAA Joint Aviation Authorities (ICAO Countries)
JAR-OPS Joint Aviation Requirements–Operations/ICAO
KG Kilogram
kHz Kilohertz
KIAS Knots Indicated Airspeed
KTAS Knots True Airspeed
L Locator (Compass)
LAAS Local Area Augmentation System
LAHSO Land and Hold Short Operations
LAT Latitude
LBS Pounds (Weight)
LCTR Locator (Compass)
LDA Landing Distance Available
LDA Localizer-type Directional Aid
LIRL Low Intensity Runway Lights
LLWAS Low Level Wind Shear Alert System
LNAV Lateral Navigation
LNDG Landing
LOC Localizer
LONG Longitude
LPV Localizer Performance with Vertical Guidance
LVP Low Visibility Procedures
MAA Maximum Authorized Altitude
MAG Magnetic
MALS Medium Intensity Approach Light System
MALSF Medium Intensity Approach Light System with Sequenced Flashing Lights
MAP Missed Approach Point
MAX Maximum
MB Millibars
MCA Minimum Crossing Altitude
MCC Multi-crew Co-ordination
MDA Minimum Descent Altitude
MDA(H) Minimum Descent Altitude (Height)
MEA Minimum Enroute Altitude
MEI Multi Engine Instructor
MEL Minimum Equipment List
MMEL Master Minimum Equipment List
METAR Meteorological Aerodrome Reports (Aviation routine weather report)
MIL Military
MIM Minimum
MIN Minute
MIRL Medium Intensity Runway Edge Lights
MLS Microwave Landing System
MM Middle Marker
MNM Minimum
MOA Military Operation Area
MOCA Minimum Obstruction Clearance Altitude
MODE C Altitude - Encoded Beacon Reply
MORA Minimum Off-Route Altitude (Grid or Route)
MRA Minimum Reception Altitude
MRO Maintenance, repair and overhaul
MSA Minimum Safe/Sector Altitude
MSL Mean Sea Level
MTOW Maximum Take-off Weight
MVFR Marginal Visual Flight Rules
N1 Gas Generator Speed (Low Pressure Compressor, Indication of Trust)
N2 Second Stage Turbine Speed (High Pressure Compressor - Tachometer)
NA Not Authorized
NAP Noise Abatement Procedure
NAS National Airspace System
NASA National Aeronautics and Space Administration
NAVAID Navigational Aid
NDB Non-Directional Beacon/Radio Beacon
NE Northeast
NM Nautical Mile(s)
No Number
NoPT No Procedure Turn
NORDO No Radio
NOSIG No Significant Change
NOTAM Notices to Airmen
NTSB National Transportation Safety Board
NVG Night Vision Goggles
NW Northwest
OAT Outside Air Temperature
OM Outer Marker
OPS Operations or Operates
O/R On Request
OVC Overcast
P Prohibited Area
PAL Pilot Activated Lighting
PAPI Precision Approach Path Indicator
PAR Precision Approach Radar
PARK Parking
PAX Passenger
PCL Pilot Controlled Lighting
PCN Pavement Classification Number
PHAK Pilot's Handbook of Aeronautical Knowledge
PIC Pilot In Command
PIREP Pilot Report
PISTON Piston Aircraft
POH Pilot Operating Handbook
PRA Precision Radar Approach
PROB Probabiliy
PROC Procedure or Procurement
PROP Propeller Aircraft
QDM Magnetic bearing to facility
QDR Magnetic bearing from facility
QFE Height above airport elevation (or runway threshold elevation) based on local station pressure
QNE Altimeter setting 29.92" Hg or 1013.2 Mb.

Abbreviations

QNH Altitude above sea level based on local station pressure
R R-070 or 141R (Radial Course from VOR Station)
R Restricted Area
RA Radio Altimeter, Resolution Advisory or Rain
RADAR Radio Detection and Ranging
RAIL Runway Alignment Indicator Lights
RAIM Receiver Autonomous Integrity Monitoring
RAPCON Radar Approach Control
RCO Remote Communications Outlet
REF Reference
REIL Runway End Identification Lights
REV Reverse
RMI Radio Magnetic Indicator
RNAV Area Navigation
RNP Required Navigation Performance
RNP AR Required Navigation Performance Authorization Required
RSA Runway Safety Area
RTF Radiotelephony
RVR Runway Visual Range
RVSM Reduced Vertical Separation Minimum
RWY Runway
S South or Southern
SAR Search and Rescue
SCT Scattered
SE Single Engine or Southeast
SEC Seconds
SEL Single Engine Land (pilot rating)
SID Standard Instrument Departure
SIGMET Significant Meteorological Convective Information
SIM Simulator
SM Statute Miles
STAR Standard Terminal Arrival Route
STC Supplemental Type Certificate
STD Indication of an altimeter set to 29.92" Hg or 1013.2 hPa (Mb) without temperature correction
Std Standard
ST-IN Straight-in
STOL Short Take-off and Landing
SUPP Supplemental/Supplementary
SVFR Special Visual Flight Rules
SW Southwest
SYS System
TA Transition Altitude- ICAO/EASA
TAA Terminal Arrival Area
TBO Time Between Overhauls
TACAN Tactical Air Navigation (bearing and distance station)
TAF Terminal Area Forecast
TAS True Air Speed
TCA Terminal Control Area
TCAS Traffic Alert and Collision Avoidance System
TCH Threshold Crossing Height
TDZ Touchdown Zone
TDZE Touchdown Zone Elevation
TEMP Temporary
THR Threshold
TMA Terminal Control Area
TODA Take-off Distance Available
TORA Take-off Run Available
TRSA Terminal Radar Service Area
TS TS . . . Thunderstorm (followed by RA = rain, SN = snow, PL = ice pellets, GR = hail, GS = small hail and/or snow pellets or combinations thereof, e.g. TSRAPL = thunderstorm with rain and ice pellets)
TSA Transportation Security Administration
TWR Tower (Aerodrome Control)
TWY Taxiway
UAV Unmanned Aerial Vehicle
UHF Ultra High Frequency (300-3000 MHz)
UNICOM Aeronautical Advisory SERVICE (Frequency)
USAF US Air Force
UTC Coordinated Universal Time
V Velocity
V1 Take-off Decision Speed
V2 Takeoff Safety Speed (Applicable to Larger Multi-engine Aircraft)
VA Maximum Manoeuvring Speed
Vref Final Approach Speed
Vso Stalling speed, minimum steady flight speed in the landing configuration
Vx Best Angle of Climb Speed
Vy Best Rate of Climb Speed
VAR Magnetic Variation
VASI Visual Approach Slope Indicator
VC Vicinity of the aerodrome (may be followed by FG fog, RA Rain,TS or CB or SN Snow; eg, VCFG, VCTS ..
VDP Visual Descent Point
VFR Visual Flight Rules
VHF Very High Frequency (30-300 MHz)
VIS Visibility
VMC Visual Meteorological Conditions
VNAV Vertical Navigation
VRB Variable
V/STOL Vertical/Short Takeoff and Landing Aircraft
VOR VHF Omnidirectional Range
VORTAC VOR and TACAN co-located
VOT VOR Test Facility
VV Vertical Visibility
V/V Vertical Velocity or speed
W West or Western
WAC World Aeronautical Chart
WAAS Wide Area Augmentation System
WILCO Will Comply
W/O Without
WX Weather
Z Zulu Time

FIGURES:

Figure-1 Start-up Materials for Private Pilot Training...................................1
Figure-2A Private Pilot Logbook Requirements and Endorsements...........4
Figure-2B Airman Certification Standarts Coding System 6
Figure-2C Private Pilot Airmen Certification Standards (ACS) ....…..9
Figure-3 Student Pilot Self-Awareness Checklist (go and no-go).............10
Figure-4 Airplane Components 12
Figure-5 Flight and Engine Instruments 6-Pack and G1000 15
Figure-6 Flight Instruments: Steam Gouges and Glass Cockpit...............16
Figure -7 Airplane Primary Flight Instruments 19
Figure-8 The first flight in the history of the world....................................21
Figure-9 Bernoulli's Equation: Airfoil/ Lift/Pressure Velocity Relation 22
Figure-10 Aerodynamic Forces (4-Force) in Flight 23
Figure-11 L/D Ratio (Lift-to-Drag Ratio) 25
Fig-12 Design Characteristics:Stability,Maneuverability,Controllability....26
Figure-13A Aerodynamic Forces in Turns..27
Figure-13B Turn Performance...27
Figure-14 Aerodynamic Forces in Climbs and Descends.........................28
Figure-15 Traffic Pattern Procedures 31
Figure-16 Airport Facility Director- A/FD and Airspace Classifications…...34
Figure- 17 VFR Sectional Chart Symbols and Reading 35
Figure-18 How To Read A Sectional Chart 36
Figure-19A Airspace Classification 37
Figure-19B Airspace VFR Weather Minimums 37
Figure-20 Wind Correction During Taxi,Aileron and Elevator Deflection...38
Figure-21 X-Wind Taxi Technique, Aileron and Elevator Deflection 38
Figure-22 Preflight Magneto Check Key and Engine Tachometer 39
Figure-23 Normal Takeoff, Climb and Rejected Takeoff...........................41
Figure-24 Normal Approach and Landing Procedures 43
Figure-25 Go Around Procedures 45
Figure-26 Crosswind Takeoff 46
Figure-27 Crosswind Landing 47
Figure- 28 How to Find a Crosswind Component.................................49
Figure-29 Sort Field Takeoff and Max. Performance Climb......................50
Figure-30 Short Field Approach and Landing 51
Figure-31 Soft Field Takeoff 52
Figure-32 Soft Field Approach and Landing 53
Figure-33 Slow Flight 55
Figure-34 Steep Turns 56

PRIVATE PILOT HANDBOOK

Figure-35 Power Off Stall (Landing Stall) 58
Figure-36 Power On Stall (Takeoff Stall) 59
Figure-37 Accelerated Stall 61
Figure-38 Turns Around A Point 63
Figure-39 Rectangular Course 63
Figure-40 S-Turns 64
Figure-41 Simulated Engine-Out (Engine failure) Procedures in Flight ...66
Figure-42 Pre-Solo Requirements 69
Figure- 43 Pre-Solo Flight Review 75
Figure-44A Center of Gravity Limitations 77
Figure-44B Weight & Balance Sheet 77
Figure- 45 Moment/Weight Graph 78
Figure- 46 Center of Gravity Moment Envelope 79
Figure- 47 Takeoff Distance Roll 80
Figure-48 VFR Navigation Planning 83
Figure- 49 Wind Aloft Data 84
Figure-50 Magnetic Compass DeviationTable 84
Figure-51 Cruise Performance 85
Figure- 52 Private Pilot Knowledge Test 115
Figure-53 Airport Taxiway Diagram 145
Figure-54 Controlled Airspace - Traffic Pattern Communication Procedures... 146
Figure-54B Untowered Airports - Traffic Pattern Communication Procedures 150
Figure- 55 Preferred Entry to the Traffic Pattern When Crossing Over Midfield... 151
Figure- 56 Alternate Downwind Entry to the Traffic Pattern....................151
Figure- 57 VASI-Visual Approach Slope Indicator 153
Figure- 58 PAPI- Precision Approach Path Indicator 153
Figure-59 Airport Signs: Taxiway and Runway Markings 154
Figure-60 Airport Signs: Taxiway and Runway Markings 155
Figure-61 Airport Operations Airport Markings and Signs 156
Figure-62 Runway Holding Position Markings 156
Figure-63 Pilot Aviation Alphabet and Practice 185
Figure-64 TAF/METAR Abreviations 186
Figure-65 Aircraft Right-of- Way Rules 187
Figure-66 Flight Plan Log 187
Figure-67 ATC Tower Light Signals 188
Figure-68 Supplemental Oxygen Requirements 188
Figure- 69 ATC Weather Fronts, High/Low Pressure Systems 189
Figure-70 VFR Cross Country Flight Planning Checklist 190

INDEX

A
5 P's Checklist 89
6-Pack (Steam Gauges) 16
Abbreviations 184
Abeam 119
Abnormal Engine Readout 20
Absolute Altitude 17
Accelerated stalls...61
Acknowledge 119
Active Runway 119
Advection Fog 110
Aerobatic Flight 157
Aerodynamic Principles 20,156
Aerodynamic Forces 21
Aeronautical Beacon 119
Aeronautical Chart 156
Aeronautical Decision Making 89,112
Aeronautical Information Manual (AIM) 156
Ailerons 156
Airborne 119
Air Defense Identification Zone.............35,156
Airplane Flight Manual (AFM) 156
Airfoil 21,156
Airplane Structure..11
Airplane Components..................................11
Airplane Equipment 12,16
Airplane Performance..................................110
Airplane System-Related Malfunctions 12
Airport and Navigation Lighting Aids.................191
Airman Certification Standards (ACS)...................5
Airman certification standards Codes/Tasks 6
Airmanship Skills 156
Airmet (WAs) 93
Airport Data 36
Airport Facility Director A/FD.............34,120,157
Air Traffic Control (ATC) 120
Airport Traffic Patterns and Operations..... 146,154
Air Route Traffic Control Center 96,121
Airport Rotating Beacon 157
Airspace Classifications 34,38, 98,120
Airspeed 17,100
Airspeed Indicator 17
Air Taxi (Hover Taxi) 158
Airworthiness Certificate 87,88, 157
Airworthiness Requirements 115
Affirmative 120
Alternator/generator problem 13,158
Altimeter 20,158
Altitude Readout 120
Altitudes 17,100, 158
Angle of attack..22,158
Annual Inspection 158
Anti-icing/deicing 104
Approach Control, Category 120,121
Approach and landing..................................42
Approach Light System (ALS) 157
Approaches to stalls (impending stalls) 58
Area Of Operations/ Critical Tasks/ Risk Management Factors 8
Artificial Horizon 19
ATC Light Gun Signals 191
ATIS, AWOS and ASOS 92,121
Atmosphere 110
Attitude Indicator 19,158
Attitude and Heading Reference System 158

Attitude and Sink Rate Control.............................66
Autokinesis 158
Automatic Dependent Surveillance 156
Automatic Direction Finder (ADF) 158
Aviation Alphabet 187
Aviation Area Forecast 96
Axis of Airplane 24,158

B
Balked Landing 159
Bank control..19
Base 121
Basic safety concepts....................................8
Bearing 159
Bernoulli's Principle 22
Before-takeoff check....................................41
Best angle of climb (VX)............................159
Best Glide (Vg)...159
Best rate of climb (VY) 159
Blind Spot 159
Blocked 121
Bouncing During Touchdown....................159
Brakes 104
Braking Action 159
Broadcast 121
Buffeting 159

C
Cabin fire 114
Calibrated Airspeed (CAS) 18,159
Call Sign 122
Carburetor Icing 12,113,159
Carbon Monoxide Poisoning 106
Category, Class, and Type 94
Ceiling 95,160
Center of Gravity (CG) 77,100,160
Centrifugal force 28
Chord Line 22,60
Circle-To-Land Maneuver 122
Circuit Breaker 160
Clearance Delivery 122
Cleared for Takeoff 122
Cleared for the Option 122
Cleared to Land 122
Clearing Turns 55
Class A,B,C,D,E,G 98
Clear Air Turbulence 160
Climbs and climbing turns...........................28
Climb to VFR 122
Climbing turns..40
Closed Traffic 123
Common Traffic Advisory Frequency (CTAF) 122,133, 160
Cockpit Resource Management 160
Coffin Corner 160
Combustion Chamber 160
Complex Aircraft 160
Compression Ratio 160
Constant-speed Propeller.........................161
Convective Outlook Chart 95
Convective Sigmet 93,161
Control Flight into Terrain (CFIT) 108
Control Touch 161
Collision Avoidance 107
Coordinated flight and turns..................26,161
Coriolis Force 162
Correction 123

Correcting during straight-and-level flight.........40
Cowl Flaps 161
Crab Method...47,161
Critical Angle of Attack 161
Cross-Country Flight Planning 116
Crosswind Component 161
Crosswind Approach and Landing..................... 48
Wing-low (sideslip) method 48
Crosswind 123
Crosswind round out (flare) 47
Crosswind takeoff/landing................................. 47
Crosswind Component 49
Cruise Performance 85
Cumulonimbus Clouds 109,111,161

D
Datum (Reference Datum). 77, 162,177
Dead Reckoning 162
Decompression Sickness 162
Density Altitude 17, 22,162
Dense Air 16,191
Departure Control 123
Departure Procedures 123
Descents and descending turns 28,40
Descent at minimum safe airspeed...................162
Designated Pilot Examiner (DPE) 162
Detonation 13,113,162
Dew point 110,162
Directional control 47
Directional Stability 162
Distress 162
Downwash 163
Downwind 123
Drag 23,163
Drift and ground track control 63
Dynamic Stability 103,163

E
Electrical fires..114
Electrical System 104
Elevator 163
Emergency Procedures 66
Emergency approaches and landings
(simulated)..67
Emergency descents..66
Emergency landings...................................... 67,114
Emergency Locator Transmitter (ELT)..............163
Empennage 11, 163
Psychological hazards..111
Engine Instruments 20
Engine Fire In-Flight 68,114
Engine-out (failure) After Takeoff......................68
Engine inoperative approach and landing...........68

E
Electrical System 11
Engine...11
Engine Instruments 13
Engine failure 43
English Language Proficiency 10
Equilibrium 163
Expedite 123

F
Ferry Flight 163
Flare 44
Flap 10,164
Flight controls 102

Flight Instruments 13,19
Flight Following Service 123
Flight Level 124
Flight Management Systems (FMS) 164
Flight Plan 124,164
Flight Service Station (FSS) 96,124
Flight Standards District Office (FSDO) 164
Fly Heading 124,164
Fuel system..103
Full-Stop Landing 125
Fixed-pitch propellers..163
Final Leg 124

Fixation 163
Flameout (Engine-Out) 66,164
Floating during round out 164
Fog 110
Forward slip 45,164
Forces in Turns 26
Force (F) 21,164
Form Drag 164
Four fundamentals of flight 40
Fuel Injection 165
Fuel System 12,103
Fuel Remaining 125
Fuel Tank Sump 165
Fuselage 165

G
General Aviation 165
Glass Cockpit 15
Glide Ratio 165
Glidepath 165
Global Position System (GPS) 165
Go-around 46,125,165
Go Ahead 125
Graphic Weather Charts 95
Gravity (weight) 23
Gross Weight 165
Ground Effect..53,165
Ground Control 125
Ground Lessons 2
Ground Reference Maneuvers 63
Groundspeed (GS) 18,165
Gyroscopic Precession 30,165
Gyroscopic System Instruments 14,105

H
Handoff (Handover) 126
Hand Propping 167
Hard landing..48
Have Numbers 126
Hazardous Attitudes 111
Heading 166
Heading Bug 20,166
Heading Indicator 20,166
Headwind Component 49,166
High Engine Temperatures 113
High- Low Pressure Systems 109
HIWAS 111
Hold Short Yellow Lines 126,189
Hold Short Points on Taxiways 154,155
Horizon 166
Hot Start 166
How do you hear me? 126
Human factors...10,111

Hydraulic Syustem 104
Hydroplaning 166
Hyperventilation 105
Hypoxia 105,106,166
I
I Say Again 126
Icing 166
Ident 127
IFR (Instrument Flight Rules) 127
IFR Clearances 127
Ignition System 12
Inclinometer 20,167
Instrument Landing System 127,167
Immediately 127
Indicated Altitude 17,167
Indicated Airspeed 18,127,167
Induction System 11
Induced Drag 167
Instrument Flight Rules 167
Instrument Maneuvers 62
International Civil Aviation Organization 166
International Standard Atmosphere (ISA) 16,168
Intersection Departure 127
Inversion or temperature inversion................... 168
Isobar 109
L
LAHSO 108,127
Landing 43
Land as soon as possible 168
Landing GEAR 103
Landing Roll 128
Lateral Axis 25,168
Lateral Stability 26,168
Leading Edge 168
Left Turning Tendencies................................... 103
Level turns 27
Lift 23,168
Lift-to-Drag Ratio (L/D) 24,169
Lift Coefficient 168
Liftoff... 169
Light Gun Signals 191
Load Factor 30,169
Logbook Requirements 3, 86,168
Local Traffic 128
Longitudinal Axis 25,168
Longitudinal Stability 169
Lost In-flight Procedures 94
Loss of Communication 191
Low/high pressure 109
Low Approach 128
M
Mach Number 18,169
Magnetic compass 14,169
Magneto Problem 13
Main Gear 12,169
Maintain 128
Maintenance/inspection Requirements 90
Maneuvering Speed (Va) 18,56,169,180
Maneuverability... 169
Maneuvering by reference to ground objects.... 62
Manifold Pressure (MP) 169
Maximum Takeoff Weight. (MTOW) 170

MAYDAY 129
Medical Cetificate 2,87
METAR 91
Microburst 170
Minimum Controllable Airspeed 170
Minimum Drag Speed (L/DMAX) 170
Minimum Equipment List................................... 87
Minimum Fuel 129
Missed Approach (MAP) 129
Mixture Control 104,112,170
Mode C transponder 129
Moment 170
Moment Arm 76,170
Motion Sickness 106
Moisture 22
Movement/Non-Movement Area 129
N
National Airspace System (NAS) 170
National Transportation Safety Board (NTSB)...170
Negative Static Stability 170
Neutral Static Stability 170
Navigational Systems 14
Negative 129
Negative Contact/ No Visual Contact 129
Newton's Third Law 21
Night 170
Normal and crosswind takeoff and climb 41,46
Normal approach and landing............................. 42
Normal Category 171
NOTAMS "Notice to Airmen" 96,130,171
O
Oil System 102
On Course 130
Oral/Practical Exam 115
Out 130
Over 130
P
PAN-PAN 130
P-Factor 29,171
Parasite Drag 171
Parking Gate 130
Passenger-PAX Briefing 94
Payload (GAMA) 171
Performance Charts... 80
Pilot's Discretion 131
Pilot Qualifications 115
Pilot Logbook 86
Pilot's Operating Handbook (POH) 171
PIREP (Pilot Report) 93
Pitch and Power.. 29
Pitch Control 40
Pitot-static System 14,104,113
Piston Engine 102,172
Pivotal Altitude 62,172
Pneumatic Systems 172
Porpoising 48
Position Lights (Navigation Lights) 172
Positive transfer of controls............................. 108
Positive Static Stability 172
Power Control.. 16
Powerplant and Related Systems ...11,101,102,172

Power-off Stalls 58
Power On Stalls 60
Practical Exam 3,117
Precision Approach Path Indicator (PAPI) 171
Primary Flight Controls 101
Precipitation 172
Preflight Planning 88
Preflight assessment of the Aircraft................. 116
Preignition 13,172
Preparation and Preflight................................. 117
Pres-Solo Preparation 69
Pressure Altitude (PA) 17,21,172
Pressure Effect on Density 22
Pre-takeoff procedures.....................................118
Preventive Maintenance....................................172
Prior to takeoff... 117
Private Pilot and Limitations 86
Profile Drag 172
Progressive Taxi 131
Prohibited Area 35,172
Propeller 11,102,172
Pushback 131
Q
QNE/QNH 173
R
Radar Contact 131
Radar Service Terminated 132
Radar Summary Chart 95
Radio Communications 137
Receiver Autonomous Integrity Monitoring 175
Rate of Turn 173
Read Back 132
Recent Flight Experience 86
Rectangular course 63
Registration Certificate 87,173
Rejected takeoff 43
Relative Wind 173
Remote Communication Outlet (RCO) 96
Report 132
Right-of-way rules 112,190
Risk and Risk Management Checklist............. 8,89
Roger 132
Rotation and lift-off 41,181
Roundout 44,47,173
Rudder 28,29,173
Run-up Checks 40
Runway 173
Runway Centerline Lights 173
Runway Centerline Markings 173
Runway Edge Lights 174
Runway End Identifier Lights (REIL) 174
Runway Incursion 108,132,174
Runway, Taxiway Markings 154,155
Runway Threshold Markings 174,189
Runway Visual Range (RVR) 174
S
"S" Turns 64
Safety considerations.......................................118
Say Again 133
Say Altitude and Heading 133
Secondary Flight Controls 102
Track 178
Sea Breeze 112

Search and Rescue 174
Self-Announce Position and/or Intentions 133
Separation 175
Service Ceiling 175
Severe Weather Reports 93,112
Short Approach 128
Short-field approach and landing...................... 52
Short field takeoff and maximum performance
climb 51
Sideslip..47,175
Sidestep Maneuver 175
SIGMET..93,175
Significant Weather Prognostic Chart 95
Single Pilot Resource Management 88
Slow flight.. 54
Soft-field approach and landing......................... 51
Soft-field landing...53
Soft/rough-field takeoff and climb......................51
Skid 28,175
Speak Slower 133
Slip 28,175
Slow Flight 55
Stability...103
Stable Air 109
Stalls 58
Stall awareness... 8, 101,117
Student Pilot Certification Standard Checklist 6
Steep Turns 56
Stress and Fatigue 106
Spatial Disorientation 105,175
Special (Ferry) Flight Permit 87
Special Use Airspace (SUA) 35,88,175
Special VFR Operations (SVFR) 33,94,175
Speed margins.. 17
Spin awareness... 8,101,117
Spin and Recovery.............60,76,100,101, 117,176
Spiraling Slipstream 29,103,176
Squawk and Ident 134
Stability 25,176
Stabilized approach......................................43,176
Stall characteristics 57.101, 176
Stall 57,101
Stall Training and Recognition.....................58,62
Standard Airport Traffic Patterns................ 30, 141
Stand by 134
Starting, taxiing, and runup............................... 30
Start-up Materials for Private Pilot Training 1
Steam Gauges 15
Standard Atmosphere 16,176
Standard Empty Weight 176
Standard Rate Turn 134,176
Static Stability 176
Station 177
Steep Turns... 55
Sterile Cockpit 177
STARs 134
Student Pilot Certificate 3
Straight-in Approach VFR 134,147
Stop and Go 134
Straight-and-level flight..................................... 29
S-turns across a road 64
Surface Analysis Chart 95

198

Supplemental Oxygen	104,177,190
Swept Wing	177
Systems malfunctions	114

T

TAF, METAR	91,188
TCAS	136
Tailwind	134
Takeoff and Climb	42
Takeoff roll	135,177
Taxi	135
Taxi-Back (Back-	
Taxiway	135
Taxiway Lights	177
Taxiway Turnoff Lights	177
Temperature Effects on Density	22
Temporary Flight Restriction (TFR)	97,83.135
Terminal	136
Tetrahedron	136,177
That is correct	136
Throttle	177
Thrust	23,177
Thunderstorm	109
Torque Effect	29
Total Drag	24,177
Touchdown	136
Touch and Go	136
Touchdown Zone Lights	177
Tower Control	136
Traffic Alert and Collision Avoidance System	136
Traffic Pattern (TP)	30, 137
Traffic In Sight	136
Traffic No Factor	137
Trailing Edge	178
Transition	137
Transponder	137,178
Threshold	136
Tricycle Gear	178
Trim Tab	178
True Airspeed (TAS)	18, 81, 85, 178
True Altitude	17,178
T-Tail	178
Turbocharging	178
Turbofan Engine	178
Turbojet Engine	178
Turboprop engines	178
engines	178
Turbulence	109,179
Turning Error	14, 179
Turns Around a Point	63
Turn Coordinator	179
Turn and Slip Indicator	19,179
Turns to Headings	41

U

Under the Hood	179
UNICOM	137,179
Unstable Air	109
Unusual attitudes versus upsets	7, 61
Unusable Fuel	179
Upwind/Departure/Takeoff Leg	31, 138
Urgency	179
Useful Load	179
Utility Category	179

V

V-speeds	19,180,181
Vacuum System	13
	13
VASI	180
Vectors	138
Velocity	180
Verify	138
Vertical Axis	180
Vertical Speed Indicator (VSI)	20,180
Vertical Stability	25, 180
VFR, MVFR, IFR, SVFR	94
VFR Flight Instrument Requirement	90
VFR Navigation Log	81
VFR Navigation Checklist	101
VFR Not Recommended	138
VFR Reporting Point	37
VFR Weather Minimums	38
VHF Radio	138
Victor Airway	138
Visibility	37, 94, 139
Visual approach	139
Visual Flight Rules (VFR)	138,180
VOR	61,181

W

Wake Turbulence	107,181
Weight	23,182
Weight and Balance	76, 100,182
Weather Briefings	112,139
Weather Depiction Chart	95
Weather Fronts	111,192
Weather Information	
	115
Wide-Area Augmentation System (WAAS)	181
Wilco	140
Wind-check	139
Wind Correction	39
Wind Correction Angle. (WCA)	81,182
Wing	182
Wing Span	182
Windmilling	65, 182
Wind Shear	93,182
Windsock	182
Wingtip Vortices	182
Wing Twist	182
Wires Strike Avoidance	107
Words Twice	139
Written Exam	1,114
Yaw	183
Zero Fuel Weight	183